THE CRAZY LIFE OF A KID FROM BROOKLYN

BILL MORGENSTEIN

ISBN: 1493691082
ISBN 13: 9781493691081
Library of Congress Control Number: 2013920871
CreateSpace Independent Publishing Platform
North Charleston, South Carolina

FORWARD

This book is written by a generally shy and quiet person who believes that you learn by listening and observing. Normally my decisions are made quickly but the decision to finally write the story of my life only came after some persuasion from friends. What I hope comes out of reading this book, besides the humor is not only the love of life but the extreme dislike for injustice and tyranny. I realize that some laws and rules are necessary but I am firmly convinced that we have far too many regulations. Economic laws especially end up having cross purposes to their original intent. A well known economist and ex chairman of the Council of Economic advisers under President Reagan told me once (and also wrote about it in one of his books), that virtually all economic laws that were passed had the opposite effect as to what they were originally intended.

I dedicate this book to my wife, Sylvia, my children, their wives and my grandchildren. We all normally speak with them a number of times a day and we are all a very close knit family. Sylvia and I have been married for over 60 years and although we have our differences she has my highest respect. Sylvia is the rock of the family, making sure that everyone is cared for and safe in every way. Highly cultured, she is a perfectionist, whether cooking a gourmet dinner, throwing a party or making sure that every article of clothing matches (including mine). She is also an extremely loyal and caring friend and she is a person that goes out of her way to be fair. Sylvia is also not afraid to speak her mind without offending. She is also honest to a fault. In all of the years that I know her I can't ever remember her being late to any engagement or appointment.

Both of my sons are successful. Lee being an IT director for a well known accounting company and Barry a world class head shot photographer with studios in Manhattan. We are also blessed with two talented grandchildren; Mike and Dan. One is already at the University and the other in high school, both destined for successful careers.

I thank those who encouraged me to write this book and all of my friends who either participated in our at least laughed at the stories. A special thanks goes to Al Kravit who helped edit, structure the book and make many valuable corrections. This took countless hours and his dedication is appreciated. Thank you also to the editors of Createspace whose corrections and suggestions were virtually faultless. Hopefully you will enjoy reading this as much as I enjoyed writing it.

MY BEST FRIEND LOUIE

It was 1933, in the middle of the Depression. Sam, my father, had found out in October 1929 that his entire fortune was wiped out. He would need to liquidate his successful curtain-rod factory with six hundred employees to pay for the margin call.

Sam was a moderately religious Jew, he did not fit the stereotype of that period. And although he was born in the Fort Greene section of Brooklyn (on farmland with a pedestrian toll bridge going to their property), he spent some time up in Norman, Oklahoma. My father was an excellent horseman and could rope a steer. Otherwise, he was the gentlest person that I had ever known. He was also an expert on nature and animals, and he knew the Latin name of almost any tree or plant.

I am told that one day when I was very young, he took me on a trip to a small town outside of Norman, and he had me on his lap on the horse. Suddenly the horse stopped cold and refused to move. When I was old enough to understand and heard my father relate the story to friends, I learned that some animals, especially those that are domesticated, have a special sense of danger. When we got back to Norman, Dad's friends couldn't believe that we had survived the tornado that had leveled the town that were supposed to go to.

Although he studied medicine, he was offended by the crude practices of the medical profession at the time, especially what he perceived to be the uncaring treatment of children in the hospitals. Still, he had surgeon's hands and could slice meat or turkey paper thin. During World War II, he did volunteer work for the Red Cross, and he did research for DuPont. Dad was a superb fisherman and outdoorsman. On weekends he would take me to Kensico Reservoir in New York, where we would fish for bass. I even learned how to find and handle copperhead snakes, once bringing one home to my mother in the trunk of the car. I was saved from a beating, but Dad got yelled at.

Jeanne was my mother, and she had a sister and two brothers. One of her brothers came back from World War II, having survived the Battle of the Bulge and with no interest in going into the family business. Another brother, Sam, led an unbelievable life. At age twelve, Sammy was hit in the eye with a snowball that had traces of a diseased horse in it. This caused him to get horribly sick. He had set a record up to that time for the greatest number of diseases residing in one person's body. Although Sam survived the ordeal, his eyes and his eyesight were destroyed completely. With the support of his family, he graduated college, played the saxophone, married, and had three fine children. Sammy refused the use of a seeing eye dog, and he managed to get around with a cane. Eventually he opened up a newsstand on Forty-Eighth Street and Broadway in Manhattan. He ran this stand successfully for many years, traveling back and forth by subway to his home in the Bronx. He was a great fan of the Yankees baseball team, and he would sit in front of the TV set (why not the radio we never really knew), always claiming that he could out manage whoever the current manager was.

I was born on Henry Street in downtown Brooklyn, which today is quite an upscale neighborhood. Mom came here from Paris at the age of two, and Dad was born in Brooklyn. It was said that my grandparents had to leave Paris very quickly, as my mother had pushed a bottle of milk down from their second-floor windowsill, killing a horse standing in front of the building. They could be characterized as Roaring Twenties flappers.

My family's friends were truly international. They included people from Mexico, Syria, Lebanon, Hungary, Latvia, Ireland, and Italy, and my mother cooked in all languages. The Syrians especially came for her baked kibbe, which they said was better than they had had in Damascus.

The Metres family, whom I considered my aunt and uncle, was fascinating. Theresa was a living angel. Her father was a general in the Mexican army. She eloped with Jim Metres, who was from Syria, and the Mexican army chased them to the border. Uncle Jim would honor me in later years by allowing me to play pinochle with him and my father. Aunt Theresa made the best chicken mole, which, when made right, I love to this day.

During the Depression, my parents fed many a jobless and very poor family.

From there we moved to the Bronx, where my grandparents had a well-known appetizing store on Allerton Avenue (smoked lox, sturgeon, beluga caviar, homemade pickles in a barrel, fancy canned goods, and exotic candies and nuts). If I had been about five years older, I probably could have run my grandparents' appetizing store.

The pickle barrels were out front. When you entered the store, there was a long counter on the right with the lox, sturgeon, caviar, herrings, and pickled herring. The lox was sliced tissue-paper thin. Everything was the best. On the left side was a table with halvah and trays of exotic candies and nuts from all over the world. As you went toward the rear, there were cans of premium-brand sardines, anchovies, salmon, tuna, and chickpeas. The Peacock brand was wrapped in a fancy purple cellophane paper. In the rear were a large freezer and a room with a table and chairs for the extended family to eat.

Grandma prepared the pickles and pickled herring in the basement.

We lasted only a little over a year there because my mother found out the building was infested. Not by bugs or vermin, but by communists. So it was back to Brooklyn in a nice neighborhood in the Flatbush section. I was in the fifth grade, and PS 92 was around the corner. I remember a cool day when we were lined up in the school yard. The line was moving slowly (I've forgotten where we were going, but it was probably to register). This guy behind me started kicking me in the back of my shins every once in a while. Finally I turned around and glared at him, and he smiled and said: "Can't you talk?" So that was the beginning of our long friendship.

It turned out that Louie Dinolfo Jr. (Louis to his family) lived diagonally across from where we lived. His family had a house, and my family had a fifth-floor apartment.

Until I went off to college, we spent lots of time at each other's houses. We adored each other's families. At one point we put up a wire across Clarkson Avenue attached to tin cans so that we could talk to each other without phones.

We had lots in common, from baseball to getting in trouble—Louie was ALWAYS the instigator. In school I was in trouble from day one. Louie sat directly behind me and would manage to get me in trouble with our homeroom teacher, Ms. Breslin. There were large ink bottles to be used to fill the inkwells in the desks. (This was before the ball point pen era) Ms. Breslin loved her plants, which were near the windows to the left of our desks. Louie's idea was to have me pour the ink into the plant dirt, and he would warn me if the teacher turned around. So what did my friend do? He told me to go ahead just as she was staring down at me. Hell to pay. She marched me into the principal's office, and my mother was called.

My mother was the only person I feared on earth. In those days there was no such thing as "time out"; you got smacked. But even she had to laugh when Ms. Breslin shouted: "It's either HIM or ME who's leaving this school."

Things calmed a little bit, and although we were both Yankee fans, the Dodger stadium (Ebbets Field) was just a few blocks from where we lived. The bleachers were fifty-five cents, and sometimes a kind usher would let us sit in the grandstand. Even better, my synagogue (Judea Center) and his church (Holy Cross) gave out free tickets on alternate weeks. So first Louie and I lined up at Judea Center and got our tickets, and the next week we went to Holy Cross church.

Louie said that when the nun with the tickets came to me, I should ask her if we could get better seats. (It took me a while to learn that Louie always had something planned.)

The nun was in front of me. One hand was holding the tickets, and the other hand was holding a twelve-inch ruler. What in the world was she going to measure?

I smiled. "Sister. Is there any chance that we can get better seats?"

She gave me a fierce look that I can picture to this day. "Hold out your hands." WHACK! She slammed the ruler with that metal piece inserted (I guess to draw lines with) on my hands, and the stinging was unbelievable. I knew there and then that there was no way I would ever become a Catholic. The memories of the games that we saw were great, however.

After school, weather permitting, we played all kinds of ball games with a pink ball that we called a Spaldeen. A Spaldeen was a little smaller than a tennis ball, but it had a lot of bounce. It was especially effective when you played stoop ball, a game in which you threw the ball at the point of one of the steps on the stoop. That, along with marbles, hide-and-seek, and ringaleevio, Johnny on the pony, stickball, punchball, and others was what we enjoyed.

One day it was just the two of us playing stickball. Louie hit one over the fence into a yard (Louie was an excellent ball player). This little, mean-looking kid picked up the ball and put it into his pocket.

"Hey! Throw that ball back over here," we yelled.

"You want the ball? Come here and see if you can take it from me."

Well, he was kind of small, so it wouldn't take the two of us to get the ball back. (Of course, who do you think was egging me on?)

Now Louie and I were, of course, known in the neighborhood as two wild characters. Didn't this guy know that? We were now face to face. All of a sudden the blows were coming from out of nowhere. This little runt was beating the crap out of me. Louie was laughing hysterically.

We didn't get the ball, and I realized that street fighting was not boxing. I decided to take boxing lessons and eventually joined the Boys Club on Avenue A and Tenth Street in Manhattan in order to learn the art of boxing. Even though I was slow on my feet and my father and mother advised me against it, I paid them no mind. In fact, one night I came home from a match with a bandage over my right eye where I had received a cut. My mother was playing cards with her group. She looked up at me as I walked into the apartment, and she told her card group that she would be right back. Mom then stood up, motioned me to the bedroom, closed the door, and from the floor her hand came flying up and hit me across the face. As I went reeling across the bedroom, she then stated that my boxing career has just ended. And so it did.

Both Louie and I were great Babe Ruth fans. The Babe was dying of cancer, and he was giving a farewell speech at Yankee Stadium. It was a sunny mid-June day. Our seats were in the grandstand. His voice was pitiful, and his uniform hung sadly over what were once very broad shoulders. It was sad, but we were glad that we went. During our late lunch at a Chinese restaurant, we commiserated over the fact that despite his foibles, he would have made a great manager since he had an instinctive knowledge of the game and its players.

Louie and I had many adventures. The superintendent of our building was a mean Norwegian Nazi. There was a large table in the center of our apartment building, and Louie lifted one end and then let it down with a large bang. Mr. Nelson, the super, came running out and smacked me across the face.

We then did everything we could to torture him, from hitting him with snowballs and even getting our friend Sid Gordon (New York Giants), who was a famous ballplayer who lived across the street, to fire snowballs at his head, to turning over the garbage cans filled with used coal, which he brought from the basement.

When we were creating mischief, sometimes the police would chase us, but we knew every back alley and hiding place in the neighborhood. They never could catch us.

Louie got me fired once from my job delivering dry cleaning. He grabbed the clean clothes and dumped them into a garbage receptacle, so when I delivered the dry cleaning, it stank like you wouldn't believe. No surprise that I was immediately fired.

On Fridays I would load up on candy from the money that I had received as tips. There was this local candy store on the corner where were well known and friendly with the owner. One Friday Louie was bragging to the owner that I could eat a dozen ice-cream sundaes with nuts, whipped cream, and Fox's U-bet chocolate syrup. Joe, the owner, said that if I finished them within an hour, they would be free and I'd get a couple of dollars to boot.

Joe obviously didn't know whom he was dealing with. I finished them all with five minutes to spare. I wasn't feeling too well, but our crazy friend Fitz (Fitzpatrick) got so excited that he ran into the street (Bedford Avenue, a busy street) and was nearly was run over by a car. Amazingly, he ended up stretched out under the car, and he was unhurt. Eventually Lou would end up in the air force and I in the army.

Lou continued to hound me. We went to different high schools, Lou locally at Erasmus High School (where my sister Eleanor went) on Flatbush Avenue and I in Manhattan on East Fifteenth Street. Stuyvesant was and still is one of the best high schools in the country, graduating many famous scientists. Few who applied were taken, and it was then an all-male school, which never made any sense to me.

Lou had gotten me a job in the summers delivering wool in the garment district. It was a very boring job, but I loved the lunches: a fried egg and a minute steak on a Kaiser roll. Stuyvesant was rebuilt and moved uptown a few years ago. Ralph, a local friend, tells me that it was so filthy in those years that he couldn't take it, so he transferred to Seward Park High School in Lower Manhattan.

Talk about being filthy—Louie and I had a friend we called Fink. He wasn't much on bathing, and my mom barred him from getting any farther than the hallway of our apartment. Fink was a very strange guy, and if there was a radical cause, he was into it. Not surprisingly, he became a well-known radical in later years and also an accomplished photographer.

His dingy apartment was on the first floor, up the block from us. It had no AC, of course, and one summer the small TV was perched on their windowsill. Louie thought it would be great fun to set off a firecracker just behind the set. Somehow the Fink family didn't see that as fun.

Louie and I were never separated for long, and we went to all of each other's affairs—weddings, bar mitzvahs, christenings, etc. Louie flew down to Birmingham for my wedding, along with some other good friends at the time. And I remember commenting at his son's wedding that those in the church, outside of the wedding party, were dressed very casually. Louie explained that if they were too strict they would never get them back into the church.

He was always a very loyal friend. Louie supported me through some very, very tough events. When the games, tricks, and jokes were over, there was nothing that we wouldn't do for each other and our families. Louie was a hard worker and had the same job in the back room of a Wall Street firm for many years, but he was a very heavy smoker. Sadly, he contracted cancer and died very quickly, way before his time. It is a rare day that I don't think of him and his family. We know his lovely parents, aunts, and uncles, and we are to this day still in contact with his wife Mary and her family.

My dream then was to play baseball for the New York Yankees. I was on the Stuyvesant baseball team, but because of my working hours, my playing time was limited. I was a pitcher, partly because I was a very slow runner. But I did have a good fastball, though it was a little wild (actually a lot wild). I had been schooled by Pop Sekol, who ran the Ice Cream League. It was called the Ice Cream League because Pop would buy ice cream for the players on the winning team.

We played in the Parade Grounds in Prospect Park in Brooklyn. Many famous ballplayers played there. In fact, the famous Sandy Koufax pitched in Pop's league.

One late afternoon I was pitching. It was a tie game and due for extra innings. Pop was the umpire and wanted to stop the game because of darkness. After much convincing and cajoling, Pop agreed to let me pitch to one more man in order to get the final out. I decided to throw sidearm so the pitch would come out of the darkened shade. The poor hitter never flinched as the ball smashed into his elbow. That ended the game, and it was also the end of Bill in the Ice Cream League.

Years later we were both in the shoe business and Pop would tell stories at the shoe shows of Sandy Koufax or Bill Morgenstein's wild pitches.

Once every two or three weeks, if the weather was clear, I loved walking so I would walk from Clarkson Avenue in Brooklyn to East Fifteenth Street (near Union Square) in Manhattan. That was probably close to eight miles, and it took over two hours. It beat taking the crowded and smelly subways.

Besides gym, my favorite courses were history and chemistry. Shop class was fun until the teacher threw what I had labored on at me. He thought it resembled a penis (I forgot what it was supposed to be).

Of course I got into trouble in chemistry. We had been given a project regarding "household dangers in the kitchen."

I like to experiment and discovered that if you mixed a brass cleaner call Noxon with Clorox, you released hydrogen, which was explosive. So when the teacher (he was a PhD in chemistry no less) called on me and I explained this, he laughed and said it was nonsense.

I then proceed to pour the Noxon into a beaker of Clorox. BOOM! Nobody got hurt, but we did have to evacuate the classroom. Now was that my fault?

My two buddies Mike and Schneiderman (we called him Abercrombie, but don't ask me why) figured out how to make smaller explosions without those cumbersome materials. We learned about sodium. Sodium is a soft metal that can be cut like cheese. If exposed to air, it burns. If put in water, after a few minutes it produces a small hydrogen explosion. We found a chemical store on Canal Street in Chinatown that sold it by the pound. They kept it in oil in large jars.

First we took it to Prospect Park Lake, cut off pieces, and flipped them into the water. Explosions all over the place.

When the cops arrived, we acted very innocent. "You damn kids playing with firecrackers?"

"No, officer. We don't have any firecrackers."

"What's in dat jar?"

"That's cheese, officer."

"Well, if youse kids see anyone with firecrackers find us and tell us."

OK, so now we had a plan for school. After you drop the sodium in the water, it takes about thirty to forty seconds for the hydrogen to separate from the oxygen. Then the reaction heats up, and the hydrogen explodes.

That gave us enough time to put about eight small slices of sodium in the men's room and get out into the hall undetected. We blew up about eight toilets that day, and the whole school had to be evacuated.

Otherwise, I did well in school. And I ended up with a Gold PSAL medal for athletics, although with my oversized flat feet, I wasn't a great athlete.

I failed Latin, not only because I told Dr. Coyle that it was not a spoken language and it was useless, but he caught me looking over at another student during the finals. He gave me a grade of 27.

The prom was nice, as Blossom was my first official date.

Louie had previously fixed me up with Bea C (name changed to protect the innocent) on a blind date. My god, was she ugly, and Louie's was no better. We resorted to plan B. We met the girls in front of the BMT subway station and were supposedly going to go to Manhattan, but when the train pulled up on the other side of the platform, Louie and I ditched them and jumped in just before the doors closed and had ourselves a good laugh.

We had other diversions, of course, such as harassing the communist speakers in Union Square (famous for weirdo speakers, jugglers, and clowns, both intentional and unintentional). Also we would cut school to see Frank Sinatra at the Brooklyn Paramount. I participated in a school strike organized by the coaches because the city or the school wanted to cut their extra curriculum pay. That made the *New York Daily News*, with a picture of someone my mother said was me in front of the march— for which I got a beating when I got home. I also witnessed my first fatal stabbing that day (glad it wasn't me). I never did find out why the fight started.

Bob Malach lived across the street, and we formed our first company—the M & M Fixit Men. We cleaned and repaired venetian blinds. Although we managed to secure a few jobs, this venture lasted only a few months, mostly due to Bob's decision to join the army and my clumsy lack of mechanical aptitude. I even get flustered walking into a hardware store. If I have to hammer a nail, I will invariably smash my thumb, and if I have to use a screwdriver, my lack of patience makes it an exercise in failure.

I managed to get a job as an usher in the Patio Theatre on Flatbush Avenue in Brooklyn. Before minimum wage was put in, there were many jobs that no longer exist, such as ushers and elevator operators.

In addition to the movies, the Patio had shows with some good comedians, such as Lord Buckley, and famous singers. My favorite (whom we were to become friendly with years later when she bought shoes in my wife's store) was Kitty Kallen.

There was a long fire escape on the side of the building, and I would leave the side balcony door open so that my friends could sneak in.

That wasn't why I got fired, though. One day the manager wanted me to check out the competition, and he gave me money to buy two tickets at the famous Kings Theatre on Flatbush Avenue, near Church Avenue. The idea was to buy a ticket around 11:00 a.m., when they opened, and then another one around 6:00 p.m. Since I wanted to play stickball, I decided to buy the two tickets at once. It was a pretty stupid thing to do, but I did it. I was fired the moment I turned the tickets in.

ACCEPTED TO THE
UNIVERSITY OF ALABAMA

I had been accepted to Brooklyn College, NYU, Oklahoma University, and the University of Alabama. My dad suggested that I go to an out-of-town school in order to meet different cultures and get a broader look on life. He had heard that 'Bama' had a good commerce school. Since their baseball team was pretty good and I was interested in business, this was the place to go. It turned out that because I had to work to defray some of the costs, playing on a college team was out.

'Bama' was quite a place, with the only disadvantage and downside being that it was still the totally segregated South. The policy was mean, uncalled for, and downright stupid. 'Bama' wasn't integrated until the sixties, but the year of my graduation, there was an informal poll in which the student body voted 50.4 percent to 49 percent segregation. (Autherine Lucy enrolled in January, 1956 and then was promptly dismissed after segregationist rioting)

My courses in banking and finance, although not up to the status of Wharton, were very much acceptable. There were also some very interesting courses in journalism (which I have to wonder today whether many so-called journalists take) and criminology. Our class toured all of the Alabama prisons and found that every inmate was completely "innocent" and needed a few bucks for a better lawyer.

This was not only noted as a fun school socially (which it certainly was), but it was also noted for its sophisticated practical jokes, such as the time we convinced a student that the New York militia had attacked the New Jersey militia. First there were whispers in class, then some flyers, and then fake radio broadcasts. There was no CNN or Fox News then. Johnny, the victim, was warned that until hostilities ceased, he should not make any outgoing telephone calls. Poor Johnny took this very hard, as his family was in New Jersey. Taking pity, they designated a group to take him to the "Little Cookie", which was a small hangout restaurant in Tuscaloosa, and break the news that it was all a clever hoax.

Hoagy Carmichael was coming to stay at the Delta Kappa Epsilon house (very snotty and traditional). Word was sent to the DKE fraternity that he would arrive by train on a Saturday. Actually Hoagy arrived on a Friday, and Sigma Alpha Mu fooled him into thinking that they were the DKE fraternity picking him up. They plied him with drinks at their fraternity house, which had fake banners with DKE on them. He entertained and played the piano all weekend. By the time that DKE found out, he had to return to the train station. Since Sigma Alpha Mu was almost all Yankee, we almost had another Civil War.

At the time this was my fraternity, but I was thrown out not too long after because I knocked our master (president) cold because he was an arrogant bully and wise guy. But that's jumping ahead.

It was my freshman year, and we were getting ready for the prom. I didn't have a date yet, but I had my eye on a very pretty, young, typical-looking Southern belle who had the pick of any of the football players (which I obviously I was not). At the frat house, there was lots of bantering going on, including teasing and asking me when I was going to get a date for the prom. My cocky response was that I could get any girl on the campus to go out with me. There was lots of laughter. They then asked, "How about Fannie? She's one of the prettiest on the campus. In fact, we have her number if you have the nerve to call her."

I responded that sure, I would call. We had these dial phones that made a clicking sound as it spun around. Wow, I was delighted that she answered.

"Fannie, this is Bill Morgenstein from the "Sammy" house, and it would be my honor to escort you to the prom weekend."

At first there was a scary silence, and then she asked if I was the one who wore Western plaid shirts on campus.

"Yes, that's me."

She responded, "Oh, I'd be happy to go out with you."

I rushed downstairs to shout to the guys: "I got the date because you see, fellows, you just don't know who you are dealing with here."

My dear friend Abercrombie, who by the way was the ringleader, said that it was not proper to take a girl to a prom weekend without dating her first. That was fine with me, and I then made the date with Fannie. Since he had a car, we picked a weekend night for the date. I was in the back, and he picked up his date at one of the female dorms (remember, this was the fifties).

We had decided on a quiet restaurant off campus from which we could adjourn to Hurricane Creek, which was the local necking area. Necking in those days was kissing, petting, and not usually much more. So we went to pick up Fannie at her dorm. The rules were very strict: you had to check in at the front with the housemother, who then called for the girl to come downstairs. I was expecting a luscious beauty, but what did I get? OMG! Even from a distance, this girl was a fright.

Now I saw their plan, but I was trapped. Well, at least the restaurant would be quiet. For a few minutes, the four of us were alone…and then out of nowhere, the door busted open, and a bunch of my fraternity brothers arrived. They explained what a coincidence it was and said I should introduce them to our dates. I don't remember how the meal tasted, but this was far from having fun.

Now we were back in Abercrombie's auto, and I begged him not to go to Hurricane Creek. This was fun for him, and besides, he had a pretty girl in the front seat. We got to the creek, which was in the woods, and suddenly Fannie grabbed me and hugged me. Even in the dark, I noticed that she had one brown eye and one blue eye. Worse, she had horrible bad breath. Truly a nightmare.

We finally dropped them off and returned to the frat house, where everyone was laughing hysterically. After a little calm, I said: "OK guys, you had your fun, but you can't expect me to take this dog to the prom!"

They made it clear that I had no choice since once I made the commitment, I couldn't dishonor the fraternity or the brothers. It was two weeks to the prom weekend, and I was going out of my mind.

When the day came, I felt as sick as if I had food poisoning. What to do? Of course Abercrombie was going to be the driver, and I was going to be in the backseat again with the "human hog"…and for a whole weekend. We arrived at the Cotillion Room at the hotel in Tuscaloosa, and I headed for the punchbowl, which, unbeknownst to the university officials who were in attendance, was grandly spiked.

In any case, I had already polished off a flask of bourbon that I had in my jacket pocket. I had to be polite, so I danced with Fannie. This was torture, sheer torture, looking at her mismatched eyes and enduring her horrible breath.

I spotted an older couple dancing, and it turned out to be the university dean, Noble Hendrix, and his wife (both eyes matched, by the way). I cut in and twirled her around the dance floor. Those who saw this opened their mouths, and they were flabbergasted.

The dean was standing there grinning when my frat brothers rescued me (or his wife, not sure which) and dragged me away. "You've got to spend more time with your date—HONOR," they growled. What followed was fuzzy in my mind.

If you remember the movie *The Lost Weekend*, you can imagine what was next. I was bamboozled out of my mind. I remember that I was trying to make conversation with a very attractive girl named Laura. I didn't know it at the time, but she was a real gold digger and a bitch.

I don't remember much else, but I was told that when we got to Hurricane Creek, to continue the partying, I jumped off the dock into the water—tuxedo, high hat, and all. When we finally got back to the frat house, the brothers congratulated me for being a great sport and a real gentleman.

It wasn't over yet, however. I was getting ready for class on Monday morning and went to shave. Taped to the mirror was a large photo of me with my arms around Fannie, which I tore to shreds. But when I went to each class, every door had our picture taped to the front of it. It was unbelievable how they had pulled this off, so I decided to have lunch in town. You guessed it: the picture was on the front window of Katzenhiemer's Deli (where I was planning to eat), and also on half of the store windows in town. Luckily, Tuscaloosa was then a rather small town.

Herb Morris was the master of Sigma Alpha Mu Fraternity, and he was a bullying, arrogant guy. I was resting on the couch, and he started picking on me. After a while, I got fed up. We had a fight. It seems that if you get into a fight with the fraternity president, you get thrown out of that fraternity. I was summarily bounced. That, of course, was before I became a member of AE Pi and had the incident I related previously.

After the Sigma Alpha Mu disaster, I started dating this lovely Southern belle, Sylvia, whom I met at the "Supe" store (supplies and coffee on campus). I married her while we were both at the University of Alabama, and we have remained married for over sixty years. Sylvia had previously gone to the University of Miami, where she says the "pickings" were not too good. Morris, her father, said that he didn't want to waste any more money and that she was to do some serious studying at Alabama. I guess she did for another year until she met me, and we got married.

Meeting Sylvia

I nstead of living in the dorm or the fraternity, I shared a room off campus on Seventh Avenue in Tuscaloosa with my roommate, Sy. Sy had been a classmate in Stuyvesant who latched on to me. He was unsophisticated and came from a very poor family, but he was a decent, friendly guy. My family helped them with the college application, transportation arrangements, and shopping for clothes, as both he and his family were completely lost.

The Ruggles, who were our landlords, couldn't have been nicer. They rented us a long attic room with a small adjoining bathroom. I kept a BB rifle in the room and took target practice on a wooden board in front of the attic window. One day I come back from class and saw my favorite bright-yellow silk shirt in front of the board by the window, full of holes. I was naturally furious beyond words, so I dumped his clothes outside the door and locked it. I guess we weren't too close after that.

After the Fannie debacle, I met a cultured, high-class, attractive young lady by the name of Sylvia. She was born and bred in Birmingham, and she had just transferred from the University of Miami. We had a couple of nice dates, and then she informed me that she was going to New York for the summer and that perhaps we could meet somewhere. It was a bit of a dilemma, as I had a job lined up as a counselor at a summer camp in Pennsylvania. Hey, what the hell. I could always get a job in New York, so I agreed that we would meet.

I did land a job as a soda jerk in a Walgreen's on Eighty-Sixth Street in Manhattan. In those days Woolworth's and Walgreens had soda fountains. I was enjoying the job, and my section was always the busiest because my customers knew that I made the ice cream sundaes with extra whipped cream and an extra cherry.

One day the district manager came waltzing in and told me that since everything was "portion controlled," I must follow the protocol. To no avail I tried to explain that my extra little bit of whipped cream was bringing the customers back. El Jerko left, and in two days he was back. My corner was filled with customers with sundaes piled high with whip cream. Guess what? I was fired on the spot.

Sylvia was staying with a cousin from Jasper, Alabama, who had an apartment on Bank Street in the Village. Maybe it's an exaggeration, but I like to say that she chased me all over New York. Anyway, we had a delicious Italian dinner in a little trattoria in Greenwich Village and sat on the stoop in front of the apartment (no air conditioning). Sylvia then proceeded to plan out our whole life together, including where we were going to get married (Birmingham), number of children (two), and many other uncanny things that ended up coming true.

This was getting serious, so I thought it might be a good idea for my folks to meet her. I told my mother, who was hoping it would be a nice Jewish girl, and she invited her for a Friday-night Sabbath dinner. This would be Sylvia's first introduction to Brooklyn.

The traditional meal consisted of the usual chicken soup, noodles, kasha (buckwheat), and boiled chicken. All went very well, as they all hit it off quite nicely. Later Sylvia would write a glowing letter telling Mom how much she had enjoyed the food and the family (half of that was true).

When I told my parents that we wanted to get married even though we were barely eighteen, my mom asked my grandparents what they thought and what their advice would be. When my grandparent reminded my mom that they were fifteen when they got married, that settled that.

Anyway, sometime after our marriage, Sylvia told Mom the truth. She hated boiled chicken and was no big fan of chicken soup (today she does like the Vietnamese version, pho ga). For years afterward, Mom would pull out the letter that Syl wrote, and we would all have a good laugh.

So the wedding was on. This being the Deep South, there were twenty-seven engagement parties for Sylvia, and we finally got married on June 8 at the Fairmont Club in Mount Brook, Alabama. It was a very hot, humid day, and I was in an itchy wool suit, no less. It was a large wedding, and then we were off to our honeymoon in Miami.

One of Syl's rich cousins lent us his Cadillac convertible. The first hotel we went to had nasty help. I remember that even the valet was nasty, so when we left, I gave him two pennies, which he flung at us.

The stay at the Shore Club was much better. When we went back for our Fiftieth Anniversary, it was redone and completely unrecognizable. We asked for our old rates, which they thought was quite humorous. We settled for a bottle of champagne.

On our honeymoon we did have good food, fun shows, and nice weather. Then we flew back to Tuscaloosa, where we rented an apartment for forty-plus dollars a month. We always did like going back to Miami, and in later years, we went there with our kids and our dear friends Gary and Jackie.

Jackie was Sylvia's friend from her childhood days. Gary was from Atlanta and was a big, jolly fellow. He had a funny answer to everything. Once in a restaurant, a waiter asked him if there were people with him (we were all standing next to him). His response was "These really aren't people, but they are camels in disguise." Another time, we went with the kids to the Rascal

House in Miami. No matter what time you arrived, day or night, the line stretched around the corner. The line finally got to the front of the restaurant, and we got in. Gary looked around and said to the maître d", "This place is filthy."

The maître d', who was a tall dude with a mustache, looked up and said, "Isn't it," then turned and walked away.

Gary and Jackie owned a real-estate company in Atlanta. They had hired mutual friend, Frank Rockstroh. Frank was a genius and could do, plan, or invent anything, except nothing ever worked out. Luckily, his wife Erica was a school principal, or they would have been lost. The purpose of Gary's hiring Frank was for Frank to sell for their real-estate company. Although Frank received leads, he never sold anything. Gary liked to call him his "star" salesman.

When we got back to Tuscaloosa, after our honeymoon our friends and fraternity brothers would come over to what was for them a unique setting. One day they thought that they would needle me by telling me a story of a young lady who was sent to the fraternity as a gift from one AE Pi fraternity chapter to another. The young lady arrived at the frat house in Tuscaloosa and exhausted the members. After three days they sent her on to the frat house at Ole Miss (I never knew how they got this past the housemother).

One day we had some of our friends over. They were cousins from a small Alabama town called Summit. They hadn't spoken to each other for a number of years. Our job was to bring them back together and end the feud. Everything was going magically well when I gave them a cigarette that I had (although I really wasn't a cigarette smoker). I had forgotten that I had placed what we called a punk charge in some of the cigarettes, as a joke to play on some unsuspecting victim. Without thinking, I innocently gave the pack of loaded cigarettes to the cousin. I then suggested that he give a cigarette to his "kissing cousin" as a peace offering. It was peaceful, all right. It blew up in her face. No amount of explaining or apologizing could bring them back together again, and of course Sylvia didn't talk to me for days, thinking I had done that on purpose.

Sylvia had a very close cousin in Florence, Alabama, who was married to a very fastidious person. They had just bought a white carpet, and when we arrived at their home, I was ready for some fun. I had told Syl what I was planning, and she saw no harm in having some fun with her stiff cousin's husband. I had brought my bag of items that I had purchased from the local "joke" store. First was the inkblot. The dark blue spot on the white rug sent Shirley's husband Bill into a panic. Dinner was served on fine China, so when they heard the crash (metal plates that sounded like dishes), both Shirley and Bill screamed. Finally, when I put the ice cube with the fly in the drink that was too much for Bill to take. He immediately retired to his bedroom.

Syl and I never saw him again, as they were divorced not long afterward. It seems that Shirley had a wreck in their new car. Bill rushed to the scene, but instead of inquiring about Shirley's health, he wanted to know how much damage there was to the car. Shirley later married George, an oil man from Kansas who was related to Ken Stabler, the famous football quarterback. We all met them one night in Manhattan and I remembered George having the waiter line up six shots of bourbon, and then downing them all in a matter of minutes. The guests in the surrounding tables couldn't help but notice since George was wearing a tall cowboy hat, all during dinner.

ROTC

The university used to put on shows, and the best entertainer was a singer with a marvelous voice and comedian by the name of Jim Nabors, whom you know, of course, as Gomer Pyle. Jim had trouble with his accounting and needed at least a C to graduate. Jim asked me to tutor him in accounting, which I did. He came over our house for a couple of evenings, received a C, and was graduated.

While he was at the house, we asked Jim what he was going to do after graduation. He said that he was going to become a big Hollywood star. Laughing to ourselves, we asked how he intended to do that. Well, he said, one of two ways: his aunt was a well-known costume designer for the stars, and with her influence, she could help him. The other way was that he would just work at various clubs until he was discovered. Again, we laughed—to ourselves, but the laugh was on us because he ended up doing just that and more. He had asthma and moved to California and then Hawaii, where he became rich by growing Macadamia nuts. It was a long road from Sylacauga, Alabama, to *The Andy Griffith Show*.

Two other famous people (whom I know of) went to the university at the same time. There was Gay Talese, the famous author, whom I seem to remember being very well dressed. Gay went on to do some fine writing. I particularly liked his stories about Joe DiMaggio and Frank Sinatra. Then there was Bart Starr, the football player. Bart was famous at the Green Bay Packers, but I don't remember him being that exceptional at Alabama except for his performance in one of the bowl games and the fact that he was a good kicker until he hurt his back punting.

The University of Alabama was a Reserve Officers Training Corps (ROTC) school. You selected whether you wanted to enroll in the air force or army, and if you passed the four years of military courses and was graduated, you received a commission in the branch that you picked. I chose the air force, and later on, that turned out to be the wrong choice.

History and especially military history intrigued me, and although I did well in the courses and made A's in the military subjects, I didn't like the regimentation or the rules and was not fond of following orders. Twice a week we had to attend and march in full dress marches with the military band and "pass in review". I hated that uniform, as it was made from heavy, itchy wool. The whole experience was a royal pain. The only break came when the weather was bad. Then there was a good chance that they would call off the march; however, every so often regular noncoms wouldn't announce it until after we got to the parade ground.

As with many of the typical military systems, common sense was not the order of the day. During one particularly cold and wet week, I got completely fed up and decided to find my own way to cancel the march and the parade. Early on the day of the parade, I called the "officer of the day" (regular air force) and said the following in a very gruff voice: "This is Captain Rogers. I happen to be aide-de-camp to General Dykema" (the general in charge of the Air Force ROTC throughout the entire country; he was stationed at Maxwell Air Force base in Montgomery, Alabama, about one hundred miles from Tuscaloosa).

That seemed to wake him up. "YES SIR. What can I do for you, sir?" the lieutenant responded.

"Where the hell were you guys this morning?"

Now he was stuttering. "What, sir? What do you mean?"

I responded, "Didn't you get our telegram? The general flew into Tuscaloosa Airport (a very small airport at the time), and there was no honor guard to meet him. In fact, NOBODY (screaming) was there, and the general was so pissed that he got into his plane and flew back to Maxwell!"

At first there was stunned silence, and I heard some unintelligible mumbling, which I suspected was him talking to someone else while covering his mouth. "Sir," he said, "we never received a telegram, and we deeply apologize, so what can we do?"

"Lieutenant, I want you to assemble all regular military in full dress uniform with medals. No ROTC personnel at the airport, and cancel all ROTC activities for the day, including any scheduled parades. I'll see if I can get the general to fly back. And remember, we don't want to see any ROTC cadets on the field."

"YES, SIR. It will be taken care of."

The announcement was made: "Today's parade is canceled, and the cadets are informed not to come to the parade grounds."

Now I was reflecting on what I had done, and I was too scared to go to the airport for obvious reasons. The next day the campus was abuzz. Remember, 'Bama likes a good practical joke. Apparently every regular officer and sergeant got into his dress uniform, went to the airport, and stood at attention in the pouring rain for two hours waiting for General Dykema to arrive. Arrive he didn't. No general. So now this very bright regular air force officer sent a telegram to General Dykema in Montgomery expressing their sorrow at not being at the airport earlier that morning, and not only that, they begged for him to return to Tuscaloosa.

We later found out that the general received this, and he was absolutely furious. We didn't know his exact words, but they were pretty damn raw. He was very sure that that the officers had been on some kind of drinking binge and that they all must have been drunk out of their minds. He called the base and threatened every one of the officers with a court martial. In their mind, the general was angry because of the missing telegram and the fact that they had not been at the airport.

Everyone wanted to know who had pulled this off. There were those on campus who wanted to congratulate the person, and there were those in the military who wanted to hang the person. For the next few weeks, I was absolutely scared to death every time the phone rang (thank the Lord there was no caller ID to trace my original call). Any time my name was called when we were in formation, and every time an officer or regular NCO looked at me cross eyed, I thought it was over. I was a complete nervous wreck, with only my wife to comfort me, as I knew that if I was caught, I would not only be discharged from the AF ROTC but thrown out of the university—if I wasn't first hanged by the officers. Until sometime later, I didn't even dare mention it to my fraternity brothers at AE Pi. Luckily, with all of the investigating, they never did find the perpetrator.

Opening a Business

The studies went on, and after no repercussions from the General Dykema incident, we agreed to ease the imposition of our parents supporting us. We decided to open up a business. Jack Hirsch was our good friend from Atlanta. Just a side note: In the mid-fifties, the populations of Atlanta and Birmingham were close to the same. The Birmingham Airport Authority placed a high tax on plane landings, while the Atlanta airport reduced their taxes. Of course, the rest is history. Atlanta swelled, and Birmingham remained stagnant. Anyway, Jack had just become the youngest CPA in Georgia's history, and he came on to become a silent partner and help us with the details of setting up a new company. Jack and Gladys had been recently married, and Gladys, who is a sweetheart of a woman, is still carrying on strong today. Sadly Jack passed away a few years ago.

Jack arrived on a brutally hot night. Of course, we had no air conditioning and discovered that instead of lying on the couch, Jack was sound asleep in the bathtub. Afraid he might drown, we immediately woke the poor guy up. Our plans continued throughout the night.

Now it turned out that the big problem was that we were planning to open up a telephone answering service. In order to do that, the extension system and paired lines had to be within a short distance of the Southern Bell) phone company. The manager of the office was a man by the name of Mr. Plant (no joke). He was not at all cooperative, the reason being that he wanted to open up a telephone answering system himself. He insisted that the location would have to be within a quarter mile of the phone company on University Avenue, and there was nothing available that he knew of. We left his office and stopped for a bite at Pete's Restaurant. Until Pete's closed, it was a landmark for students for many years. We met with Pete and told him of our dilemma.

Pete smiled and said that he had great news for us. He owned apartments in the back of the store. The third floor was vacant, and it was just yards from the phone company building. Pete had a simple lease form, which we signed forthwith.

We ran to Mr. Plant, who was obviously irritated and not at all happy. (What happened to Southern hospitality?) He very reluctantly agreed to install the extensions that we needed, but it was apparent that he wanted this for himself and made sure that we were constantly harassed by the phone company.

One of our customers was an American Indian couple who equally hated the phone company. One night they invited Syl and me for dinner. The portions were enormous, as they were pretty large people themselves. They had large extra freezers in the back of their house. Imagine steamed potatoes piled a couple of feet high, with tremendous steaks. And for dessert we had a half-gallon bucket of ice cream for each of us. They finished theirs, but we didn't, although I came close.

Anyway, we agreed that the only revenge that we could impose, since lawsuits were not in vogue in those days, was to bring wheelbarrows loaded with pennies to pay the bill. The law at the time was that you couldn't refuse legal currency when offered. When the phone company objected, we reminded them of this and took great glee when they had to count out the pennies. We enjoyed watching the chaos as extra young ladies were brought from the back to help with the counting. I'm pretty sure that we heard the muffled voice of Mr. Plant growling in the background.

Being new to the business world, we were not very sophisticated in vetting our employees. Our training program was mostly verbal and lasted a couple of hours, and since we had a night shift, we put up signs in order to help guide the operators on how to answer the phones. One sign, for example, read: "Good morning; this is Dr. Cronkite's office. How may we help you?"

One of the operators was on duty at 11:00 p.m., and when she received calls, she would say, "Good morning." When we questioned her, she responded that that was what it said on the card.

We had another young man who turned out to be insane. He sadly ended up at Bryce Mental hospital in Tuscaloosa. Besides cursing some of the callers, he was making obscene calls to nurses at the local hospital. We visited him in the hospital, and we felt sorry for him. Johnny apologized profusely, saying that he was sorry. He appeared calm and spoke normally, but when he asked us when he could come back to work, we left the hospital quickly, shaking our heads.

As the proud owners of Prompt Answering Service, we did some local advertising and had a folded brochure made stating that phone answering was done by direct extension: "When your phone rings, your extension line rings in our office. We file the name and phone number of each call to you and keep them on file for your future reference. We can also sell for you, locate you in emergencies, take messages, accept credit applications, and dispatch your servicemen. All at a price that you won't believe."

We also had a wake-up service, which had me waking up in the middle of the night making phone calls.

This went on for a number of months, but between the phone company's harassment and the fact that we had a hard time collecting our monthly fees from those who were friendly but apparently in bad financial shape, we had to close Prompt Answering Service. It was sometimes fun while it lasted, and we certainly got an education in business and human nature.

31

So as I indicated before, if the Southern Bell harassment had happened some years later and we had gotten a hold of a fine attorney, this would have been a different story. We probably could have sued them for millions and collected. We also heard later on that Mr. Plant had opened up a telephone answering service of his own and that he was doing quite well with it.

SALES TUTOR

M oe was a friend at school, and one day he approached me and asked if we could find a way to make some money. We had been going to the hospital every month and selling a pint of our blood for twenty dollars. A glass of orange juice, a little rest, and you were fine. Moe was a nice, simple guy. He was honest and the type of person you liked immediately. He knew nothing about selling, but he was in my opinion a quick learner.

That same week, I was sitting on a bench in an area of the campus that was called the quadrangle. This was the center of the campus, where you could congregate or simply walk to class. Picture this thin, pockmarked guy coming up to me and explaining that he had invented a revolutionary sterling silver cleaner. I called him "Slim", and since he had a carton of bottles with him, which he called No Dip, and since it had a pretty good odor, I took a dozen bottles, along with his phone number in case I sold all of them.

When I showed the No Dip to Moe, he seemed a little bewildered. So I told Moe to just watch me, and he would learn some selling techniques (which actually I was yet to learn). Now, in those days, you went from door to door, and people were generally friendly, especially in the South. We picked a decent-looking, tree-lined street, and at the first house that we hit, a nice-looking housewife answered the door. We were in luck!

I started my spiel: "Mrs. Johnson, we have a revolutionary product that cleans your silverware. May we demonstrate it? It will clean all of your sterling, and there will be no charge and no obligation on your part."

Mrs. Johnson proceeded to take us to her silverware cabinet, which was a fancy felt-lined box. There lay the blackened, tarnished silver. I proceeded to open a jar of No Dip, and both Moe and I were rubbing, rubbing, rubbing. Nothing was happening. The silver was the same as when we had started. Moe gave me that scared-to-death look.

I laughed and asked Mrs. Johnson, who was watching us with a curious, quizzical look on her face, "Mrs. Johnson, do you have any Noxon in the house?" Noxon was a silver polish cleaner that was sold in the grocery stores.

She looked under the sink in a cabinet, and lo and behold, she found a jar of Noxon. We then proceeded to polish all of her silverware and did a fairly nice job of it. Our lovely housewife obviously felt sorry for us and bought two jars of our revolutionary silver cleaner.

"You see, Moe, I told you that selling was easy."

Moe went back to his studies. I knew that a career change was necessary, so I answered a help-wanted ad for a chain-link fence salesman (ads were not gender neutral then). The company was the Alabama Fence Company, and Bob Shockley was the owner. Bob hired me and explained in his thick, Alabama, real-country-boy (which he certainly was) accent that he was going to teach me the chain-link fence business. That included measuring, installing, digging fence-post holes, anchoring and cementing the ends, and stretching the chain link over the posts. Most importantly, selling chain link fences, which would be the most interesting part.

Bob was short, stocky, and solidly built, with a perpetual smile on his face. He wore a checkered shirt and always had a large cowboy hat on. Ready to go. We got into Bob's old Chevy, and off we went. I was to just watch Bob and learn and ask questions only after the sale was made (he was quite confident). After all, I was sitting next to the best fence salesman in the entire world (and so he was). He caught me grinning, so in order to prove his point, he said that while he was driving, I should point to any house, and he would proceed to sell the occupants a fence.

Since there was FHA financing available at the time, even for home improvements such as fencing, and since FICO wasn't even invented then, it took little if any cash to make the purchase. Now, you know that I wasn't going to let this opportunity pass, and when I saw a dilapidated house, I told Bob to stop so I could get my laugh of the day in. "Bob, let's see if you can make this sale," I said in a half-fit of laughter.

We screeched to a halt, and I was thrown forward since seat belts had not been invented yet. I got out and walked to the front door, which had large holes in it. I could see clear out to the backyard. We knocked on the door, and I commented that if we were to sell the fence, it would be worth more than the whole house, excluding the land.

This didn't bother Mr. Shockley, but then nothing really did. A woman in an old-fashioned print housecoat opened the door. With a dramatic flourish, Mr. S stepped back. She invited us into the dusty, dingy house and made another dramatic gesture.

Mr. Shockley grabbed his large hat from the top with his oversized hand and dropped it in the center of the living room on the soiled floor. I was thinking, is this guy nuts?

What had I gotten myself into? We were seated in two large rocking chairs, and he proceeded to explain to this woman why we were there. He saw her two lovely children playing in the back…(a prolonged silence) and that made him extremely sad. If you looked closely, there was a tear in Mr. S's eye. The poor woman was a little bewildered, and she offered us a glass of water, and of course she wanted to know what was making Bob so sad.

He responded: "Well, ma'am, I happen to be in the fence business, and just last week, I went to a home just like yours on Highway 78 near Leeds, Alabama, and that poor family felt that they couldn't afford a fence. Don't know if you read last week's Birmingham News about the two young kids who were killed on Highway 78?"

The poor woman didn't know where to sign first for a fence all around the house, and yes, the fence was worth almost as much as the appraised value of the house. I was stunned, but I still needed to know why he had acted the way he did.

Bob explained as follows: "When you knock on a door and a woman answers, you must know that a woman is very protective of her house and family. Most salespeople push forward, and the woman will resist; however, a woman being naturally curious, when I stepped backward to move forward, she wanted to see what I was carrying."

"What about the hat on the floor?"

"Dropping the hat that sits on your head shows that you respect the woman's housekeeping, and that gives her the confidence to trust you."

Bob taught me many things about selling and human nature, and I did well with him. That is, until one day when I got a lead in Mountain Brook, which was a ritzy suburb "over the mountain," as it was called, with some of the finest and prettiest residential areas in the country. Mrs. J wanted a chain-link fence. Her house was really gorgeous, but you had to walk up a hill with a lot of steps. I made it up the steps and knocked on the door, and then I was absolutely stunned. I laugh every time I think of this. A tall, funny (only way to describe her face)—and I mean funny-looking—older woman with a long, meaty, pockmarked nose and face opened the door.

I stood there dumbstruck, afraid that I would go into paroxysms of laughter. So before I completely cracked up, I waved at her, got back down the stairs, and waited while I composed myself. I just couldn't. Every time I started to climb the stairs,

I started laughing until there were tears in my eyes. Once I got near the door again, I was afraid that Mrs. J would come out.

On the fifth try, I gave up, went back to the office, and quit the job. That ended my chain-link-fence selling career.

We were going to drive to Brooklyn, to visit my folks, anyway, as summer was about to arrive. Our first car was a '48 Dodge. This was the first car with fluid drive, but I didn't find out how to use it until about two weeks before I sold it, when I finally realized that it was possible to take your foot off the clutch without the car stalling.

We were taking along a couple of fraternity brothers to possibly share in the driving, and we were going to drop them off in Newark, New Jersey. This was before the Eisenhower east-west, north-south highway express system was built. There were a few four-lane highways but no freeways or superhighways yet. There were mostly two-lane roads, so if you drove without stopping, it was about a twenty-six-hour trip. Also, there was no air conditioning, so every time we stopped for gas, we'd wet our towels, and while driving; I would hang my left arm out of the car with the towel over it. That lasted about an hour, after which the towel was dry and I would be sweating again. The dust was awful, especially if we were on a dirt road.

We were young, so we had a good time, and we laughed at silly things. At one point we came to an area where they were repairing the road. We were sitting and sitting, and we noticed that there wasn't too much traffic going the other way. Every once in a while a car would come, and this guy would wave the oncoming car through. Blowing the horn didn't help, so my friend Sandy got out and strolled over to this guy and said: "Shay, shonny, you guys ain't too shmart. How about letting the young'uns through." They looked around, shrugged, and let us through.

Gas was probably twenty cents a gallon, and they washed your windshield front and back and checked your oil. A bottle of Coke (no cans) and a burger were about a dollar. Summer driving was hot, and winter driving was foggy and treacherous. When you finally got to your destination, you were completely exhausted, but you were sure glad to get there. My parents were happy to see us arrive completely safe. After resting a bit, we went out and celebrated at a good Chinese restaurant.

Graduating and Going to Work in Hillbilly Country

I was finishing my studies, and I was getting ready to graduate and then to become a second lieutenant in the air force. We suddenly got a notification that due to newly imposed quotas, the only openings were for those who qualified for pilot training. Unless I became a pilot, I would be dropped from further participation in the program.

I would have loved to become a pilot. When the Korean War broke out, my dearest friend, Louie, and two other buddies went to the Marine Corps recruiting station (which I believe was near Prospect Park in Brooklyn) to volunteer. Louie and I were not accepted, but our other buddies were. Sadly they were both killed in hand-to-hand fighting when hordes of communist troops (who were told they would immediately go to heaven if killed in battle) overran their position at the Chosin Reservoir.

Anyway, the problem was that my wearing glasses disqualified me from becoming a pilot. I then got some encouraging news. Since my ROTC grades were high and I had qualified for (but had not joined) the Pershing Rifles, which was an honor guard drill team, they would find an opening for a small group of us in the Army ROTC. However, I would have to take an extra year of Army ROTC, and that meant going to summer school. OK. There went a hot summer for Syl and me.

It turned out that I got my BS in finance but no lieutenant bars, as I received another notice and another ruling. What? Why? Sorry, but the army's officer quota was already filled. I then questioned how come the idiots didn't know this before I had to take an extra year, attending marches and enduring hot weather in the summer? So it was back to Birmingham, where I would wait to be drafted.

While I was waiting to be drafted, I was offered a job with Sylvia's dad (Morris), her Uncle Max, and Sylvia's cousins, Irving and Maxie. They both had shoe stores and a wholesale shoe company on First Avenue North near downtown Birmingham. Irving was smart. He wasn't especially likeable, but he knew his business. He would eventually open up a wholesale shoe company and local chain in Dallas. Maxie, on the other hand, always had a smile, and although he was not as hard a worker as Irving, he was an excellent salesperson. He was a scratch golfer who never used a driver on the golf course (very unusual).

Sylvia's uncles Abe and Phillip were assigned to take me out in the field when Maxie was tied up in the warehouse. I remember eating some great barbecue in a mining town in Walker County.

Phillip was a no-nonsense seller but a good one. Abe wore a hearing aid, and when he laid out the line, he could never hear when the owner yelled NO! However, if the owner whispered, "Yes, I'll take that one," the pad came right out, and Abe jotted down the details. Good lesson.

I was also assigned to help with stock in the back room, where I worked with three fine black men: Wash Wilson, William Washington, and Bobby Short. This was still the highly segregated South, and although there were no segregated bathrooms—since Uncle Max was a fair and kind gentleman—a certain protocol was followed. Since I was from the North and was not really in tune with the idea of segregation, not knowing the implication, I said to Wash one day, "Boy! Can you help me move some cartons?"

William, who was a part-timer and who worked for the post office, which was one of the best jobs that you could get as a black man, was horrified. Although it was before MLK's time, this man was rightfully proud, and he called me down. I was of course very embarrassed and apologized.

Soon after that, I become the proud sales rep for Greenwald Wholesale Shoe Company, where I replaced their longtime rep, C. R. Byrd, who was retiring from the territory, after many years of dedicated work. C. R. was related to the famous Byrds of West Virginia. He was a crusty and fine Southern gentleman with impeccable manners and a very distinguished air about him. Although I was still a kid, we hit it off famously.

On his final swing, he was going to take me around and introduce me to all of the customers in the territory, including some very famous people. The territory mostly consisted of southeast Tennessee, which we called "shoo enough hillbilly country." The counties included Cumberland, Polk, Rhea, Warren, McMinn, and others. Some of these counties did not have a paved road in the entire county. The territory included towns like Jasper, Sparta, Pall Mall, McMinnville, Dunlap, Copperhill, Tracy City, and others. The hub of the area was the Sequatchie Valley.

These were some of the original hillbillies, and they were mostly "Ulster" Scots, with not so much of a Southern accent but more of a Scotch twang. They would turn out to be some of the most unbelievable people I would meet anywhere, including all of the United States and the forty-plus countries that I would eventually visit.

We would drive up from Birmingham to Chattanooga and then drive west about twenty-five miles to Jasper, Tennessee, the gateway to the Sequatchie Valley, which at one time had been Cherokee territory. After that, there was a drive on an absolutely horrific mountain road through Tracy City. You could look down the mountainside into the valley and see wrecked coal trucks that hadn't made some of the very sharp single-lane turns.

At one point, C. R. remarked that he had confidence in me and my character. In front of the people we met, he put his arm on my shoulder as a signal that I was to be accepted and that he was sponsoring me in good faith.

Before we met the customers, he took us on a side trip to meet some of the famous people in the area. Cordell Hull was the secretary of state. He was not well and it was hard to understand him. He died within weeks of our meeting. I later found out that he had a mixed and controversial record.

Next was Sergeant York, the famous World War I hero. The state of Tennessee had built a home for him, and he sold some items from the front parlor as kind of a makeshift store. Mr. York told me that he did everything by instinct, since he had virtually no education. He was most proud of the Bible school that he was building. What I remember most was that he absolutely glowed with patriotism. Spending time with a real American unbelievable hero was a highlight for me, and I will always remember it. I could never understand why the Internal Revenue bugged him as they did.

From there we went on to visit the customers. Besides some of the small general stores that carried firewood, groceries, and clothes, the largest industry in this small, poor area was moonshine! The fact that I could drive my '48 Dodge without being molested or stopped was due to C. R., of course. Strangers were not welcome.

One day I was making my rounds not only to sell but to pick up the cash that customers owed to the company. The owners paid only when I came around to collect, as they did not have bank accounts, didn't even know what a checking account was, and didn't trust banks anyway. Note that in all of the years that Greenwald Shoe dealt with this area, they NEVER lost a dime due to nonpayment. Bad debt was unheard of, but again, we had to collect when we made our rounds. Carrying around all this money made me very nervous, so when I collected it, I couldn't wait to get to the local Western Union office in order to telegraph the funds to Birmingham and not have to carry so much cash around in my pockets.

One of my assignments was to hand print in large letters signs for the storekeepers since few were literate except to read some parts of the Bible. Every store that you went into had a very large Bible (usually open) on a table in the center of the store. One sunny day, the owner of the store was alone, and he asked me if I could mind the store for him, as he had to go up to his house to do a chore, the house being on a hill overlooking the store. A customer came into the store for some eggs and bacon, which I fetched. She paid, and I made change. Holy cow! I had never seen so much cash in a cash drawer in all of my life.

Finally Mr. Daniel, the owner, returned, and I asked him why he would trust me with all that cash in the drawer. His response was immediate and simple: "Young feller, you were approved by C. R., and that is enough for me. And besides, you are well known in these parts, as is your car. If you were that foolish and took something that didn't belong to you, you'd never leave the county." He then hugged me and insisted that I stay for a turkey shoot.

A Turkey shoot is simply a party with moonshine, laughing, jokes, and a target shoot with either a shotgun or a .22-caliber rifle. A short prayer starts everything off, with the climax being the target shoot. My shooting was excellent. Apparently I solidified their faith in me, and I won their hearts. More important, they won mine. These were the finest, most G-d fearing, absolutely honest people you would meet anywhere.

On another interesting sidelight, they knew that I was Jewish, and they treated me with the utmost respect and reverence. Yes, they might mention that they liked to go to the "Jew store" in Chattanooga, but there was not an ounce of venom in that statement. I called them on it once, and they were mystified and asked what was wrong with a "Jew store," as they felt that was where they got their fairest shake.

They loved the Bible, and incredibly, they were the forerunners of the so-called Christian Right in that they truly loved and respected my people, and even though the state of Israel was very young, they were ardent Zionists. A number of times I felt truly humbled when they commented that my presence was sent from heaven to them.

You shouldn't be surprised that there was a school project, about which a movie was made, in Whitwell, Tennessee. They collected eleven million paper clips in order to illustrate to the students what it meant for millions to be killed. The boxcar was brought from one of the Nazi death camps and it serves as a well-attended Holocaust memory today.

Selling in the hill country of Tennessee was not that difficult since it wasn't really selling. The customers knew exactly what they needed or wanted, so I was really just taking orders. I was not the backslapping, outgoing type and was actually on the shy side. On the other hand, I wanted to be successful and do things right, and I was, especially later on, very ambitious. I guess since I smiled a lot, people seemed to gravitate toward me for help, and I have never been one to turn down a person who asks for my guidance or assistance, even when growing up.

Drafted into the Army

The fence selling had ended, and I wasted a very hot summer in Tuscaloosa taking extra courses in Army ROTC. Once they politely informed me that I was not going to become an officer, I was pissed as hell. When I received my BS in finance and banking, I told the university that they could mail my diploma to me since I would not attend the graduation ceremonies. It was a letdown for my wife and mother, but my mind was firmly made up. Both my father and my father-in-law (both sweet, kind men with good intentions) suggested that I become a CPA. My math skills were good, but that was boring as hell. I had almost fallen asleep tutoring Jim Nabors in accounting. I considered law school, but at the time that didn't excite me either.

I realized that my dream of pitching for the Yankees was just that—a dream—even though a scout from the New York Giants baseball organization saw me on one of my better days and offered a job in Class D (doesn't exist today), and even though I had dated Suzie Birne, whose father was a Yankee scout, I realized I still had no chance. My dad's advice had been that if I wasn't good enough for the majors, I would not only waste my time but go through hell with lousy meals and terrible buses. I remembered that the bus trips from Birmingham to Tuscaloosa were torture for me.

So I thought of becoming an FBI agent, but when I inquired, they told me that you had to be a CPA or a lawyer. Thinking of a CPA carrying a weapon struck me as funny. The Foreign Service would have been great, but I was told that you needed the right connections, which I didn't have at the time.

But! I did have a banking degree, so I answered an ad for a "bank exec wanted," made an appointment, and drove down to Montgomery to the bank, whose name I have long forgotten.

The secretary took me upstairs to an office that reminded me of a scene out of *The Time of Your Life*. This guy, who I guess was the junior manager, looked to be in his thirties. He was a tall, slim, thin lipped, snot-pug-nosed-looking twerp, and with a sneer he looked me up and down and then virtually spit out his question: "Why would you want to work in this bank? You should apply to the 'Jew' bank in Birmingham." Unlike in Tennessee, this was meant as a mean slur.

The Lord only knows what kept me from decking this clown. I did have my parting shot, however, as I stomped out in a rage, mentioning that the next time he brought someone in, especially from out of town, he should at least have the decency to wipe off all of that white dandruff from his shoulders and horrible-fitting jacket.

We moved from a forty-four-dollar-a-month apartment in Tuscaloosa to a fifty-five-dollar-a-month apartment near the zoo in Birmingham, on Lane Park Road. We got our gas at O'Connor's Shell, where the owner was a character. Along with your gas, oil check, and front- and rear-window cleaning, you had your tires painted. Syl told him once that she was in a hurry, and his glib response was, "Of course, ma'am. Most prominent women are!"

We had good friends, and they were always fun to be with. One had a wife who was not too smart. We saw her once with a bandaged hand, and when we asked what happened, she proceeded to inform us that she had tried to stop the fan on her table with the palm of her hand. This was after she was seen trying to go up a down escalator in Pizitz Department Store. Coming from the country, she had never seen an escalator before.

We were good friends with the Mays and used to go on trips together. We loved to play gin rummy. I kept my score on a pad for years, and we considered ourselves experts. One day we were discussing a gin game with another friend, Big Al Toronto, because we figured that we could con him along with another friend into a game and make some fast, easy money. Unfortunately we were losing every hand—and I mean losing—as we were getting schneidered, which meant 150 to 0, and that cost double. Within an hour we were each out over forty bucks. That was a lot of money in those days. We quickly left Al's apartment two sad and beaten con men.

I knew that I was going to be drafted into the army. Sure enough, one summer day I received a telegram telling me that I must report to Montgomery for a physical exam. Bus transportation would be provided. A hot bus again! The thought of being drafted as a private after five years of ROTC was a real letdown. I had figured that the fact that I wore glasses and had terrible flat feet could keep me out of the army. When I boxed, I could not dance away from my opponent fast enough, so I had developed a powerful punch.

So now, 175 pounds of me got off the bus, and we started with getting shots. A big fellow in front of me was blustering and joking around, and then, all of a sudden, he fainted when the needle was put into his arm. I had to help lift this two-hundred-pound lug off the floor.

Now it was my turn to go into the doctor's office. Usual routine: bend over and cough, and when I got the doc's attention, I explained that I had terrible flat feet, had a hard time walking, wore glasses, and was a married man. Very impressive. He pointed me to a room, and I walked in smiling, as I knew that I must have really conned the doctor. Surprise! There was a group of about fifty or sixty of us, and just like that, we were asked to raise our hands and were sworn in as draftees in the United States Army. A sergeant was intoning: "I encourage our honored inductees to continue to uphold the same morals and character, the same resiliency, and the dedication to serving others that our forefathers have echoed," etc., etc.

In the meantime, I thought that we would be returning to Birmingham for a few weeks and report back. No such luck. We were allowed to make one phone call at a bank of pay phones (five cents a call), after which we got on a bus for Fort Jackson, South Carolina. This was rumored to be the toughest basic-training camp in the country.

On the phone, Syl was in a panic. "What? When am I going to see you?"

"Maybe not for ten weeks."

"Are they kidding me?"

So I was thinking that since I was a college graduate with five years of ROTC, I couldn't go into the army as a buck private. Or so I thought. I wrote to my congressman but again had no clout, so nothing helped. Two years were going to be a waste. At one point I was offered officer's candidate school, but that would mean signing up for another year. No way, Jay. You can fool me once but no more than once.

Basic training was no picnic, and the rumor about drill sergeants being mean was undoubtedly true. I managed to set my mold quickly, however. One evening in the barracks, I was fooling around with this big South Carolinian monster who weighed well over 250 pounds. All of a sudden, I sent him flying across the barracks, and he landed flat on his back. It was a fluke, but everyone looked at me in a different light after that.

The next day, we were exercising or drilling in back of the barracks, and this tough Tennessee sergeant was picking on me in front of the whole platoon. We had just come from a training exercise, and it seemed that I wasn't aggressive enough for his liking. His comment to me was that Jews didn't know how to fight and that they were a bunch of cowards.

Was I hearing right? Sgt. Numbnuts obviously didn't know the Jews in my Brooklyn neighborhood. I explained to him that I was a draftee and only had two years to serve, and I didn't want to prolong my stay in an army stockade. If we removed our blouses (army shirts), however, he may find out how Jews fought.

He laughed and ripped off his blouse. I ripped off mine, and BANG! I hit him with a left hook to the jaw that sent him flying. Before he could get his composure, I hit him again.

He got up and laughed, and we shook hands. His comment was, "Well, private, I guess that Jews DO know how to fight." Later we even became drinking buddies.

Now we were back in the barracks, and it was nighttime. We were sharing it with a group of native recruits from Poland, who after serving for six years can become US citizens. I think some of them served in the Russian Army, so they thought that this was a picnic. This was their fourth basic training cycle, and they loved every minute of it. It had been a long day of hard training, and I was tired. A bunch of them were in front of my bunk staring at me. What was with these dodos? Their leader was a fellow by the name of Kazimirs, and he explained that they were watching over me to protect me.

Protect me from what? Go to sleep, fellows.

It turned out that they thought that the noncoms were going to come in during the middle of the night, drag me out of bed, and beat the living hell out of me.

I explained that this was America and not Russia, where what I had done could mean a severe beating at best and even death. Both China and Russia were known for their brutal, uncivilized training methods. I went to sleep, and the next morning I had become the hero of the Poles. From that day on, they made my bed, spit shined my shoes and boots, and pressed my uniform. When I went on to win the Expert badge with the M-1 rifle and Sharpshooter with the carbine, I had the run of "Boot Hill", as

Fort Jackson basic training was called. I could dissemble the Garand rifle blindfolded but not the trigger housing. Throwing grenades at a beat-up truck was fun.

If I remember, we had one or two weekend passes. Normally your day started at 5:00 a.m. Everything was done in squads or platoon formation. We were constantly yelled at, and the idea was to make us stop thinking like individuals (hard to do with me) and have us think as a combat unit, following orders almost by instinct. Most of us were sleep deprived. Note that digging a foxhole is not as you see in the movies. It is very, very difficult.

You also took classes such as the UCMJ, which was the Uniform Code of Military Justice, which taught you how to behave if captured by the enemy.

They took pictures when we went through the infiltration course, and I heard they made a yearbook, but I never saw it.

There was one very sad note. A couple of bunks down from me was this tall, very quiet but friendly black man. One morning we woke up to find this poor fellow cold and stiff as a stick. Apparently he had died in the middle of the night of epilepsy. Unless you were with a unit after basic training for some reason, you didn't get extra close to those who were with you, although you were friendly while you were together.

As with all things, basic training finally ended. Through some flukes and luck, I ended up being one of the heroes of the company—well respected; not being assigned to many dirty details (I had KP only once); had my uniforms cleaned, ironed, and starched and my boots and shoes spit shined—but I was still a buck private.

So where would they send me next? Normally it was an eight-week tour. I was told that the possibilities were DC; Fort Hood, Texas; and Fort Leavenworth, Kansas; but I was hoping for Chicago, where I could get an MOS (military occupation specialty) of 711.1, which was a clerk typist, since I was already a touch typist. My friendly sergeant told me that they were going to train me for a hand-to-hand-combat NCO and teach me how to kill a man fourteen ways with my bare hands. Hey, the only thing I wanted to kill was cockroaches. I was never enamored with the water. I knew how to swim but had had a bad scare at Coney Island, where I got stuck in a rip tide. Jumping out of airplanes was also not for me, so airborne was definitely out. So where did they send me?

FORT MCCLELLAN

I nstead of eight weeks of secondary training, just as in the game of Monopoly I was sent directly to GO. My orders read: "You are to report forthwith, directly by the fastest means possible, to Fort McClellan, Anniston, Alabama." Hey! That was only about sixty miles from home. I didn't know what I was going to do there, but it didn't sound like bad duty. When I arrived, I was told that it was the WAC (Women's Army Corps) basic training center. So maybe I was being sent there to teach the girls hand-to-hand combat.

No such luck, as it was also CCTC (Chemical Corps Training Command). This was devoted to chemical training involving smoke grenades, flamethrowers, decontamination procedures, and chemical warfare protection. Oh well.

After a long bus ride again, I finally arrived at what was probably one of the nicest forts in America. It had been completely refurbished about a year or so before. The buildings were in Spanish style, beautiful with manicured lawns. The men on base looked sharp and friendly. The WAC section was on the other side of the base and was pretty much closed off. When I finally got to see them, what a letdown. They were another story, as they were some of the ugliest women I had seen in some time.

Guess I'd have to find a way to live off base and get home every night. Later, when I saw more of them, there were some who were attractive.

I got assigned to a barracks and found the guys were friendly and accommodating. They introduced me to the company commander, who was a first lieutenant and a real friendly guy. We hit it off great, and he told me that he lived in Birmingham. He asked me where I was from, and when I told him that I lived just over the mountain in Mountain Brook, he suggested that we carpool together. I asked myself if this was really the army. So you know what that means? There would be no late-night details (a detail is crappy work that the military likes to dream up, and if it isn't dirty work, it is boring as hell and useless). In basic training they used to make us "police the area," which meant picking up cigarette butts and paper, or worse, dig holes and then fill them in again.

After a couple of weeks, Lieutenant Capuano made me his duty clerk, which earned me a stripe. That meant basically typing and filing. Later on I did receive a certificate of training for records management. However, the only problem now was that in the mornings, I still had to go through Chemical Corps training. Every morning after I dropped off the lieutenant—or on alternate days, he dropped me off in his convertible—I had to put on a gas mask and run through the gas bunker, which was a Quonset hut. You were supposed to remove the mask with the gas flowing a few minutes before you exited the bunker. Screw them. They must be kidding. The few who obeyed orders came out choking, sputtering, and sometimes vomiting.

After that, we lined up in formation in order to protect ourselves against the enemy, who might attempt a chemical warfare attack.

The only enemy that I could think of in the nearest town, which was Anniston—besides the KKK—was flying gnats and rodents. Anyway, you were supposed to jab your thigh about six inches above the knee with an atropine syrette (long needle, baby). Supposedly you felt no pain, as there were no nerves there, and it also prevented you from getting the effects of the phosgene gas. What the hell did I care? I was home every night, and I even gave up joining the army rifle team so that I wouldn't take a chance of losing my job with the good lieutenant. If I was going to be in the army, this should be the life.

We had a pretty good group at company headquarters, and we liked to joke around a lot. Ed McGrath was a person who was always nervous. He was a worrywart and a bit of a hypochondriac who constantly thought that he was going to catch some bug or something. Worse, he thought that he was going to be levied out to Korea. To be levied meant that you were taken from your assigned post and sent to an overseas unit.

You guessed it. I decided to have some fun with Ed. I mimeographed a set of orders that looked real. The orders read that Edward McGrath was being levied from Fort McClellan to the Far East. That almost always meant Korea. Poor guy. When he picked up the orders from his out box, he went running around the compound screaming like a mating duck. So I finally felt sorry for him and had to tell him that it was only one big joke. Unfortunately, he could not see the humor in all of this, and he said that one day, he would get his revenge on me.

Things were calming down, and they were almost getting back to normal, I sensed that for some reason, he was keeping his distance from me. About a month went by, and I saw a set of orders in my in box. "You are hereby reassigned to AFFE, Armed Forces Far East Command." I thought, couldn't Ed be more original than this? and laughed. One thing, though: he had done a better job on the orders than I had. They really looked official. You know something? THEY WERE! I just couldn't believe it. I said that I couldn't leave this cushy assignment. It had to be a joke. IT WASN'T. I checked with the lieutenant, and he confirmed that sadly, the orders were real. I had given up baseball and the rifle team for this?

On February 27, I got my installation clearance certificate from the Twenty-First Chemical Corps, turned in my cards, and received my ratings. Conduct: Excellent. Efficiency: Excellent. State of mind: Poor.

Sylvia was beside herself. Just like that, I was off to Fort Lewis, Washington, on March 8. Of course, in those days there were no direct flights to either Seattle or Tacoma, so we made four stops in nonpressurized cabins, with my ears killing me every time we landed. The third stop was Billings, Montana, at what looked like a ranch with a wooden fence around it. I thought John Wayne would pop up any minute.

I finally got to Fort Lewis in Tacoma, and except for a brief tour of Seattle and Vancouver, we saw nothing but ten soggy days of rain. I ended up leaving a civilian pair of pants and a shirt at the local dry cleaners in Tacoma. Since I have never returned to Tacoma, I never did pick them up.

Luckily, I met an old classmate from PS 92 who said that he would try to get me on the baseball team, meaning that I would go to Japan instead of Korea. On the night that we were ready to embark, there was a long line of troops going to Korea on the right and a few stragglers who were going to Japan on the left— they, of course, being the lucky ones. The master sergeant waved me to the right.

"No, Sergeant," I yelled. "I'm on the army baseball team, and I'm going to Japan."

He yelled back, "A pig's ass you are, PFC. MARCH TO THE RIGHT."

I was stunned, as was Sylvia when I made the call to her. There was no time to call the folks, so Syl would have to break the news. There was a photographer there, who stood in front of a silly background taking pictures. As if I felt like taking pictures that night? I looked and felt like a washed-out duck. Down the long, narrow passageway and onto the ship, and what a horrible, depressing feeling that was!

Aboard Ship to Korea

We had the pleasure to board the USS *General J. C. Breckinridge*, which was built in 1945 with a speed of nineteen knots and a capacity to hold over five thousand troops. It was sold for salvage in 1987.

From the looks of the old tub, it was not going to be a fun trip. When I saw the accommodations, I nearly croaked. You went to the latrine (toilet) with fifty other guys, and you showered twelve or more abreast. The sleeping quarters—ah, yes, the sleeping quarters. They were four bunks high, and the bunk was a thick, smelly piece of cloth with four chains on either side holding them up. Luckily, my first night, I got the upper bunk. This meant that I didn't have to worry about anyone vomiting on me in the middle of the night. The guy on the third bunk kept climbing up and down the ladder to go to the latrine in the middle of the night.

Our breakfast shifts started at 6:00 a.m., and I don't even want to talk about the mush that they served. They called it chow, but I called it "dog" chow. I had to figure out some way to escape this utter torture and nonsense.

It seemed that fortune was smiling upon me, as the next morning, there was a notice on a large board in the gangway that

Special Services was looking for anyone who could play a musical instrument or who was an entertainer or artist, and those who qualified should report to the NCO (noncommissioned officer) in charge of morale. It turned out there were dependents onboard who had better quarters than we had and surely didn't have to sleep four high, and the captain was planning to have entertainment for them.

So right after the morning dog chow, which consisted of imitation eggs with slop over stale bread and coffee that could have been mud from the Hudson River, I rushed down to the area where the interviews were being held. What was buzzing through my head was, what the hell am I going to sign up for without any musical talent? Of course, I knew how to use the phonograph but no musical instrument of any kind. I spotted this guy with a clipboard in his hand. He was obviously in charge of this circus.

Smiling, I approached him, and we hit it off immediately. Jim Anglisano and I would become lifelong friends. In fact, after my best friend, Lou Dinolfo, Jim is second in line. When he asked me what instrument I played, I completely broke him up with a story that my music teacher told in high school. I told Jim that I used to play the piccolo, but I gave it up. Jim asked why. With a straight face, I explained that our band (I really hadn't been part of the band) played so badly that our bandmaster, Mr. Stoffregen (stuff made out of rain), told us to take our instruments and shove them up our asses! The problem was that only mine fit since I had the piccolo.

After all but rolling on the deck, Jim asked what else I had a talent for. Thinking that the easiest thing to fake would be working as an artist, I told him that. Jim was now all excited, explaining that the captain of the ship had a big project. He wanted a large picture painted that would be hung in the recreation room in the dependents' section of the ship. Could I do it?

"Of course, Jim. Why not?"

I got the job, and he started to explain the "perks".. I would have my own cabin, either next to the bridge (where the captain and his officers run the ship) or just one level below the bridge. It got better: I wouldn't have to wait in that interminable line to get snacks at the canteen, and I would have access to navy personnel who would get me whatever I wanted or needed.

Whew. I was ecstatic, as I now had my own private latrine, showers, a table, comfortable chairs, and my own bed, escaping the smelly crap house, crowded quarters, and bunks.

Jim left me at the cabin, and I started to ponder. Yes, quite a life, but now I had to figure out how the hell I was going to paint a full-size picture. Well, that should be easy, as I would get some real artists who COULD paint, and I would just supervise the project.

I ran back to Jim's area and explained that I needed help because a painting this size couldn't be done in the approximately two weeks that we would be at sea (if the bucket didn't leak). He had me put a notice on the bulletin board asking for "accomplished artists." I figured that I needed at least three of them so that in our spare time we could play pinochle, since I had brought a couple of decks of pinochle cards from the commissary with me.

Now I was ready to interview my artists. Art Blackmon, Bob Saxman, and Carl Tronolone all claimed that they were experienced artists. What a crew I selected! The nicest guys you would ever meet—except that they were a bunch of lying bastards. Not one of them could draw a lick. Like me, they would pull any trick to get away from the dirt, seasickness, boredom, and all the rest of the nonsense. The "conner" had gotten conned.

So what did we do? We played pinochle for a couple of days until we could figure out a useful strategy.

There was a knock on the door, and it was Jim with his damned clipboard. "What's going on, guys?" he smilingly intoned.

We explained that we had problems in that we didn't have a canvas, an easel, or even paint or paint brushes, for that matter.

"Well, that's what the swabbies are for," he said, and then gave out a combination laugh and grunt.

The navy rounded up the so-called supplies, all of which were OK except that the paint was mostly the gray they used to paint the old tub.

Back to the cards, and before long, Jim came back with the news that we were going to handle the special stage effects for the Breckinridge Big Top Dance. (Who the hell were we going to dance with?) Jim would be playing the accordion, which he did very well and there will be more on that in a later chapter. Right after that, there would be a ceremony as we passed the International Date Line. During this ceremony, we would all receive "Domain of the Golden Dragon" certificates.

We were about to start our card game when all of a sudden there was a loud knocking on the metal door. It was not Jim's carefree knock. The only thing that we had on the canvas so far was some green paint to represent the sea.

When I asked for identification, the answer was "Captain Donald W. Todd, who is the freaking captain of the ship."

Cards were flying in the air, and everyone was in a complete state of panic, so I motioned for them to stand in front of the canvas. I opened the door just a crack.

"May I come in?"

"NO, SIR. Please remember that we are artists, and we can't show anyone our painting until the finished work of art is ready."

To our relief, he agreed as long as he would be the first to see it when it was finished. So now the panic really set in, as we had less than five days before we reached Inchon, Korea, or we might just be thrown overboard. What the hell were we going to paint? Since most of our paint was either green or gray, I suggested a fish scene. All agreed. We certainly did our best, but for some reason the fishes came out like seahorses. We added lots of seaweed, rocks, and green plants.

Finally, the work of art was finished, and we all had visions of being put into the brig if not thrown overboard. We asked Jim to get word to Captain Todd and explained that we promised the captain that he would be the first to see the finished product.

By the way, each of us signed the canvas in the lower right-hand corner in large, probably eighteen-inch letters. Our signatures were more prominent than the fish.

Here came the captain in his white dress uniform, gold braid, and the works. He entered, stared for what seemed an hour, turned around, smiled, and shook each of our hands. I hope he wasn't a pilot, as he must have been half blind. He actually liked the painting! We then carried the masterpiece down to the lounge and proudly hung it prominently right in the center. I've heard that it held that place of honor for many years, and I wondered if before they scrapped the old bucket in 1987 what happened to our work of art. If I could find it, I would buy it and hang it in Jimmy Anglisano's basement.

Arriving in Seoul, Korea

Finally we docked at Inchon. Inchon Harbor didn't seem like the most accessible port in the world, with its high bulkheads and very brown, muddy water. We disembarked on what I think they called wide rope ladders onto a speedboat that took us ashore. I guess the boatswain thought he was being funny as he shouted to move fast in case the "gooks" (a derogatory name for the North Koreans) started SHOOTING at us. What war? The armistice had been signed some time ago.

From there we were taken by a two-and-a-half-ton truck to Yongsan City, although I wouldn't really call it a city. From there, most of us would be sent to Seventh Division, I Corps, or the First Cavalry, all of which meant lousy food and sleeping in tents.

I was in luck, as one of my friends from grade school was in charge of assignments. Marty eventually became a bank president and is currently retired in Mexico. He managed to get me a job in Eighth Army Headquarters, working for a general. General Thomas Griffin, it turned out, was a decent, rather quiet but friendly type. The outfit was called EASCOM—Eighth Army Support Command, which was part of SAC, Seoul Army Command. It was a little complicated, but then that's the military for you.

The sleeping quarters assigned to me was a single room in a brick building right next to the JAG section (army attorneys). This was just outside of Seoul on the MSR. The MSR (main supply route) was the dirt road that went into downtown Seoul. There were no paved roads or sidewalks rebuilt yet. Being an army HQ, it was a pleasant setting of mostly brick buildings and some Quonset huts, a decent PX, and a mess hall, which I tried to avoid as much as possible. The PX was reasonably well stocked (at one point I wrote a report suggesting improvements, which were followed, although they never gave me the credit for the suggestions). Some of the items were quite fascinating. Cigarettes were vital, as they could be sold on the black market along with Ajinomoto (MSG), which was used extensively in Korean cooking. I only smoked cigars and a pipe, so the cigarettes came in handy for trade. The most fascinating items were the jars of gefilte fish. I guess the Koreans took a liking to that also, as they were very much in demand.

I was the NCO in charge of files and reports, and I was given a Top Secret clearance. The FBI did a thorough check, and I was called in and asked about my in-laws being born in Russia. I assured them that they were not communists and that my immediate family was far from that. They gave me the clearance.

The PX was just a short distance from the firehouse, and they were on one end of the base. One night, we suddenly get a red alert signal, which meant a possible enemy attack from the north. Since I had the security clearance, I had to put this waxy thing on top of the security files, and it burned all the way through and destroyed the classified documents. I didn't believe that there would be an actual attack, and if I did this every time there was a red alert, there would be no files for us to work with.

It turns out that it was a smart move not to destroy the documents on my part, as the alert was due to a fire on the base. Out went the fire trucks with lights and sirens blazing. They made a right turn (the PX was on the left) and went all around the base looking for the fire. The fire! Where the hell was it? Wait until you read this: it turned out that the fire was in the PX, and it burned completely down. If they had turned left instead of right, they would have seen the blaze less than three hundred feet away.

A couple of weeks later, a ship docked at Inchon with supplies to refurbish the PX, including enough cigarettes to fill a two-and-a-half-ton truck. It was escorted by MPs on motorcycles from Inchon to Seoul. When it arrived at SAC and was unloaded, almost half the cigarettes had disappeared. To this day, the case has never been solved. If you had asked anyone at HQ how the cigarettes disappeared, they would have smiled and pointed to the MP battalion.

Everyone in our office had a security clearance, and we were constantly warned to keep our mouths shut and never reveal anything that we read or learned. We even restricted our conversations among ourselves, and we were scared to death that we could reveal something that was confidential, secret, or top secret, which were the classifications used. The army was hyper about security, and when we read the English-language paper, the *Korean Republic*, which printed things from our files, we of course wondered where they were getting their information. Was it the Korean mama-san who cleaned our office? She seemed like such a sweet old lady.

To give you an idea of the military mentality, the enlisted men alternated serving watches at night. They were called CQs, or charge of quarters, and there was an officer who was an OD, or officer of the day—and yes, he was on duty at night. We would get a list of files to declassify, and then when the OD came on duty, he would scratch out the classification with a red marker, rendering the document safe for distribution. Breaches in security were not tolerated. One evening, a tired young Lieutenant Johnson started working on the files, and three-quarters of the way through marking them, he fell asleep. When he went off duty, he forgot that he had put the remaining files in the drawer instead of the locked classified file cabinet. Remember that technically, these files had been declassified. As his luck would have it, the next morning the CID (criminal investigating division) showed up and discovered the files. He was court-martialed, convicted, and busted to sergeant. When I think of WikiLeaks today, I wonder how things have so changed.

My job, however, was great. I had access to a jeep and even a two-and-a-half-ton truck if I needed it, along with all kinds of perks, including lots of free time to listen to records in the recreation center.

Since one of my assignments was to find billets (brick sleeping quarters) for majors, colonels, and foreign officers who came down from division, whether on leave or special assignment, I was endowed with all kinds of trading power. When I flew either on R&R (rest and recuperation), which I received often, TDY (temporary duty), or leave, I got to fly on VIP flights. These could be luxurious, and some even had sleeping quarters on them. I joined various enlisted men's clubs so I wouldn't have to eat in their illustrious mess hall, which was supervised by Sergeant "Drunken Hines."

Soon I discovered the OEC club, which was the Office of Economic Cooperation, and yes, we did give foreign aid to countries back then also. This was a civilian club that allowed all ranks as long as they had "special" status. Of course I managed to get myself and my buddies, including Lenny, Jimmy, and a few others into the club. The food and the drinks were fine.

One day we got an invite from the club to attend a special YMCA charity outdoor party to raise funds for the poor Korean children. The YMCA was just up the road from the SAC entrance. There would be games, dignitaries, food, and beer. Also, there were all kinds of carnival activities, and at one of the stands you had to throw a baseball at bottles to see if you could knock them all down. There was this guy dressed in a jacket throwing the ball all over the place except at the bottle. Being an ex-pitcher, I went up to him and gave him pitching instructions. Allie Reynolds of the Yankees he wasn't. He was very appreciative, and we all hit it off great, taking pictures and making our rounds having fun.

Now it turned out that this gentleman, Cosme Garcia, was the ambassador from the Philippines to Korea, and his brother was the president of the Philippines. As we were parting company, His Honor, Mr. Garcia, invited me to dinner at the Chosun Hotel in the center of Seoul. At the time, the Chosun hotel was reserved for generals and dignitaries. I got a kick out this, as there was no way that they were going to let a noncommissioned officer in. So I figured we would just have to find another restaurant when the time came.

The planned day arrived, and I was outside my room having a catch with the boys waiting for the gate to summon me when all of a sudden this long black limo with flags flying pulled up. It was Cosme Garcia with his driver. I was stunned and asked him how the hell he got through the gate and then drove right up to the buildings. You can't come on an army post!

He replied that as an ambassador, he could go wherever the hell he wanted to.

Yes, but not the Chosun Hotel, I told him.

He paid me no mind. We proceeded to the Chosin, and he announced that I was his HONORED guest. You had to see the startled look on the face of the enlisted doorman. Holy shit. How was I going to get out of this one?

After a brief conversation with the maître d', he pulled out his documents, and amazingly, we were seated. Facing us were four generals (unfortunately—or maybe fortunately—not the one I worked for) and their aides-de-camp. I had privileges, but that didn't include eating at the generals' mess. Major Jaworksi came storming over. "What the f— do you think you are doing here, soldier?"

I tried to explain that I was an invited guest of the ambassador, who then told the major in no uncertain terms that the major was breaking protocol. I got a very mean, steady glare from

Major Jaworski, and he spat out that he would find me and re-member me.

Sometime later he surely did. Three months before I was to leave Korea, that day did come. Len was another close friend who was stationed with us. He was an attorney and a budding professor, but his first love was the stage. In Korea, Len needed a mentor and someone who could keep him out of trouble and guide him in the ways of the world. That assignment fell on me. I performed the task with my obtuse humor. Sometimes on a Sunday, we would tour Seoul and end up at the Deoksugung Museum, one of the few buildings that had not been destroyed by the Japanese or the North Koreans during the occupation and the war. Although the museum was closed on Sundays, we would bribe the guards to let us in. On one visit, I had Len take a picture of me lying on the "King's Gold Sleeping Chamber." I still have that picture somewhere.

This was relaxing and fun, so on our next visit, I asked Len to take a picture of me lying on the queen's bed. This was appar-ently frowned upon and maybe even considered sacred territory, so he was scared to death. As he was about to snap the photo, a guard came running down the hall screaming in Korean, level-ing his rifle, and he either took a shot at us or was about to. As we raced out the exit, Len was screaming, "Don't shoot, don't shoot! I'm an American, I'm an American!" Len was not happy, and he always make it known that it was entirely my fault that he was almost shot. That was our last visit to the museum.

One day Len and I were in the PX, and he confessed to me that he was in love with one of the Korean salesgirls (they spoke almost perfect English). It was, however, against the rules for them to go out or in any way fraternize with a foreigner. It was also strictly against their tradition, and since this was a prize job for a Korean to have, they would never take the risk of getting caught.

I convinced Len that I could arrange it for him. He be-lieved me and was thrilled. The plan was as follows: About two kilometers (less than two miles) from SAC was the YMCA compound. We would meet the girl in front of the YMCA, but of course it wasn't going to be the girl from the PX. I arranged for some MP friends of mine to have the girl standing in the dark, and when Len approached her, they would jump out and arrest him, after which I would appear and save him.

A snag developed, as Len said that he would not go on the dark MSR unless I accompanied him. There was no choice, so I had to walk with him. We were happily walking along when he spotted what he thought was the girl from the PX. He thanked me and was running forward when all of a sudden he DISAPPEARED. It was hard for me to believe my eyes, and then I heard moaning. He had fallen into what was probably a deep shell hole and bruised his ankle badly. The MPs saw what had occurred and drove him back to the base hospital to get a cast put on.

The following week we were scheduled to fly to Tokyo for R&R. There would be little "rest and recuperation" on this trip, as I had to help lug him around on his crutches throughout our stay in Japan. Len swore revenge, and in the next chapter you will find out how he exacted it.

Army Acting Career

One sunshiny day I got a call from Len, whose foot had healed by then. Korean weather is extreme. It's brutally cold in the winter, especially as you get into higher elevation, and suffocatingly hot in the summer. When you took a shower, you sometimes had that "honey bucket" smell, and there was no way to get rid of it. On the road you could see the honey bucket trucks loaded with human excrement the honey bucket honchos collected from the homes. The farms used the waste to fertilize their crops, which meant you couldn't eat fresh vegetables.

Anyway, Len wanted me to accompany him to a tryout for a play the base was giving called *Sabrina Fair*, a modern comedy by Samuel Taylor. He claimed that he needed the moral support because the play was going to be directed by a budding Hollywood playwright by the name of Garry Marshall. None of this meant much to me because I knew nothing about the stage except for the fact that I enjoyed watching plays. I got this from my mother, who at one time had virtually every *Playbill* from Broadway from the twenties to the forties.

So, on we went to this makeshift studio with all kinds of people milling around. Most of them were still in their army or nurse's uniforms. We sat down on these hard wood chairs, and people were coming over to me saying that they couldn't wait for me to read the part of Linus Larrabie (Sabrina's father). I couldn't imagine who they thought that I was, but I must have looked like somebody else. I kept saying that it was a mistake and that I was only there to accompany and to give support to Len.

It seemed, however, that Len had told everyone that I was a budding actor and that after I got out of the army, I would be famous. He also told them that I didn't want to seem pretentious and publicize the fact.

This was now serious, so I tried to explain to Len that by employing this ruse, he was not doing the play or players a favor.

They didn't stop insisting, so to get them off of my back, I read the part, though not very well. Since their minds were already made up, it probably didn't matter how I read it. They gave me the part.

I asked Len if they were all crazy, but Len assured me that I couldn't let the troupe down and that they were short of talent.

Did they think that I was talent?

Rehearsals went on for a couple of weeks, and I was not performing very well, although I certainly knew my lines. I guess you could say that I was "tepid." Also, I was starting to worry because I could see the very concerned looks on their faces. I said to myself that I had better shape up rather than embarrass myself.

At dress rehearsal, I was scared completely out of my wits, and I think I would have preferred combat to doing this. The rehearsal went well, and although I improvised some lines (directors love it when you do that?), I ended up doing well.

Now we were at opening night, and after a couple of shots of Seagram's VO Whiskey (it had a gold silk ribbon attached to the front of the bottle; if you were a short-timer in Korea, you wore the ribbon around your green fatigue hat), I become as white as the driven snow when I took a peek out of the curtain and saw a full house with civilians and troops from the First Cavalry, Twenty-Fourth Division, I Corps, Seventh Army, and Eighth Army HQ. The last thing I wanted to do was make a fool of myself by forgetting my lines or fainting on stage. I was playing an old man, and boy, I really felt the age.

Once I was out there, however, I was completely transformed. Amazingly—and even today I can't explain it—I did fantastically well, and I believe that I got the loudest applause at the end of the show. The cast, including Len, swarmed all over me as if I had just scored the winning touchdown in a bowl game. We went on tour for a couple of weeks to the various division areas where they couldn't attend the opening.

In the months to come, when I was not on special duty or teaching my Korean students English, I did a number of other shows, including the End Man in a minstrel show and even a short tap dance bit for a one-and-only time. I would have loved to become either a tap dancer or a drummer a la Buddy Rich, but I just didn't have the talent. So that was Len's revenge.

After the play, it was due time for an R&R to Japan. I had been corresponding with some of my Korean students' friends from Japan. Arrangements were made to get me on a VIP flight. I had learned on a previous R&R that it was important to have the green cloth document pouch handcuffed to my wrist so I wouldn't be questioned. No matter what your rank was, classified material was available on a "need to know basis" only.

On one flight the weather was god-awful, and one of the officers—a colonel or general—ordered the pilot to take off. The pilot's response was that on an aircraft, the pilot was the commanding officer. So we didn't take off.

Anyway, on this particular flight, all was calm, and as luck would have it, I was seated across from James Gavin, the famous general from the Eighty-Second Airborne Division. We had in common the fact that we were both born in Brooklyn and we both smoked pipes, which you could do on VIP flights. Surprisingly, he opened up to me, saying that he was getting ready to retire, as he was not happy with the equipment and conditions of the current armed forces and that he could not get the administration to listen to him. He went back to the Western novel that he was reading, and he was also writing notes on a book that he was going to publish on the subject of military preparedness. The general retired in 1958.

When we landed—I believe at Camp Drake in Tokyo—we bid our good-byes and wished each other the best of luck. The general offered me a ride and any help that I might need, but I told him that I already had that set up. When I told him that, he just gave me a wink and a somewhat quizzical look.

Japan in the fifties was a fascinating place. They were finally recovering from the war. It was clean, the food was good and varied, and the shopping was excellent. The entertainment was great, whether it was the theatre, Kabuki, sumo wrestling, baseball, shrines, or the interesting small bars.

They were not always friendly to foreigners, however. One day I found myself right in the center of an anti-American riot. Since I stood out as the only target for their immediate anger, I was naturally frightened. I understood the Japanese language, as I'd studied it from army manuals and tapes, and I understood that they were not wishing America anything pleasant. For some reason they left me completely alone, and I skedaddled out of there as quickly as I could.

Often you would walk into a nice club, and you would immediately be told, "No foreigners allowed!"

Happily, I spent most of my time with the group of Japanese students who had been introduced to me via mail from Korea. We became quite friendly and close, and we corresponded for some years afterward. The father of one of the students was a professor in Hong Kong, where I eventually arrived. The professor contacted me at the hotel and invited me to dinner with his entire family, which included his wife and two children. The dinner was in a famous and in all respects magnificent restaurant (the name escapes me) on the water at the beautiful Hong Kong harbor. My appetite has always been quite large, but I couldn't believe the quantity, variety, and exquisite taste of the food. Dish after dish after dish kept coming out until at one point, it was impossible for me to take another bite. They all sighed a sigh of complete relief; I had not realized that the tradition was that they stopped service only when the guest stopped eating and had had his or her fill.

In the meantime, while I was making a glutton out of myself, the kids had taken a fascination to my smoking pipe, which I had left on the table. They somehow managed to break off a piece of the chopstick into the stem of the pipe—they had been using wooden chopsticks while we used large plastic ones.

I managed to overstay my R&R time on one pretext or another, and before I got into serious trouble, I returned to Seoul. While I was gone, they changed the MPC (military payment certificates, the currency we used in Korea). This had caused panic and riots among the locals, and I had to prove that I had been out of the country in order to exchange my currency.

I only had two pipes, so I had to find a way to repair the one with the chopstick stuck up its butt. The shop at the base didn't have a drill small enough, so I was told that maybe a small Korean shop, doctor, or dentist might have an instrument to get it out. So I took a stroll along the MSR and had gone way past the MSR toward town when I saw a two-story building with a large sign: DR. KIM'S VD CLINIC. Aha! The doctor would surely have the tools to fix my pipe. At the top of the stairs, there was a very nice receptionist who was dressed in traditional Korean garb. I tried to explain to her that I had a very embarrassing situation that I needed to speak to the doctor about. She replied that everyone who came to see Dr. Kim had an embarrassing situation to speak about, but in any case, she would have him see me in a couple of minutes.

I went into the doc's office, and he was very pleasant and with a smile bid me to be seated. I again mentioned and stressed the fact that I was extremely embarrassed to trouble him as I was having a problem with my PIPE!

He laughed and said that everyone who came to see him had a problem with their pipe.

When I pulled out my smoking pipe from the small felt bag that I carried it in, we both got hysterical with laughter. In less than five minutes, he fixed it and then refused to get paid, so I invited him for a night out at a local restaurant.

We started by drinking large bottles of Korean beer. Even then, Korean beer was very good. We finished our dinner, and a little bleary eyed, I mentioned that I was wary of what we were eating and that I was surprised that as a member of the medical profession, he didn't caution me. Dr. Kim's reply was that as an American with American standards, I should have cautioned him. Anyway, we survived and became fast friends.

My Wonderful Korean
Students

Teaching my young students at the *Chosun Ilbo* (local newspaper) was a great pleasure and an experience that I remember till this day. Mr. Nam, who was the editor and my top student, arranged it.

Since I always liked to joke around and play pranks, I would get the usual laughs, which relaxed the class. Sometimes I would bring a picture of a monkey into class, and that always broke them up, as monkeys were traditionally used to frighten away enemies. All of the Korean temples are adorned with a line of monkeys on each roof joint, from top to bottom.

There was always a great deal of giggling when I went to the blackboard. The reason was that in Korea at that time, nobody wrote with his or her left hand. Sometimes I would write with the white chalk in both hands, which really brought the house down.

During one class, I called a young female student by the name of Bo Yul Kim to the blackboard to finish a sentence. She did it well, and I walked over and patted her head. She seemed stunned by this, and as I looked around the classroom, all I saw were horrified looks. It seemed the culture in Korea—and much of Asia, for that matter—was that you not only limit your emotion, but you never touch anyone of the opposite sex in public. To touch the hair of a female was strictly forbidden. To see men walking down the street holding hands was common, and it was not considered sexual in any way.

Boy, did I have a hard time getting out of that one. Explaining that I came from a different culture with different attitudes and mores took a long time to accomplish. My abject apologies were received slowly but steadily until all was back to normal again.

At Christmas time (the cards that we sent home read, "This Christmas we are telling everyone to go to hell"), they threw a magnificent party for me in a traditional Korean restaurant. The girls dressed in traditional Korean long dresses. Songs were sung, and Colonel Kim sang "Oh My Papa" in English. Speeches were given, and the food was scrumptious: kimchi dishes, chap chae noodles, bulgogi and kalbi (meat was expensive and hard to get) and gotgoki (very spicy and even spicier than the winter kimchi). A great time was had by all.

Oh, I almost forgot: in early December, I was chatting with the fellows in the JAG office when I got a Red Cross radiogram informing me that my son Lee was born on December 2. I had prepared myself with a box of cigars and ran to Eighth Army headquarters screaming, "It's a boy, it's a boy," not realizing that I had run into General Decker's office (four-star general) during one of his meetings.

I didn't get shot, and when I ran into my office, General Griffin offered me a drink. When I got to the Red Cross unit, they had some kind of either microwave or cable system to make overseas calls. No dial tones as yet. I called Sylvia, but only one of us could speak at one time. You had to say "over" and click the button to speak. It was cumbersome but very exciting to speak to the new mother. This was one unforgettable day.

So now I was off to another R&R. This time I went by ferry to the southern coast of Japan. The crew all spoke Japanese, and my

Japanese language skills were serviceable, although my Korean was very limited. Note that in class all spoke Japanese because for many years when the Japanese were the conquerors of Korea, the Japanese language was mandatory. They gave me a nice bunk to sleep in, and the meals were "serviceable."

On this trip, I explored Japan from north to south. I loved the train ride when it arrived in the morning, and outside of the train, women were selling o soba noodles, which steamed in the morning air. A group of friends took me to a city called Kokura, where they made stainless-steel silverware. Japan went through a number of tough years before their manufacturing became modernized and sophisticated. There, at a sports center, they introduced me to a famous teacher of kendo. Kendo is a sparring sport with a long, bamboo type of training sword. Watching his students, I commented that it looked easy.

"Would you like to try?" he said.

"Of course," I said as I put on their special helmet and uniform. Before I could even move, I was hit all over the shoulders and body, standing there like a clown, never even able to move. Oh well, it's easier going back to the Shinto shrines and temples like the normal tourists do.

The only depressing part of this trip was going to Hiroshima. This was something tragic that they brought on themselves. Truman undoubtedly made the correct decision. More lives would have been lost on both sides if we had had to invade Japan. The populace was indoctrinated to fight until the end.

It was now time to go back to Korea and get back to work. I had become friendly with a Catholic priest and used to invite him to the OEC Club for drinks. He really appreciated that and reciprocated by inviting me for a weekend at this compound outside of the city, which may have been Uijongbu, north of Seoul. Also, I forgot whether it was a Jesuit or Dominican compound. Father John was extremely kind, and his only concern was putting me in a room with a large cross hanging over the bed. It didn't bother me, but I appreciated his thoughtfulness. Often I have wondered whatever happened to him.

For some reason, Halloween was a big holiday for us. Halloween was party time. You drank until you fell. The ambassador was long gone, and the last thing Captain Jim (Jimmy) and Mr. X (me) remembered was downing whiskeys at the OEC Club. Waking up out our stupor, we were in a very unfamiliar place.

Worse, our boots were gone, and walking around in khaki army socks was no pleasure. We had to get off the rocky road and into a town and then find the base. We didn't have a compass with us, and I had a notoriously bad sense of direction. After lots of aimless walking, we suddenly saw some two- and three-story buildings in the distance. Hopefully, that was Seoul.

As we approached in what seemed like an eternity, we saw a shocking sight. Flags were draped from the windows. Not just flags, but RED flags. My god, we must have wandered into North Korea. As we were now completely sober, we knew a number of things:

1. We couldn't be seen.
2. We had to head south.
3. If we were discovered by the MPs without boots, we would be court-martialed.

The sun was setting, so we figured out which way was south, hiding and frozen with fear every time we heard a sound. Feet stinging, hungry, and feeling cruddy, we walked, hid, walked, hid. It looked like the MSR ahead, which would lead to EASCOM (Eighth Army Support Command) and our base. Our luck; here was a cab. Luckily our documents hadn't been stolen, and I had MPCs hidden in my sock. "SAC Army Base!" we yelled in unison.

Since the driver was not responding, Jim went into his Turkish soldier act. The Koreans were deathly afraid of the Turkish soldiers, who all carried long knives. Jim was screaming gibberish and pounding the top of the taxi cab's front seat. "Yongsan! Yongsan! Reservation!" he yelled.

The driver sped to the post, but we had him leave us about fifty yards on the side. We were frightened again because if the MPs saw that we had no boots, we would be in a heap of trouble. When we got to the gate, we were in for a bit of luck. As we approached and showed our documents, a Korean honey bucket truck was just passing. The MPs were distracted by the noise and the smell of the human waste (which was used to fertilize their crops). Koreans are not overly fond of dogs; one of my friends from the JAG Corps saved a dog from the honey bucket brigade, but unfortunately, the smell never left the dog.

Anyway, we were saved, got back to the barracks, and told our story. Carl (who was a Harvard-trained lawyer and knew everything) laughed (one of the few times I had ever seen him laugh). Usually Carl had no common sense, but this time, he knew what the flags were about. No, we had not been in North Korea. There was a small village nearby inhabited by a small Nationalist Chinese community. It had been a Nationalist Chinese holiday! We didn't know the difference between Communist Chinese and National Chinese flags. Shame on us.

THIRTY-DAY LEAVE

I t was now April 1958, and my tour in Korea was winding down. Jimmy had already gone back to the States from the Twenty-Fourth Division due to his dad's death, so I applied for the thirty-day leave that I had accrued. This after numerous TDYs (temporary duty assignments) and R&Rs in Japan. At first I was granted a seventeen-day leave, and then it was extended. It would include the Dai Ichi Hotel in Tokyo, International Hotel in Hong Kong, the Macao Inn in Macao, the Presidential Palace in the Philippines, Kadena air force billets in Okinawa, the MAAG transient billets in Formosa, the Oriental Hotel in Bangkok, Rangoon Hotel in Burma, the Majestic Hotel in Saigon, and finally, the New Cambodia Hotel in Cambodia. I was scheduled to return at the end of July.

The last visa that I had to obtain was from the Philippines. Entering the consulate, I was met by two tough-looking, unsmiling gents. "What is the purpose of your stay?"

"Well, since I am friends with Mr. Garcia, the ambassador to Korea, I wanted to learn more about the country and possibly see about a master's degree in economics at the university."

They were for some reason not pleased with my answer. "Where do you intend on staying?"

I answered that Mr. Garcia mentioned that I could stay at the presidential palace. The two stone-faced, thug-looking characters got up and left the room for what seemed like hours (probably ten minutes). When they returned, they stated that I would be staying at the Manila Hotel in Manila and that I was NOT to mention Cosme Garcia's name, nor was I to inquire about him.

"OK," I said as they loudly stamped my visa on the table. I've always wondered in my travels throughout the world why customs agents got such a large thrill out of stamping the passport with a loud bang. They must feel that they can exercise their sense of power during the day and then go home to their meager pay and their subservience to their domineering wife.

I believe the first stop was Japan, where I would return for the final leg back. I arranged with my friends, who owed me favors, for another VIP flight to Tokyo, after which the trip would be mostly on commercial Pan Am #1 (the flights that went around the world).

There were six of us, and the two lowest-ranking were a navy lieutenant and I, the only enlisted man. I got friendly with Lieutenant Schwartz, who was a history buff and somewhat of a mystic. We decided to visit various cities that I had missed in my numerous trips there. Our conversations tended toward history, religion, and philosophy. His views were quite pronounced and sometimes even a bit scary. When we spoke about the death camps in Europe and I mentioned how shocking it was for a civilized, educated population to commit such crimes, his comment was that in the future, these crimes would be denied by some— although they would not go so far as saying that the Jews murdered the Germans, just that it never happened. Shocking me further, he stated that at one point Jews would be compared to Nazis. And this without a lot of drinking on his part.

We then discussed Americans as occupiers and civilized soldiers who would tend to shield women and children. The lieutenant then made an astounding prediction that hounds me to this day. He said that our next war would be in Southeast Asia to keep communism from spreading further and that during this war, US troops would commit a massacre against civilians. Later, whenever I would hear something about My Lai, this conversation would come to mind.

I was getting depressed, so I asked for lighter conversation. He proceeded to tell me about the person who spent months trying to track down the Dalai Lama of Tibet. The person went through all kinds of hardship and drama, climbing mountains and getting bum steers along the way. Finally he was directed to a cave where the Dalai Lama was meditating. "Your Highness," he said, "I have traveled many, many miles to find you, and I have only one question."

"What is that, my son?"

"WHAT IS THE SECRET OF LIFE?" he asked.

The Dalai Lama pondered this for a long time and finally answered: "Life is a fountain."

Dumbfounded, the person could only repeat the answer as a question. The Dalai Lama looked at him with puzzled eyes and responded: "SO LIFE ISN'T A FOUNTAIN?"

At this point the lieutenant was roaring with laughter as he explained that it was all a joke. So at least he had a sense of humor. At some point we got separated, and maybe it was for the best, as who knows what other predictions the good lieutenant had.

On to the Philippines

I hate the heat, and Southeast Asia at this time of year is a horrible inferno. This was 1958, and there was no AC. We landed in Manila, and as I stepped off the plane, the blast of heat hit me like a wave. I grabbed my bags and was in luck, as there was one empty taxi right there at the curb. What a break. "Manila Hotel," I called out.

His response was in clear English: "Yes, sir, my pleasure." This guy seemed quite friendly, and we seem to hit it off quite nicely. So after a while, I asked him how I could find a friend of mine who may be working for the ruling Nationalista Party and happened to be the brother of President Carlos Garcia.

"Why would you want to meet him?" the cab driver asked impassively.

"Well, he's a friend of mine from Korea, and he was the ambassador, but I lost track of him."

"Sorry, I can't help you."

We pulled up to the Manila Hotel on Dewey Boulevard. My reservation was in order, and while they were preparing my room, I went to the Jungle Room Bar for a nice, cold Filipino San Miguel beer. My room was ready, and I was starting to get ready for a shower when all of a sudden there was a loud banging on the door—and I mean loud.

"Who is it?" I asked, and the answer sounded like something military.

I ran to the phone and tried to call down to the desk, but no one answered. More loud banging, so I opened the door. There were two mean-looking gorillas standing there in their dark-green military uniforms. They shoved their way in. This was a little scary, to say the least.

The biggest one did the talking. "Weren't you told in our consulate that you were NOT to inquire about Cosme Garcia or the presidential palace?"

Apparently all was set up with the taxi driver, and there was obviously something serious going on with the brothers.

Since it looked as if they would be following me wherever I went, it was best to adhere to their wishes. I said that I understood and apologized. They left, and I needed a shower and a good stiff drink.

After cleaning up, I wandered down to Dewey Boulevard and stopped at the World War II museum where the Japanese held, tortured, and murdered civilians. It was right in the center of town. It was a dark, scary museum where you could almost hear the screams of the innocent men, women, and children.

I wandered into this raucous bar that looked like something out of an Old West movie except for those long, colored shirts that they wore. On the left when you walked in was a room that looked like a large coat-check room. Only you didn't check your coat and hat, you checked your .45 pistol. It was quite a sight, seeing rows of .45s and holsters with little white tags hanging down. Manila was apparently a bit of a rough place.

I did not have a great night's sleep in the hotel, as real or imagined, I thought I heard gunshots throughout the night. Later on I was to find for the most part that the natives were friendly and hospitable, and they loved Americans. The food was excellent, especially the *kare-kare* and the *arroz caldo*, which was a chicken-and-rice soup.

I was told the best place to cool off was Baguio, up in the mountains not far from Luzon. I got a cab (no questions about Cosme this time) in front of the hotel and told him that I wanted to go north. On the trip, something was mentioned about the Luzon jungle, and I said that I would love to see a jungle, as I had never seen one before. OK. Jose would be my guide.

We arrived at the forest (jungle) and got out to walk. It didn't resemble a jungle like the ones I had seen in the movies; it was just like walking through an overgrown forest. "Any wildlife or wild animals?" I asked.

"Yes. If you look at the branch above your head, there is a python!"

I glanced up and couldn't believe my eyes. There was this bright-green snake (I think he called it a python lizard) about twenty feet long and a few inches thick staring down at me.

"OK. Jungle tour is over; let's go on to Baguio, I say."

He **dropped** me off at a lovely hotel restaurant and told me I would have no trouble getting a cab to go back. In a way I felt safe, as with the authorities following me, I was sure the cab would be a legitimate one. As I approached the hotel, I was met by a family with a couple of kids who asked if I was an American. We would become fast friends after I related the python story, and they would eventually take me to their home in a small town and drive me back to Manila.

From there it was on to many other counties in Southeast Asia. They were all fascinating, with magnificent scenery, interesting people, terrible heat, and very high humidity. I couldn't get off the plane in India because I hadn't received a yellow-fever shot. It seemed that I had had every shot in the world before I left, but apparently they had missed one.

I've forgotten many of the various incidents, but in Thailand, the memory of the extreme friendliness of the people remains, along with a tour of an opium den. We were brought into a dark, large, smoky room, and the sight of very old women huddled in a corner was enough to cure me of any thoughts of using drugs or smoking pot. I'll stay with good cigars and pipes.

I usually managed to stay in decent hotels in the various countries, as I had saved up money from my sales of Ajinomoto (MSG) in both Japan and Korea. I had purchased the MSG in the PX in Seoul. In the Orient, MSG is commonly used in cooking to flavor food. In America, it seems that a doctor once felt ill after eating in a Chinese restaurant, and he publicized the fact that MSG was not good for you. Maybe it does affect some people, but I know it has never affected me in any way. Then again, with my stainless-steel stomach, I can eat almost anything without having any after effects.

The only place that I didn't feel comfortable in was Okinawa, where I felt a distinct atmosphere of resentment; this in spite of my wearing civilian clothes.

Korean Inspection Tour and the Major's Revenge

At some point while working for General Griffin at Eighth Army Support Command, I became friendly with a lieutenant colonel who, when he came down from Division, wanted brick accommodations instead of the tents that he was used to sleeping in. I was able to provide the accommodations that he wanted, and he became one of those who introduced me to noncoms who could get me jeeps and VIP flights.

He was also my protector from Major Jaworski, who, ever since he saw me at the Chosun Hotel with the Korean ambassador, had a real hate for me. The problem now was that his tour was ending, and I would have a few months without protection. General Griffin, although friendly, was too preoccupied with his duties. General Decker had four stars, but after I burst into his office during his staff meeting (after I had gotten word of my son being born), I kinda stayed away from him.

The colonel would be spending the next few months at HQ in Seoul, and since I was out of assignments, he asked if I could be temporarily appointed as his aide, which he was able to arrange.

The timing was good because right after that, the CO left, and Major Jaworksi took over as company commander. Oh, oh.

The colonel said not to worry, as he was going to take me on an inspection tour of the Korean II Corps as a nonspec. A nonspec means that you wear your uniform but show no rank. He had to show that I had some special importance, as we were meeting with a well-known Korean general who had been a hero during the war.

So off we went in our jeep, heading northwest, with the colonel driving since he knew the way. We had our pens and clipboard, as this was going to be an inspection tour. We finally got to the Korean HQ base, and we were greeted and saluted like celebrities. There was no time for a pass in review, although it would have been nice to have a parade in our honor. The inspection seemed to be going well, and it was getting close to retreat time, which is when the flags are lowered at dusk with a brief ceremony and bugle call.

That was when I was told to inspect the ammo dump. Upon entering, I first noticed that there were wooden cases of carbines on one side and rust-coated wooden boxes on the other side. I didn't know whether to freeze or run. My God there were GRENADES inside those boxes! As my blood drained, I ran outside and tracked down the colonel.

"Not to worry," he said. "We will give the general a perfect score, but tell him to dispose of the grenades."

Dispose he did. The general had everyone go to the far side of the base. After about thirty minutes, we heard pops and explosions. Our illustrious general blew up the ammo dump, and he came to us smiling and acting like one happy guy. His interpreter told us that in our honor, he was having key personnel from all over the division for a banquet. We were told that we would be honored and given a Korean medal, which I have long since misplaced.

Since it was considered a combat zone, it was OK to come in fatigues, which of course we did. The colonel, being in Army

Intelligence, knew a lot about this commander, as he always did his research before meeting with anyone. We were seated at the head of one of two long tables where we are in the *L* on one end and the general at the other end. Along with our uniforms, we were required to wear our hard hats (helmets). Remember, it was a combat zone, even though there hadn't been any combat in a few years.

Some of the Korean troops were showing up from the surrounding areas, and some of them didn't know the details of the general's habits. A few started to remove their hard hats. The next thing I knew, the general took off his helmet and smashed one of the poor fellows across the face. The point was taken very quickly and everyone got the message.

We were now ready for dinner. The large bottles of Korean beer were on the table, but we were served something called Mool first, which was a milky alcohol drink. Then winter kimchi (very hot) was served with appetizers and pickled vegetables, which is traditional. Then the barbecued flank steaks, which were quite good.

There was lots of belching as the dinner was winding down, as this is considered a polite sign telling the host that the food and drinks were good. The colonel then nudged me. "Whatever you do, don't take out a toothpick."

I didn't have one and don't use them but couldn't understand the comment. As I said, the colonel knew the general well. The next thing we knew, the general stood up, took his helmet off, and started smashing people on the side of the head. It didn't take long for the troops who didn't know him to realize that toothpicks were verboten.

We had a good laugh on the way back to SAC, but I thought about what kind of honor the Korean general would have given to me if he had found out that I was a noncom and not some officer from an inspector's general unit. I kind of felt like Danny Kaye in that very funny move *The Inspector General.*

After the inspection of the Korean II Corps, it was a relief to get back to SAC (Seoul Area Command), as that eerie experience seemed to haunt me on the drive back. Just a few months to go, and I'd be back home to see my wife and young son, get discharged, and assigned to reserve training for a couple of years. But I figured it would be a boring few months, as most of my friends from JAG who bunked in the same building had already been shipped home. The colonel was about to leave, and our company commander, whom I had gotten on well with, was gone, replaced by my nemesis, Major Jaworski.

My Korean friend Mr. Ro was in Pusan investigating a large, very suspicious fire. Mr. Ro was a short, thin, jolly fellow with a twinkle in his eye. He had good connections and worked as a translator. I suspect that he may have even become president of South Korea in the nineties. He'd watch me at work or sometimes we went to a restaurant in Seoul. His favorite comment was: "You are majoring it again," which meant that I was acting like an officer. Of course I was frustrated that I wasn't one.

Then there was Major Kim. This Korean marine major was tall and tough, with a chubby, smiling face that belied his toughness. No doubt he saved my life. One evening I decided to walk by myself along the MSR, which was the unpaved road to Seoul. As I was walking, I overheard a very loud commotion and hollering inside a large Korean MP station. I remember the large doors and the brightly lit interior. As I walked in, I was horrified to see a soldier holding his pistol to the head of this kid, maybe sixteen years old if even that, and the soldier was screaming away in Korean (naturally) at this poor young fellow. I'll never know why I did this because I am anything but the brave type, but I pulled out my .45 pistol and told the soldier to put his weapon down. Whether he understood the words I don't know, but he apparently understood the meaning, and he lowered his weapon.

At this point this giant of a Korean came out, and it turned out that he was the Major Kim. He jerked me outside and pushed me around the corner away from a streetlight and asked me (in English) if I had completely lost my mind. "Do you love communists?" he screamed.

"No, I don't love communists. Anything but, and the army wouldn't have given me a top security clearance if I had been one. But this is a young boy and not a combat soldier."

"OK." And he burst out laughing and said, "Let's go for a beer."

We went to this Korean bar that had large bottles of beer. When the beer neared bottom of the bottle, they poured it on the ground under the table. Also, because I was an American, there was no way they would let us pay for anything.

Major Kim and I became great friends after that, but somehow I lost track of him.

Since I didn't have a real assignment anymore, there was little to do except go to the OEC Club with the few friends who were left or the library and listen to jazz, show tunes, and popular music records.

Two or three times a week, I was teaching my young Korean students. That was always a great joy. One Saturday I checked the bulletin board, perhaps not too closely, as I didn't expect any assignment on a Sunday. I didn't notice anything, so I went to my teaching class on Sunday. As usual, they were bright, fun to be with, and quick to learn. After dinner, I returned to my bunk, and there was a note from the sergeant major instructing me to report to his office at 0800 hours. What in the world could this be about?

I sensed trouble, so I put on my well-creased dress uniform, spit-shined shoes, and shiny buckle, and I proceeded to his office.

"Soldier, you missed your duty assignment yesterday, and that means that you were AWOL, and that means either a court-martial or an article 15."

I explained to no avail that I had checked the board on Saturday.

I was told to report to (you guessed it) Major Jaworski at 1500 Hours (3:00 p.m.), which I did with a very sharp salute. "Reporting as ordered, sir." My explanation fell on clogged ears.

With his piercing eyes, he just stared at me for what seemed like an eternity and then blurted out: "I knew that I would finally get you, soldier. I always get my man!" He offered me either the court martial or the article 15, and I had forty-eight hours to decide.

Most of my JAG buddies had gone, but I asked one of the attorneys his advice. "Article 15 is company punishment," he said, "and you will probably get thirty days' restriction to the base."

So that was what I decided to take. I reported back to the major, and without looking up, he growled, "Loss of two grades and loss of pay." (Wait until my wife gets her next allotment check—which she did and nearly croaked).

I was now a PFC! I was obviously set up, but there was nothing that I could do.

The major had finally gotten his revenge.

HOME FROM KOREA

The last few weeks before I was to be shipped back to the
United States, I found it to be very sad to be saying good-
bye to my wonderful students, but the thought of going home
and seeing my son for the first time (he was now nine months
old) was so exciting and overpowering that it was all that I could
think about. Some of these students were Lee Kuhn Hong, Ho
Sang Lee (Korean Agricultural Bank), Keun Hong Lee, Ki Young
Nam (editor of *Chosun Ilbo* newspaper), Ho Sang Lee (Korean
Agricultural Bank), Keun Hong Lee, Ki Chung Kim, Lee Kuhn
Hong, Kim Chul Kim (ex-minister of finance), Sung Yul Kim,
Han Ock Young. There were others, of course, but these are the
names that I have from their correspondence that we carried on
for a few years. Sadly, after a couple of years, I lost track of them.

I would be leaving the "Land of the Morning Calm," which
was founded well over five thousand years ago, and its deep, long,
and often tragic history.

The trip back was on the SS *Patrick Henry*. This was one of the
Liberty ships built in 1941. By 1957 it was an old tub, and I believe
it was decommissioned shortly after my return. I managed to get
a good job on the ship and had my own room, the only problem

being that I was close to the foghorn. Due to the lousy weather, it went off every twenty seconds or so. The blast was unbearable, and to this day I can't take loud noises except blues music and jazz. Any excuse to get into the interior of the ship brought great relief.

As we approached Adak, Alaska, the sight of tremendous whales was truly unbelievable. I was never much at taking pictures, so I missed out on some really great shots from Alaska to Vancouver. We stopped briefly at Adak, Alaska, but we weren't allowed to leave the ship. Since I was to be discharged in Fort Hamilton, Brooklyn, I was put on Capital Airlines (if I remember correctly) for a four-stop, nonpressurized flight. If you have a sinus condition or excess mucous in your nasal cavity, the pain becomes excruciating when you take off and land. You keep swallowing in order to clear your ears, but somehow it doesn't work, and for about an hour after you land, you can't hear a thing. So now, from coast to coast and with multiple takeoffs and landings in propeller planes going around 225 miles per hour, we finally arrived at Idlewild Airport (which around 1963 was to become JFK).

Some years later, Sylvia and I were looking for an address in Queens, and since I have never gone anywhere without getting lost, I took a road next to the airport, and somehow there was an opening. Amazingly, we ended up on the runway near a taxiing plane. Don't ask me how I did that. Today, of course, that would not be possible to do.

In those days, you could walk on or near the runway and greet the arriving passengers. You can imagine the thrill when I departed the gangplank, and there in front of me was my mother, my father, my wife with our nine-month-old son Lee, my sister Eleanor, and her husband. Upon seeing me, Lee started to bawl like a baby (he was a baby!). I guess that I would cry too if I saw a 175-pound, five-foot-ten-inch monster coming at me to kiss and hug me.

Off we went to Mama Leone's Italian restaurant in midtown Manhattan, where we had gone the night before I departed for Fort Lewis, Washington, two years prior. The restaurant was known for hearty Italian pasta, tremendous portions at very reasonable prices. It was certainly more fun having dinner there the second time around. I saved the menu, which was very large in stature, and it showed all of the various food items with their incredibly low late 1950 prices. Some years later, however, I gave the old menu to Mama Leone's granddaughter, who had a restaurant with the same name in Florida, only to find out that she was on the outs with her family, especially her grandmother, whom she claimed was a mean witch.

After a brief stop at Fort Hamilton to process my discharge (honorable), I was on my own. I was placed in the reserves for a few more years, but for some reason, I never had to go to any meetings or field trips.

My parents still lived on Clarkson Avenue in Brooklyn, and we eventually moved into a ground-floor, two-story house just a few doors from their apartment building. The owners, the Carimellis, were a lovely family. We had a garage in the rear and a backyard in which we used to barbecue together, along with their son and their daughter. We didn't have a signed lease. When I met and sat with Mr. Carimelli, we looked each other in the eye and mentioned simultaneously that we were "old school" and had learned from our parents that when you stood face to face and looked into someone's eyes when you were going to do business, you could get a pretty good idea of that person's character. In this case we were right; in all the time that we were there, neither of us had any kind of problem with the other. It certainly would be nice if things worked that way in today's climate. Obviously you just can no longer rely on a simple handshake to do business.

Also, by this time Syl was getting used to Brooklyn, which was far from the country-club style that she had been used to. In Brooklyn, you carted a wire wagon down the street to the

Flatbush Avenue shopping area, where you did your shopping. The first time my mother presented Syl with the wire wagon, Syl wanted to know if she expected her to drag it down the street. My mother's reply was that "finer women than you have done this, and therefore, so will you!" And she did sometimes run over the ankles of women on crowded Flatbush Avenue.

There was a famous bakery by the name of Ebinger's Bakery, but the help was so intimidating and brusque in their New York accents that Syl was afraid to ask what anything was. For dessert we had red-frosted cupcakes for weeks afterward, until she finally had the nerve to ask for something else. We did get settled quickly, however, and I was now ready to go out into the working world.

THOM MCAN SHOES

My job search didn't take long. I went for an interview in Midtown Manhattan on West Forty-Third Street. Thom McAn was a division of Melville Shoe Company, which eventually became the Melville Corporation, a conglomerate with many well-know companies, including Marshall's, T.J. Maxx, Bob's, Vanguard, KB Toys, Linens 'n Things, and CVS. Most were eventually sold off, and Melville in later years became CVS. In the various companies, there were thousands of stores, which included a famous shoe chain called Miles Shoes.

The job was management training, and I was chosen along with four other bright-looking recruits.

Jet planes were just starting to fly, and we all got excited with the idea of flying on jets, especially me, as I could now avoid the ear problem on takeoffs and landings. We were flown to Boston and then driven to Maine to see how their warehouses and factories operated (Thom McAn made most of their shoes in their own factories in New England). It was all new and fascinating.

After that, our training continued at the Westchester Country Club in Larchmont, New York, where the famous management guru Peter Drucker lectured us on management procedures. He was dynamic and memorable, and I could see why he had become so noteworthy. His management techniques and writings are still valid, and he is still considered our top management guru.

After the tours, orientations, and training, the five of us were split up with the idea that we learn each job function from the bottom up. That meant that we started in a shoe store as a stock boy, which is how they characterized the job in those days. My first store was on Forty-Second Street in Manhattan. As a stock boy, I put away shipments onto the shelves, put back the shoes that the sales people had left by the stools, dusted the displays, straightened the socks, and swept the floors.

Soon I was promoted to salesperson. The stores had an "up" system, which meant that we lined up in the back, and when a potential customer entered, whoever was next up approached the customer. The new guy was put last, of course, although if it looked as if a loser was coming in, they would designate me to approach him (it was a men's store).

They were a ravenous and very competitive bunch. Many of the customers were old-timers who knew what they wanted and were quite easy to deal with. You still had to bring out extra styles. If there was any hesitation, you had to exercise a T.O, (turn over), which meant you called another salesperson over to finish the sale on the pretext that he was the manager or something. Actually, it worked pretty well. The crews, although greedily competitive, were both friendly and helpful. The managers especially were diehard loyal Thom McAn supporters. Many of them had been with the company for many years, and they liked to brag that Mr. Melville didn't fire anyone during the depression. On the other hand, the pay was meager, and Mr. Melville demanded loyalty coupled with 100 percent honesty out of his workers.

Ward Melville formed Thom McAn in the 1920s, and although the name was fictitious, many customers would claim that they knew Thom. Melville was extremely charitable. He founded schools and gave away four hundred acres in Long Island, where a town was named for him. I was clearly working for a class company.

Because this was a management training program, we were moved along quickly, and the next step for me was assistant manager. I was transferred to Astoria, Queens, where the manager was Greg Simonelli. Greg was a pro, and he went out of his way to teach me about the company, selling, and store management. His friendliness and enthusiasm boiled over to those around him. As assistant manager, I had to work most weekends and nights, but that was to be expected.

I was soon transferred to the border of Brooklyn and Queens, where my manager was Frank Santangelo. Frank was one of the old-timers, and he was a perfectionist and a pro. We became quite friendly, and he invited us over to his family's house for a traditional Italian dinner. Although I was familiar with the procedure, it was new to Sylvia. Starter bites first, then salads, and then pasta. Sylvia thought the dinner was over, but then they then brought out the main course, which was a large roast beef. Syl couldn't believe her eyes. I was enjoying the wine and then the grappa. Of course, later on, when they brought bowls of fruit, salamis, sausages, and pepperonis, Syl turned grass green, and I laughed as I told her that she could wash it down with espresso. We left this nice, old-time Italian family a few pounds heavier.

Frank's district manager was a real old-timer. He was crusty and highly suspicious of his managers. There was a cemetery across the street from the store, and Tony would hide behind one of the mausoleums to see when the store opened. Heaven forbid that the manager or the assistant came one minute late. Luckily we never did.

It looked as if I was now ready to become a store manager. This meant that I would have full responsibility for the personnel, the sales results, the entire store inventory, and the cash. The store that they gave me was a small one in the Inwood section of the Bronx in a quiet neighborhood. I was there for about four months. Business picked up, and when the auditor

103

checked me out, I was $3.99 over. My district manager (DD), of course, questioned why it wasn't perfect, and frankly I wondered also.

Next was Fordham Road, also in the Bronx. Only now we were talking about a very large, active store. My DD came in after a couple of weeks to tell me that they were promoting my existing assistant to manager. They had a new candidate to take his place, but there was one problem with him. What was the problem? Well, it seemed that at his previous store, he lost a "drop." A drop was a heavy cloth bag with a zippered lock on top that you placed your cash in. It could be deposited during the day if the cash receipts were substantial, but you always deposited the drop in the bank after you closed the store. Tony said he made the drop, but the bank couldn't find it the next day.

Would I interview him? Of course, I responded. I met Tony, and he swore that he never took any money. I believed him and liked his personality, so I gave the OK for him to be my assistant manager. In the meantime, I cautioned him about my rules when handling money. The important one was that whenever he made the drop, he must have another person accompany him. That way, he would have a witness.

Everything was going fine, and business in the store was picking up. One day Tony was on the late shift, and he was also due to open the next morning. I got a frantic phone call from one of the salesman saying that I had to rush down to the store. There was panic all around. Tony was white with fright and bawling like a baby. "It happened a second time!'

I told him to calm down, and I asked him if he made the drop with a witness. He did, so I told him to come with me to the bank across the street. We went to the teller, who told him that the drop did not show up. I asked if they had checked the chute for obstructions and got a nasty reply that they weren't going to tear down the bank wall to look for a nonexistent drop. He also stated that if the drop was made last night, it would have shown up in the morning.

I had had enough of this twerp and asked for the manager. Mr. S came out, and I informed him that if the drop was not recovered in one hour, I was going to inform the FBI since there was a witness that the drop had been made. Oh, I forgot: I had canvassed some of the neighboring stores quickly before I went to the bank, and the Ripley Men's Store, which was right next to the bank, had a missing drop just a month before. I was now thrilled, and I said to Tony that he nothing to worry about and that the news was great.

I did contact the FBI, and the money was found. It turned out that the teller was embezzling money from the bank in various ways, including stealing the two drops. He may still be in jail for all I know.

Tony couldn't praise or do enough for me, although I felt it was just simple common sense. He did well after that and went on to a successful career with Thom McAn with no further blemishes. The office and my DD were happy.

Soon after, I was given a promotion to the largest store in the chain on Forty-Second Street in Manhattan, in the same store where I had started as a stock boy (now they are called stock persons). I was less than a hundred dollars short when I checked out, which was fine for a large store.

The Forty-Second Street store was quite an experience. Not only was this a high-crime area with every kind of hooker, grifter, con person, and thief you could think of, but also the wildest-looking and wildest-acting nut cases you ever saw. Still, it was a busy store, and we had fun and took most everything as a joke and with a smile.

I got friendly with a guy who would sit on the sidewalk near the store with his legs folded under and his crutches at his side. At the end of the day, he would stand up, tuck his crutches under his arm, and walk to his hotel nearby after a pretty good haul. He took me to his hotel once and introduced me to the men and women con artists, all of whom roomed at that hotel. Most of those who were blind could see, and most of the cripples could walk. They got quite a kick of the naïve tourists they encountered. Meeting them helped because for the most part, they kept the cons and the crooks out of our store.

One day, however, I was near the cash register when this sharp-looking fellow was buying a sixty-nine-cent pair of socks. He gave the cashier a twenty-dollar bill and a penny and then proceeded to thoroughly confuse her. I knew she was about to lose twenty dollars, so I rushed over and grabbed all of the money on the counter and told the cashier to call the cops.

The guy was screaming, and I told him that his choice was to leave and never set foot in the store again or get arrested, as the police were on the way. What he didn't know was the pay phone was all the way in the back. To save money when making a call, we would stick a wire in the phone, ground it, and then get a dial tone. A customer had to put the dime in the slot. (In any case we hadn't actually called the police).

Another time, a young fellow walked in and nervously sat on one of the front seats (already a bad sign). He asked the salesperson for a size 10½, tried it on, and all of a sudden was running out of the store with the salesperson running after him—but to no avail, as the thief disappear into Times Square.

It turned out OK, though, as he left a brand-new pair of Flagg Bros. shoes, which was only two doors up from us. I went to their store and got a refund of $10.99. The shoes that he left were $8.99, so we ended up with a $2.00 profit.

One day it was pouring outside. A strange-looking dude walked in and asked for a cheap pair of rain shoes. He said $2.99 was too high for him, so they discovered an old style that was just $1.99. This was still too much, so using the "T.O." system, they called me over. The only thing that I could think of was that in the trash there were some of the plastic bags that some of the better shoes were wrapped in. I pulled two of the bags out of the trash, slipped them over his shoes, and tied a knot at the back.

"How much?" he wanted to know.

I told him that they were free, as we wanted to service our customers.

The guy was ecstatic as he danced out of store stomping his feet. He continued to stomp, looking like Gene Kelly in *Singing in the Rain* as he laughed and stomped down Seventh Avenue, splattering water as he went.

Finally, there was a commotion at the front desk. It seemed that this old gentleman wanted a refund. The problem was that the shoes were clearly marked "Florsheim." I tried to explain that I couldn't give a refund on someone else's shoes. He wasn't buying it, as he only bought Thom McAn shoes and had never been in a Florsheim shop, and further, he knew Thom McAn. I couldn't help him.

About a half hour later, I got a call from the main office, which was around the corner on Forty-Third Street. It was one of the vice-presidents, Richard McCarthey. He said that he had this nice gentleman in front of him who wanted a refund, and he was surprised that he was refused.

I said to Mr. McCarthey (we were formal in those days) that I didn't think that it would be fair to the company to give a refund on someone else's product. His response was that the man in his mind thought that this was our shoe and that we should give him a refund to keep him out of our competitor's store. Florsheim was next door, so maybe it was easy to confuse the two.

After the refund incident, Frank Rooney, the president of Melville, came into the store with a man from Spain. All of our shoes were made in America, and most at TM plants in New England. Mr. Rooney wanted to know whether Spanish shoes would sell in the store, and if so, which styles?

I told him definitely, even though they were a buck or so higher than the styles we were currently carrying.

Mr. Rooney asked why I picked a particular shoe. I replied that we had a large Italian clientele, and this kidskin ankle bootie would remind them of the "gator"-style slipper they liked to wear.

We got a couple of cases delivered, and they sold out in a week, which for a men's shoe was very unusual. Mr. Rooney came into the store all excited and wanted to know how I knew and what I done to promote the style. I explained that I had noticed the customers' habit of looking at the front display and then walking toward the door on the opposite side of the vestibule, so I placed a pair prominently in the front and again in the rear by the door. It worked like a charm. Thom McAn was now starting to import shoes.

Two weeks later I got word that I was going to be transferred to a new flagship store, which was the old Globe Theatre on Forty-Eighth Street and Eighth Avenue. I didn't check out of this store too well, as it turned out that my assistant manager was stealing. In a way, I was lucky, as the shortage was held to about $1,200—not a small amount at the time, but under the circumstances, it could have been worse. What was bad, however, was that he had a boyfriend who had persuaded him to borrow our black-and-pink Mercury. After I lent him the car, they both disappeared with the money and the car.

I had a friend at the FBI at the time. I called him and told him that our car had been stolen. He questioned me as to the circumstances, and when I told him that I had lent the car to John, his response was that if I gave John the keys, it would not be considered a stolen vehicle. However, as a friend, he would find the Mercury for us.

A few weeks later, I got a call from the FBI, and they wanted to know whether I trusted my in-laws. Trusted my in-laws? What kind of question was that? Well, it seemed that the Mercury was left at the Birmingham Airport, of all places. We called our in-laws and told them to bring it to their house in Mountain Brook and that we would explain when we got to Birmingham.

Anyway, back to the store. Charlie Drucker was the new manager. Charlie was one suave guy, also a Thom McAn old-timer. Charlie was cocky and knew everything. In checking him in, I tried to explain that this store was like no other in the chain, but he viewed me as the kid and was paying zero attention. I had just finished explaining that our biggest worry as far as theft was concerned was the large counter of socks in the front, where we happened to be standing.

As I was trying to explain the techniques the crooks used, this tall bum came waltzing in. He was wearing an old, dirty camel-hair overcoat that he had obviously found, as it was too long for his body and was dragging on the ground. I knew this was trouble but waited to see Charlie's reaction.

No reaction as the bum slipped an armful of men's socks into the coat's upper side pocket.

"Charlie," I screamed, "this is your inventory, and you are about to lose mucho dinero on your first day" as I reached into the bum's coat and pulled out the pile of socks that had been sitting on the sock rack.

Charley sheepishly apologized as I threw the bum out of the store and threatened to call the cops.

Before I go on to the Forty-Eighth Street store, a quick word about the Fourteenth Street store, where I had also worked. I got some of my best training there. Besides that, it was perfectly safe since we had a large back room where the police from the precinct took their breaks and had their coffee. Tony Morales was from Puerto Rico and was a great manager. Eventually he was promoted to Rio Piedras in Puerto Rico as district manager, and he turned the Puerto Rico district into the best and most profitable area in the chain. Sylvia and I used to love going to Puerto Rico, where we would often have a fine dinner at Tony's home (except for the plantains, which I didn't care for). We also enjoyed the better restaurants, clubs, and casinos.

NEW STORE: FORTY-EIGHTH AND BROADWAY

I was being moved to a new Thom McAn men's store that would be located in the old Globe Theatre on Forty-Eighth and Broadway (Broadway, baby!). HQ expected a dramatic opening that would be advertised in all five boroughs. It was scheduled for just before Thanksgiving, and they were going to bring in a team of managers from all over to service the crowds. A betting pool was set up to see who could guess closest to the number of shoes sold in the four-day scheduled opening. My guess was ten thousand pair, with the next highest guess being less than four thousand. Nobody in the history of the men's shoe business had ever sold that many shoes in so short of a period of time. They all shook their heads and laughed at my crazy prediction.

They didn't realize that I had a plan. Our policy was that anyone could exchange a purchase in any Thom McAn store, even without a receipt. So my instructions to everyone were to tell their customers that to save time, they should just take any pair of shoes and exchange them at their local store.

We were ready to roll, but when I entered the store in order to start setting up with the crew, I couldn't believe how small it was. There was a small stage in the rear and a front foyer that had room for the registers, a large sock rack, and a notions display, but there was room for only eighteen chairs.

So now I had to check to see that my plan (scheme) was re-inforced. I pounded it into all of the crew again: "Give the customer any shoe, any size, and tell them to exchange it in their local store."

It was opening day, and the crew was all there gawking at the long line that stretched around the block. There were police, some mounted; reporters; and execs from the office, who were all talking about the scene on this cold November morning. There were four days of chaos, fun, and, more importantly, unbelievable sales that went on until midnight Saturday.

Celebrations were in order. I wanted to have a party with the crew in the basement, but because of the strict moral climate of the management, liquor of any kind was a no-go. Not even a cold beer was permitted, so we commemorated the occasion with sandwiches and soda. The final count of shoes sold: 10,028. I won the pool and was a hero. When asked by the bosses and others how I had known, I just smiled and told them that I had a complicated formula to figure it out.

OK, we'd had our fun, and now we had to do business without promotions and giveaways. In the ad for the opening, we had offered a shoeshine kit as the giveaway, and that apparently had helped the promotion. The store was open until 11:00 p.m. every night, with the busiest period being when the Broadway shows let out. People passed the store in droves, and those who came in bought lots of socks but few shoes. I had to find a way to get them to sit down.

I had a solution. I called my good friend from the army, Jim Anglisano, and told him that I needed him onstage to play the accordion. Jim, being the showman that he was, readily agreed, but I first had to get permission from Gus Caminiti, who was my manager.

Now Gus was a good man, but he was not what you would call either an experimenter or a forward-thinking person, so I knew I was going to have a little battle. Sure enough, he had all kinds of reasons why it was a bad idea. I insisted that the only way we were going to get business in that store and pay the high rent was to do something dramatic. Gus finally said that he might agree, but the law said that you had to be a union member (I think I was a member of Local 1260) to entertain in New York.

So I asked Jim, and sure enough, he was a member of the musician's union. Without telling Gus, I booked him, and he arrived around 9:00 p.m. on a Thursday evening and began to play his accordion. He was good, by the way.

I told my assistant Ralph to keep the door open. Sure enough, they came flocking in and bought not only lots of hosiery but also shoes.

All of a sudden Ralph froze. Who was standing there but the executive vice-president, Dave Hermann. Mr. Hermann had a tough reputation, and he was feared by everyone. Ralph fled to the rear of the store, and I greeted Mr. H.

"What's going on here?" he barked.

I explained that I had to pick up business, and it seemed to be working. He asked for the records before Jim arrived, and then he wanted to see the sales after Jim arrived. The records showed a very dramatic increase.

"Good job, son," he intoned and left the store.

I told Ralph that he could come out from the back now. The next day, I got a call from the TM VP, Richard McCarthey. "I hear that you had a visitor last night."

"Yes, sir."

"Did you clear this with Gus, the district manager?"

"Well, not exactly, but I did make sure that the accordionist belonged to the union."

"I hear your figures are way up."

"Yes, sir."

"Great job." And the crusty VP hung up, as he wasn't going to go over the head of the executive vice-president.

The Globe Theatre had moved down to Forty-Second Street and Eighth Avenue, where they showed porno movies. (The answer is no. I never set foot in that theatre.)

When Jim couldn't play anymore, I had to find other ways to pick up business. We did everything from handing out business cards to having my assistant either act as a mannequin in the front window or put on live fashion shows. The Actor's Fund in Englewood, New Jersey, also had an agreement with the store to send out-of-work actors and actresses to the store to obtain free pairs of shoes. I had the autographs of such people as Milton Caniff, Robert Ruark, and Fred Allen.

We did anything to get business into the store, and before long HQ notified me that they were moving me to a job as a troubleshooter and assistant district director of the Chicago area.

They moved Charley from the Forty-Second Street store to become manager of this one (smaller volume but greater prestige). I tried to explain the uniqueness of the store and what had to be done to create business, but Charley was still not listening. Some months later, Charley was not making his figures, and he called me up in a panic wanting to know "what the hell you did." I tried to explain to him that this was a unique store, and he had to be very creative.

On our move to Chicago, we found a house to rent in what was then a small, mostly farming community outside of Chicago called Addison. But before we left, I scraped the side of the car rushing Syl to the hospital in order to give birth to our second child.

I went on to Chicago before the family came, as they needed me there urgently. It seemed that a manager and an assistant had both quit at the same time and angrily sabotaged the store by pulling out every shoe from both the wall shelves and the back-room shelves and tossing them into the center of the floor in the front selling area. What a mess! The auditor arrived shortly after I did and promptly announced that he had never seen anything like this and that there was no way that he could audit the store.

With the crew that we had on hand, we took off our shirts and went to work placing all the shoes back in the walls. I worked almost forty-eight hours straight with just short breaks to eat and go to the bathroom.

The phone rang, and it was my very agitated spouse. "I just wanted to know if you are alive," she shouted into the phone. Bang! She hung up.

It took us almost a week to straighten things out. I went to a barber for a shave and haircut, and when the office complained that I put that on my expense account, my response was, "I grew the damn hair on company time, and you're going to pay for it." They did.

The store was located in Berwyn, Illinois, which was near Cicero (a very rough city where the bartenders kept baseball bats, which they didn't hesitate to use, under their counters for unruly patrons). Berwyn was a city of mostly people of Czech descent. Their homes were spotless, with perfectly manicured lawns. They all worked and came into the store from 6:00 p.m. on. This meant that we hired mostly part-timers because the rush lasted only a couple of hours. The customers all had very wide feet, and they knew exactly what they wanted. After trying on the shoe, they would stamp their foot twice and go up to the counter to pay with no further fuss. You couldn't find easier (as long as you had what they wanted) customers anywhere.

We were ready to reopen, and they sent me Tony G over from another store to manage the Berwyn store. Tony was kind of rough around the edges. The crew was lined up in the back, and I gave them instructions to start by thoroughly cleaning up the place. I grabbed a broom and started sweeping the vestibule in the front of the store, and I gave Tony a mop and told him to start mopping the floor.

He scowled at me and said that he was no God damn janitor, so I immediately decked him. "What did you do that for?" he asked, but it seemed to set the tone because everyone moved like lightning, even this giant truck driver who I was afraid was going to deck me! He was a part-timer, and he was absolutely fabulous with children.

The other stores didn't have these problems, and except for the fact that it was the hottest summer on record up until that time, all went reasonably smoothly. I even enjoyed the lunches in Berwyn, as the restaurants specialized in game, venison, and the like.

Addison at the time was not the most exciting place. It seemed that the housewives sat around and gossiped while they snapped green beans. Syl and I would occasionally go to downtown Chicago, where the restaurants were varied and top notch. We saw a few shows and got to watch Shelley Berman in person.

Winter came, and it was the coldest damn winter that they had ever experienced, especially in the suburbs. When I took out the garbage in the rear of the house, the wind was so bad that I ended up putting the garbage in the neighbors' garbage cans three doors down from our house. We went thirty days with temperature never reaching above zero. To start the car, I had to heat up the distributor cap with a lighter and then take it to a local heated garage to warm up.

It was not only the cold, but there was one snowstorm after another. One night a blizzard dropped twenty inches of snow or more on an already-existing pile of snow. I got up in the morning only to find that I couldn't open either the front or the back door, as the drifts of snow had piled up against them so that they couldn't be opened. It was very depressing.

As we sat there feeling very lucky that we still had electricity, the phone rang. It was the home office. It seemed that I was being promoted to the distribution office in Clifton, New Jersey, and they want to know how soon I could leave. My answer was simple: "Just as soon as I can dig my way out of here."

When I hung up, Syl wanted to know what the job was. I had no idea, and we didn't care just as long as we got away from the Chicago winter. As soon as I could dig out of the mess, I got into the car and drove through snow, ice, and mud from Addison to New Jersey. There were times when I was the only one on the road.

Syl and the kids soon followed by plane. They sat her next to a cranky old guy who complained that he had to sit next to an infant. A young Catholic priest saved the day and took the old coot's seat. My young son never gave out a peep, and the priest and Syl joked all the way to Newark.

When I got to the office, I discovered something that I hadn't known or realized, and that was that along with the promotion, there would be a large drop in salary. I had been one of the highest-paid people in the field, but since I was moving from a field position to a staff position, my pay was cut by around $130 per week. In the 1960s, that was a lot of dough.

CLIFTON, NEW JERSEY, DISTRIBUTION CENTER (CNJ)

One of our close University of Alabama friends who was living in the area at the time told us that Teaneck, New Jersey, was a nice place to live, so we found a garden apartment on Teaneck Road across the street from a Carvel and a Popeye's Chicken, both of which we loved. The office—CNJ, as it was called—was a combination warehouse, distribution center, and buying office. My assignment was to distribute the women's footwear from the warehouse to the stores in the most expeditious manner. There were no computers, but during that time, I had an excellent memory and knew all of the store numbers (hundreds) and their characteristics. This was a great help as it saved time and helped me do my job more efficiently.

My boss at the time was Bill Rossiter, who was the brother of a famous historian. In just a couple of months, he called me to come into his office to promote me to merchandiser, which was the next step to being a buyer.

"Wait a minute," I announced. "I don't know if I can afford another promotion. How much is this promotion going to cost me?"

Bill explained that this promotion was free! I ended up writing all of the merchandising procedures, spending time with the various buyers, and going to the shoe shows in the New York area. I again did well, and I was soon promoted to women's shoe buyer, as the current buyer had decided to retire after many years with the company. I even received a nice raise in pay.

At this point, we decided to buy our first house, on Northumberland Road in Teaneck. It cost around $23,000, and we were both scared to death thinking about how we would ever be able to pay the mortgage.

My new boss was Bill Muckley, who was a vice-president with a very officious and serious manner. Bill was always having closed-door meetings. My desk was in the open not far from his office, and everyone would make fun of Bill's antics, especially the door closings. One day I was working late and Bill had already left, so I removed the door from its hinges and put it in the warehouse, out of sight. Mr. Muckley came in the next morning, and the first thing he did, which he did every morning, was sweep his hand where the door would normally be and start to march into his office, not yet realizing that there was no door in his hand. Out he popped, and now he discovered that the door was missing.

Everyone was waiting for his reaction. Bill knew right away who the culprit was, especially seeing a wide grin on my face. He barked, "Morgenstein, put that damn door back!"

The whole place cracked up, and I retreated to the warehouse to retrieve the door and put it back on its hinges. Naturally he then called me into his office, closed the door, and lectured me on decorum.

In the meantime, our business was excellent. Frank Rooney had been named president of Melville, which was owned Thom McAn. Melville as a conglomerate was growing, as were its divisions.

Our social life was good. I had become friendly with the postmaster of Teaneck, and in fact, when he was assistant postmaster,

I wrote a letter on his behalf to President Kennedy. This was a few months before his assassination.

We received the stunning news late Friday afternoon, and all we did for the next three days was sit pasted to our TV set. If I recall correctly, there were few if any commercial breaks.

Larry Friedman, the postmaster, was a fine character. He had been an officer on the *Wasp* aircraft carrier during World War II, and then with his wife Clara was stationed in postwar Germany, where they acquired a taste for fine food. They also brought back some fine tableware, dishes, and crystal.

Larry was also a member of the Toastmasters Club in Ridgewood. He invited me to some of the meetings and then announced that he was forming a Toastmasters Club in Teaneck. I knew of no better way to learn how to become a public speaker, and I became active to the point of eventually becoming president of the club and then area governor.

At some point it was New Jersey's three hundredth anniversary, and I was appointed to the New Jersey Tercentenary Committee, where I learned about New Jersey's history and made speeches to various groups promoting the state. One of the statistics that I still remember and that always intrigued me was that New Jersey was almost one-half woodlands, which is an impression you do not get driving down the New Jersey Turnpike.

With good neighbors and good friends, we were feeling quite at home where we were, but there was a rumor going around that we had outgrown our space in Clifton and might be moving to Worcester, Massachusetts. I'd miss the lunches at the famous Rut's Hut, with its famous deep-fried hot dog, called the Ripper.

Sure enough, they were going to build a completely new Thom McAn complex on a hill in Worcester, and everyone was expected to make the move. Neither Syl nor I were thrilled at the prospect.

I asked for a meeting with Frank Rooney, which he readily arranged (his door was always open). Frank, in my view, was an unheralded great executive, and he looked every inch the part.

He was always impeccably dressed. He also expected all his employees to be the same. No sport coats or short sleeves were permitted. Hair had to be cut at all times and shoes well-shined (we learned to spit shine them at the Forty-Second Street store). Men had to be clean shaven and wear a clean white shirt. I wore a pink shirt once, and Bill Muckley went wild and told me never to wear anything but a white shirt in the future. That doesn't sound like today's world, does it?

Frank explained that everyone had to make the move. I then brazenly asked him what was in it for me. He explained that this would be an expensive operation and all expenses would be paid, but if he gave me a raise, he would have to give it to everyone in the company.

I said that I understood, but unfortunately I would not be making the move and would be looking for another job. Frank said that he didn't want to lose me under any circumstances and that he would work something out. In the meantime, I was to go to Worcester for a couple of weeks in order to set up the women's departments and put in the systems.

I of course complied. Worcester is not the most exciting town in the world, although it is near enough to Boston. Flying in to Worcester is scary as hell, as you come in over a mountain to a very narrow airport. They built a beautiful, long, sky-blue building with a lot of modern attributes for its time.

I finished my assignment and flew home. There was a message waiting for me to call Frank, which I did immediately. He told me that they had just developed a new discount shoe division and that the discount department stores would be leasing out departments to us. The office was located on Fifty-Eighth Street and Tenth Avenue, which was across from the Fordham Law School adjunct building. I was to go and meet the executives of Miles Shoe Stores, which was a chain that they had recently acquired. Miles would be in charge of this new subdivision, which they called Meldisco.

In this way I would be kept in the Melville family, and it was the first time that anyone had been transferred from one division to another. It would be sad to leave Thom McAn, as I had made some very fine friends there and had enjoyed virtually every minute of it. In any case, I had made my decision. So off I went to find out what this was all about, not knowing what or who I would find on the west side of Manhattan.

MELDISCO

The west side of Manhattan on Tenth Avenue was mostly low office buildings, especially close to or on Fifty-Ninth Street. The Miles offices were unexceptional, with basically a long corridor with offices on the sides and the executive offices in the rear. I first met with Spencer Ottinger (ex–navy admiral), the executive VP. He was apparently very sharp. He spoke to the point and was very enthusiastic about this new division. He mentioned that they had some good existing contracts with major discounters for their leased footwear departments and that I should go to one of them, which was at the Major's Discount store in Staten Island. After that, I should come back with a full report and then meet my new boss, Bob Kuhn.

Bob was a quirky guy who obviously wanted to prove that he was smarter than anyone in the room (or the company, for that matter). He was also a perfectionist who was void of any sense of humor. Boy, was this new to me! Everything in the store was on tables and racks. The shoes all smelled of plastic except their big cloth item, which was called the Woolworth shoe. Maybe I should have gone to Worcester. It all looked like cheap crap to me. I noticed the women would hold onto their shopping cart with one hand and try on the shoe with the other. I thought that this would never work. When I returned to the office and announced that the division would never be a success (a blunt statement but not very smart, and as it turned out, not very accurate either), Spencer laughed, and Bob scowled as they brought out the sales figures, which were tremendous. They would soon expand to many of the discount chains that were famous in its day, such as Zayre and Spartan Stores, with the largest being K-Mart.

They started me out as a merchandise coordinator. Getting into the swing of things quickly, I wrote up an SOP (standard operating procedure), which Howard David, who was another co-ordinator, purloined and eventually claimed as his own. Howard D went on to become a very famous retail consultant.

Soon after this, I was again promoted to women's buyer of shoes and handbags. Bob Kuhn micromanaged everything and he was a stickler for detailed planning (on long spreadsheets by type, color, monthly sales, area, etc.). Bob had to approve and sign off on every buy, and before he did that, he would grill you unmercifully so as to find some mistakes or weakness in your presentation.

Since I knew his tactics, I would always leave something for him to correct because if by chance you had everything perfect that would greatly upset him. As you can see, he was a bit of a nut case. My figures turned out to be dramatically greater than those for the plan that he had approved. That meant my sales were terrific. No matter, however, as when I went over them with Bob, he wanted to know why I was such a poor planner.

To give another example of his obtuseness, one day I went out with our most important supplier. His name was Al Brief. We called him Alfie. Alfie was a legend, as he had an unbelievable eye for picking winners and doing research, and he was the most successful salesperson for a company called Lawrence-Maid. They were the largest manufacturer of women's sport shoes and casuals in the country. We became close friends, and he became one of the keys to my success. On a Saturday, we made the rounds of the stores, not only to see our shoes but also to see what the competition was doing. Alfie was pleased with what he saw and complimented me on what I was doing, and of course he was pleased at the styles that I had picked (there were many from his factory).

I also knew that Bob Kuhn would be making the rounds to see what he could criticize on Monday morning. Sure enough, Monday came, and he called me into his office and notified me that he was disappointed in finding one of the same styles that we carried in our competition's store. "Why didn't we have exclusivity?" he asked.

Since you couldn't argue with this guy, I just apologized and said that I would straighten it out in the future.

Then, the next thing I knew, I was promoted to assistant merchandise manager in addition to my duties as shoe and handbag buyer. That, of course, meant even more contact with my crazy boss.

One Friday, he made the announcement that we were to prepare our detailed plans for the coming season (about two weeks earlier than usual). I hurriedly called a meeting of all the buyers and merchandisers and explained to them that if we didn't want a hellish day tomorrow, the plans and spreadsheet would have to be perfect and add up from top to bottom and across.

We worked until the evening, and I checked to make sure that everything was perfect. Unfortunately, I had forgotten my rule of leaving at least one mistake for Bob to correct.

The next day, we were waiting for Bob, and he arrived late, obviously to make us nervous. Were we ready? Of course! We all went into the boardroom and laid out all of the plans by department. He was peppering each of us with questions. How many tan sandals would be left in inventory in June? What was the total buy for white sneakers? On and on, and each question was answered without hesitation.

All of a sudden Bob got up and stormed out of the room, heading toward the rear where the bathrooms were. We waited and waited and waited. Finally I sent my assistant Harvey in to see if he was all right. He came back and said that Bob had disappeared.

An hour went by, and no Bob.

I suddenly figured out what had happened, and I got up and announced that I knew where he was and why. Because we had answered everything, Bob got so upset that he couldn't take it, and he went home. I called his home, and his wife answered. When I asked for Bob, she responded that he couldn't come to the phone, and he would see us all on Monday! We all left the office shaking our heads.

Bob was brilliant and well educated in private schools, and he had loads of money. His father and cousins were associated with Miles Shoe Company, which Melville had purchased, and then they started the Meldisco Division. I guess that they gave him the position where he could do the least harm.

Otherwise, Meldisco was a pleasant company to work for. We all got along except for Harvey S, the athletic-shoe buyer. He was sneaky and had the reputation of being a spy for Bob. One day I caught him rifling though some of my papers. I grabbed him and threw him out into the hall and told him that if he ever came near my office again, I would tear him apart.

During the lunch break, if we ate with a buyer, we would go to Fifty-Seventh Street to the 400 Delicatessen, where the food was excellent. If not, we were allowed (I forgot why, but think it was an arrangement between our respective companies) to go to the CBS cafeteria in their old broadcast building on West Fifty-Seventh Street. The food was very good, and the prices were subsidized, so they were unbelievably low.

Many of those who worked for this extremely fast-growing company became quite successful in the shoe business. At least one, we suspected, got very wealthy taking bribes, but generally it seems, unlike the garment industry, to attract people on a higher moral plane. Technically it is very complicated, and the variations of a shoe can get mathematically very complex:

- Style
- Fit
- Color

- Length
- Width
- Material
- Matching left and right (Only gloves fit that criteria)
- Timing
- Heel height
- Sole material

Put that all together, and you have a lot of complex decisions to make.

Besides the above-average person the industry attracted, it also had its very fair share of "characters".. We were unfortunately ending an age of creativity before the accountants, computers, and paper pushers took over. The numerous shoe chain stores that existed came from the turn of the century, when in order to survive, you had to be very tough. Many of them started as auctioneers buying up bankrupt stocks and then opening stores, which they expanded when they did well.

We've forgotten the names now, but until the early sixties, National, Simco, Father & Son, Miles, A. S. Beck, Kitty Kelly, and many others were famous. They survived by being hard and innovative, yet there was a great spirit of camaraderie. When in need, they tried to take care of one another, and that included helping a competitor in one way or another. In 1939, unemployment was over 17 percent. Just outside of Boston at 210 Lincoln Street, there were over three hundred shoe companies. Some of them decided to pass the hat to help those who didn't have enough to eat. So the 210 Foundation was born, and it still exists today. "Shoe People Helping Shoe People." It is the only industry organization of its kind. It binds those in the industry with a certain respect and a desire to help those who fall on hard times.

We used to call it the "Old Shoe Biz." That meant lasting friendships, drinking, good restaurants, and carousing.

Some of the Characters

Joe Miller had a casual-shoe factory in Maine, and both Thom McAn and Meldisco were good customers of theirs. He would come down from Maine to New York with his wife once in a while. Syl and I would have dinner with them, as they were a very pleasant and interesting couple. On one of his trips, Joe mentioned that a close friend of his wanted to meet me. It seemed that the merchandise manager of Montgomery Ward was retiring. Joe had recommended me for the merchandise manager's job, and his friend Henry had an inside tie to management.

Ward's offices were on Thirty-First and Seventh Avenue, and Jack resided in the hotel across the street from the office. We met for dinner at the Waldorf Astoria, and this old guy (I was young then), Henry Hermer, seemed pleased with my answers to his grilling and said that he would like me to meet Roy Kendrick, who was Ward's merchandise manager, the following week.

The food was pretty good, but Henry had different ideas. He had ordered a whole flounder, and when it arrived, it was headless and tailless. In his deep, loud voice he screamed, "Where's the tail? Where's the damn head? Get it from the kitchen if you have to."

I thought that if I got the job, I sure didn't want to have to deal with this old fool. The meeting with Roy Kendrick seemed very positive. After the meeting I was walking toward the elevator, and I spotted him waiting there. "Hello, Roy. I want to thank you for taking the time to speak with me."

There was a mumbling under his breath, and he didn't even look at me as we went down in the elevator. Joe Miller called me the next day, and it seemed that I didn't get the job because I called Roy by his first name instead of Mr. Kendrick. Damn. I always called Frank Rooney Frank, and he was a much bigger shot than Roy would ever be. All turned out well, as that kind of atmosphere would not bode well for me anyway.

Then there was Bill Battersby. When you went out with Bill, you had better have lined your stomach with solid food, as there was going to be a lot of drinking. Between drinks, Bill was an excellent salesman with a good command of the market and what was happening.

Syl and I got a call that Bill would be coming in from New Hampshire in a couple of days, and he wanted to take us to Trader Vic's. This was a famous Polynesian restaurant known for its exotic drinks. We got to Trader Vic's, and Bill obviously had had a bit of a head start in the drinking department. He ordered a coconut rum barrel drink, and I had something with fruit and a colored flag on it.

Suddenly Bill got up and told me to follow him to the kitchen. I thought something may have been wrong, so like a dummy, I followed him. I saw he had a pad and pencil in his hand, and as he opened the kitchen double doors, he bellowed that "we are here to inspect the kitchen." Bill had the kitchen staff line up and started inspecting their fingernails. I couldn't believe what I was seeing.

He then handed me the pad and swiped his hand on this large insulated pipe just above us. "Mark it down," he said. "Dirt on the pipes!" He then stormed out of the kitchen, calmly sat down, and finished his meal. To this day, Syl and I wonder how we weren't arrested or stuck with a large kitchen knife by one of the chefs.

Bill was very much like the other shoe salesmen of that era. For the most part, they were happy and easygoing, and they told jokes that were always topical and sometimes hysterical, and they obviously loved good food and drink.

Eddie Myer was a character supreme. Eddie was the original Meldisco sport-shoe buyer. He was extremely talented and effective, but he was as eccentric as they come, and sadly in his later years apparently suffered from severe mental illness. He was a great buyer, so Bob Kuhn tended to tolerate him. His working habits were bizarre, as, for example, he would disappear for a few days at a time, going to the airport counter and asking what flights were going out. Detroit: "OK, I'll take that one." You could do that in the sixties. He would then proceed to shop the fashion stores, take pictures, and look at the competition. He would sometimes forget where he parked his rented car and just leave it and then tell Hertz to find it. Other times he would drive up to the departure gate, leave the car, and tell the rental company to pick it up out front.

Eddie was notorious for making appointments with sales people and then either showing up late or not at all. One day he got a call from Dave Brilliant from a company called Sporto. They had never called on Meldisco before, and of course they knew about Ed's reputation. The appointment was for a Tuesday morning at 10:00 a.m. Dave was on time, expecting a very long wait, but within ten minutes, he was called into Ed's office. He laid out his samples, and Ed asked all the right questions: Who did they sell the shoes to? Why did they think they would sell in a discount store? Which were the best styles? Best colors? Etc.

Ed liked the answers, picked out some styles, and planned them out on his spreadsheet. He told Dave that he was going to buy some of them as a test and write the orders, but he had to get approval from Bob first. Ed went into Bob's office, where he got the usual grilling ("Why are we buying from a new source? What do you know about them?" Etc.), but Bob gave Ed a grudging approval to buy the shoes.

Dave was amazed and asked Ed to go to lunch. It was a winter's day, and there was slush on the ground, but the 400 Deli was only few blocks away. They had a very decent lunch. Eddie was lucent and spoke well about fashion, politics, and sports. Dave was astounded. He said that he would catch a cab out front. "Ed, can I ask you something without you getting offended?"

"Sure."

"You had the reputation of not keeping appointments. You were right on time. You picked the right styles and made the buy with no fuss. Some even say you're flaky, yet our conversation was perfectly normal."

Ed interrupted and acted as if this were all news to him, but in the middle of his talking, he announced that he had to go back into the restaurant to get his shoes. He was standing in the snowy street with just his socks on!

On another occasion, the company had a large store opening in New Bedford, Massachusetts. Bob Kuhn sent a large crew of assistant store managers and distributors up to set up the store. This was a hard few days' work. Both in gratitude and with the thought of getting preferential treatment, the store manager arranged for some hookers to entertain the guys. When they returned to the office, Bob had already gotten wind of this and immediately fired those employees involved. Although we couldn't prove anything, we were sure that Harvey Shafler was the snitch.

Bob called a somber meeting of the entire Meldisco staff. He went on about propriety, ethics, and morality. In the middle of this very reflective moment, Eddie Myers raised his hand.

"What is it, Eddie?" Bob impatiently bellowed.

Eddie stared for a few moments and looked Bob straight in the eyes. "I have one question for you: Bob, do you really have anything against f–king?"

That was the end of that meeting, as Bob first just stood there and stared in disbelief at what he had just heard and then suddenly stormed out of the conference room.

Everyone in the room roared with laughter. The pandemonium broke up the meeting. That episode got around the entire shoe industry in a matter of hours.

One day, Eddie invited Syl and me to his home for dinner in Long Island. It was obvious that Eddie and his wife did not get along. Ed and I went out to look at the stores in the area while his wife complained bitterly as to how she hated him.

It turned out they were ordering Chinese food to be delivered to their home. We were about to return to the house, and Eddie stopped at a hot-dog stand and ordered a couple of frankfurters. I asked why he was doing this, as his wife had ordered Chinese food, which we would have in less than an hour. He said, "Screw that mean bitch."

We couldn't wait to leave. The Chinese food was served in cartons and no dishes. Syl and I always loved Chinese food, but we didn't eat much that night.

Some years later, there was a shoe show in the New York Coliseum. Due to a bomb scare (yes, bomb scares even in the early seventies), we had to evacuate the entire building in the middle of the show. Eddie showed up at every show, but he was nowhere to be found on this day. We weren't sure what pissed him off, but it was unanimous: Eddie had done it.

He went downhill, and he became a recluse and, we guessed, somewhat of a homeless person. For a while in later years, he would show up at my office. I felt sorry for him and would give him money until he became irrational, and when he started to rail against the Catholic Church and their conspiracies, I asked him to stop coming. Eddie Myer was a very talented person, but he was certainly a weird one.

There were others, such as Ralph Barr, who would come down every couple of weeks from his factory in Maine to our office. I would make sure that he was the last appointment so that we could go to the Regency Hotel on Park Avenue and have a drink. Everyone knew us—the manager, the hat-check girl, and especially Kurt the piano player. The place was always jammed, but they always held a table for us.

Ralph looked the part of a very classy, impeccably dressed man-about-town. As soon as we entered, Kurt would play one of my favorite tunes at the time—either "Rhapsody in Blue" or "No Other Love Have I" by Richard Rodgers. Kurt had been a very famous piano player in Czechoslovakia. All were well tipped. Kurt also used to send some very attractive ladies to sit with us. That was great for him, but eventually I had to get back to New Jersey to get some rest and get ready for another day.

In the meantime, things were going well on Fifty-Eighth Street. I had made sure to maintain my reputation as a straight shooter—incorruptible—and I was lucky enough to have outstanding sales figures. This was drawing attention, and other companies were starting to approach me. At first I ignored them, but my goal was to be the president of a company before I was thirty-five years old. This couldn't happen at Melville, which was large and getting larger. The move to the top there would be a long and unwieldy process. The other factor was that we were thinking of buying a larger house. Sure enough, the opportunity would soon come.

KITTY KELLY

S ure enough, the day soon came. I received a call from Irv Shirline, who was president of Kitty Kelly Shoe Company. It was a chain of thirty-plus shoe stores in the New York metro area, the Midwest, and Miami. Both he and his wife Shirley wanted to have dinner with Syl and me at Delmonico's, which was a famous restaurant in Lower Manhattan. Often you could meet celebrities (I wouldn't know one from another) and politicos there, although I don't think we saw any that evening.

The food was delicious. Syl had a lobster, and I had Delmonico's famous steak (very rare). We all hit it off immediately. Irv was a character (of course). He liked to joke, and if he were around today, he would have been fired and sued for his comments, especially the sexy ones toward women. Funny, though: he never meant anything by it, and you could get away without a lot of politically correct nonsense that we have today. He used to call Syl BT because of her well-endowed stature. We all laughed and loved it.

Irv had nice things to say about what he had heard about me and my performance. Before the evening was over, he offered me the job of running the buying and merchandising department as a senior vice-president, with a substantial increase in salary.

When I mentioned that my goal was to become a president of a chain of stores before I was thirty-five years old, he mentioned that it was a good possibility, as he thought that he would go on to other things within a year.

It didn't take much for Syl and me to make up our minds, as we were now ready to buy a larger house in Teaneck. We eventually did buy that house. It's a four-bedroom house in the best part of town with a pool, deck, fireplace, and the works. Here again, though, we were scared to death thinking about how we were going to pay the mortgage. We did, of course.

Actually, the pool came later. We were on vacation one summer in Montauk, Long Island, and we were shown a piece of property on the bay. The lot was $12,000, but we decided to put a pool in our house instead. That property probably eventually jumped in value to well over $700,000.

In any case, I had to be accepted by the chairman of the board, Mr. Kellner. He was very gracious, which he could be when he wanted something. Mr. Kellner liked to tell stories (so do I), and he talked out of the side of his mouth in a very gruff voice. After about an hour, he called Irv in to finalize the agreed-upon details and congratulated me on being hired. Now, I had to give proper notice to Meldisco.

I explained to Bob Kuhn that this represented not only a higher-paying position with more responsibility but the opportunity to become a president of a company in a short period of time.

Bob looked shocked and said that he didn't want to accept my resignation. Within a half hour, I got a call from Frank Rooney. He was not happy, especially when I told him that I had no chance to get his job any time soon.

So I left Meldisco, and Frank refused to talk to me or acknowledge me when we ran into each other at shows. It was as if I had abandoned the family.

I fit into KK right away with their fine crew. Sol Pollack was my assistant, and I liked him because he would "tell it like it is";

and he was not a "yes-man". He and his wife Fran became very close friends of ours.

Herb Stone ran operations, and he knew his stuff. Irv treated me as if I were the boss, and I was sometimes even embarrassed by the deference that he gave to me.

Quickly I noticed that Mr. Kellner had some very strange ways. He could be very generous, such as the time he bailed out Gene Rubin's factory in Boston. Gene and his father had gone into Chapter 11, and whenever Kitty Kelly bought shoes from their factory after the reorganization, they tacked a little something extra onto the cost in order to help them. The Rubins were unusual people in that they decided to eventually pay off all of their creditors in full.

We became very close to Gene, his wife, Natalie, and his family throughout the years. Once we were having lunch at Gallagher's Steak House, and I ordered steak tartare as an appetizer for the table. He started eating it, but when I told him it was raw chopped meat with a special sauce on it, he turned white, and he never forgave me for doing that.

We still remained very close. Some years later in a Florida shopping mall, he said that he was thirsty. I saw a water kiosk selling water for a quarter. Sounded good to me, so I put the quarter in, not realizing that you needed to bring your own container. All I could do was cup my hands and offer the water from my hands. He laughed hysterically and told both stories whenever we met.

Unfortunately Gene suffered a serious stroke, and a few years ago, the TSA pulled him out of the line in front of the gate for a flight to Boston in order to strip-search an eighty-year-old, obviously very sick man. DISGRACEFUL! Gene passed not very long after that. It was very sad to lose a great friend.

Back to Mr. K: He had many contradictions. He was brilliant at picking locations and negotiating leases. After five years in the course of the lease, he would meet with the landlord and tell him that he wanted to increase the rent immediately. In exchange, he wanted a fifty-year lease. In most cases the tactic would work. Long leases were an asset in the retail business. On the other side, he was not easy to get along with and could be downright nasty and mean. He was also a very heavy drinker.

Luckily for me, he was very fond of me, and he liked my work. He was divorced, and he had fired his son because, he said, his son had put Kitty Kelly into Chapter 11 just a couple of years before I came onto the scene.

One day Irv and Mr. K went to lunch at a restaurant that they frequented a couple of times a week. Mr. K was known there, and although sometimes he would act up, especially if they didn't make his Rob Roy correctly (very dry with just a touch of Vermouth), he was a very big tipper, which in his mind may have compensated for his rudeness. Every time someone would bring his drink, he would pull out a five-dollar bill and thrust it in his or her hand. Five dollars was lots of dough for a tip in those days.

One day Irv had sensed that he wasn't in too good of a mood, as he had just had an argument with his ninety-year-old sister Elsie. Irv knew that there was going to be trouble because their regular waiter was out sick. The replacement could do nothing right. Although Mr. Kellner wanted his Rob Roy to have Scotch and just a dash of dry vermouth, the waiter brought the Rob Roy with sweet vermouth. "You damn dummy!" he screamed as the folks at the neighboring table looked on in horror.

Then the food came out wrong, and he berated this poor guy terribly. Irv was mortified, and when they asked for the bill, the owner came over. "Mr. Kellner," he said, "you have been coming into my restaurant for a long time, but I am going to tell you this here and now: I don't want to see your damn, ugly face in my restaurant ever again. If you do try to come in, I'm going to throw you right out the door."

They both made their quick retreat and went into the hallway to wait for the elevator. Mr. Kellner looked at Irv and screamed, "What an idiot that guy was. I'm never going back there again."

Not long after that, Irv came to me and said that he had had a big fight with the boss and that Mr. K had accused him of all kinds of things, which, incidentally, I knew that he hadn't done. Irv had just done a brilliant job opening up a high-grade store on Fifty-Seventh Street called the Booteria, and it was the jewel of the chain. Ironically, Irv used to just about kiss his ass, cater to him, take him home when he was drunk, and take care of his family in many ways.

Irv then said that I was now the new president and that we were going to announce the news in the papers tomorrow.

As much as I wanted that job, I said, "Look, I'm not going to take care of his personal affairs, as I have kids at home, and besides, that's just not my personality."

Irv explained that he had already told Mr. K that, and he fully understood. I was then called into Mr. K's office, and he told me that he knew that I would make a fine president.

The building was on the corner of Nineteenth Street and Park Avenue South in Manhattan. We had the entire ground floor, which included offices and a warehouse in the rear. If you faced the building, there was a large window on the right, with the entrance doors in the center and a large window on the left side of the building. Behind those windows were two executive offices. One was for the chairman of the board, and the other was for the president. BK (Ben Kellner) asked me if I wanted to redecorate my office, and I said no because I wouldn't be spending much time there. I would be visiting stores, and although I was making Sol Pollack the merchandise manager and VP, I would still travel with him overseas.

I got into the swing of things right away. Our operations guy, Herb Lewis, was afraid to visit the Harlem store, so I would go to 125th Street, double-park, and have one of the salespeople watch the car. I would visit with the crew, check the competition, and buy a paper called *Mohammed Speaks,* which I carried prominently for all to see. I never had a problem of any kind and in fact asked the store manager if I could promote his cashier to work for us.

One of the things that I changed was to eliminate secretaries per se and use the pool of clerks for letters and documentation. Ms. Raines thought I had moved her to the office to be my secretary, and I explained that I wanted her for the operations manager because the crew at the store had told me that whenever there was a problem at the store, she solved it, even if she had to call a plumber out in the middle of the night. She was incredibly talented and efficient. She was also an excellent executive.

After a short while, because of her extraordinary performance, I decided to make her the vice-president of operations. When I told BK about the promotion, he went absolutely wild. "You can't make a colored person a VP. Are you crazy?"

I responded that I was the president, and if he thought after three months it was really such a terrible mistake, we would review the decision. Janet Raines went on to work wonders in her job as vice-president of operations.

After a few months, Mr. K called me into his office with these astounding remarks: "Bill, don't you think it was brilliant of me to promote this girl to vice-president?"

"Of course, Mr. K."

Although I didn't view it as such a big deal, word got out that we were breaking ground in race relations, and we received a call one morning from an organization, which I believe may have been the Urban League, asking if we would help and promote minorities. Of course we would.

One of our vendors was a fellow (another character, of course) by the name of Harry Feldstein. Harry was very intuitive in coming up with ideas, which he said he could find anywhere. He once took me into a hardware store and picked up some screws that he was going to adorn his styles with. That style turned out to be quite a big seller.

As with many of the shoe "dogs," as we called them, he liked to drink. His son told the story of Harry getting completely drunk on a Christmas Eve. They were returning home together on the subway when Harry started to vomit right on the train. The passengers were horrified when Harry looked up, smiled, and said, "What's the matter? Haven't you ever seen Santa Claus before?"

Harry was completely bald, and I used to call him Skin Head. He would call me and tell the operator that he was President Eisenhower, or the governor, or the mayor, or anyone else who was famous. So shortly after the Urban League call, the operator said that David Rockefeller was on the phone. "Hello, Skin Head," I bellowed on the phone.

There was silence. "Is this Skin Head?"

"No, this is Mr. David Rockefeller."

I was shocked and astounded that David Rockefeller would be calling me. I tried my best to apologize and explain the background and that I would never really expect a call from such a very important personality. He was very cold, a no-nonsense guy, and I never heard from him again, although we did do our part for the Urban League.

Janet Raines did go on to open some successful dress shops shortly after I left the company.

Soon after, Kitty Kelly was approached by a conglomerate from Kentucky that had originated in the coal business. After a series of meetings, they decided that they wanted to add our company to their group. All seemed to be going well when they asked for a special meeting with the board, which consisted of Seymour Field (the CFO), Herb, Sol, and me, except that for some reason Mr. K wasn't invited. That was strange until they told us that Mr. K was getting old and useless, and they would get rid of him within a year.

I was appalled, and I left the room to go to Mr. K's office to inform him. He immediately went wild. The deal was off, and we threw them out.

Mr. K next made Sol and me members of the Tammy Brook Country Club in northern New Jersey, which he belonged to.

That, of course, meant that not only did we have to play golf with him on Sundays, we often had to have dinner with him on Saturday nights, dance, and go to the New Year's Eve party (corsages for the women, which Syl hated).

One day he called Syl at home, since I was just returning from a trip, to tell her he was having a party on Sunday night. She said that she wasn't sure she could get a baby-sitter on short notice.

"You get one," he barked.

We went to the party, and he was drunk as usual. He had brought Elsie, his sister. Elsie disappeared into the ladies' room.

"Go find my damn sister," he told one of the girls.

When she arrived, he told Sol to dance with the old fart (loud enough for her to hear), and off to the dance floor they went.

The company also bought me a Buick. I had had the car less than two weeks when Mr. K invited the board members and their wives on a Saturday night to a restaurant called Asti's in Greenwich Village. Syl and I picked up Sol and his wife, Fran. Sol put his golf clubs in the car, anticipating that we would play golf at the club on Sunday, and I had the trunk loaded with clothes that I had picked up at the cleaners.

The Italian food at Asti's was only fair, but the entertainment was fun, as the waiters would sing opera while they served the food.

We had luckily found a parking spot near the restaurant. The only problem was that when we left the restaurant, the car was gone. The police station was around the corner. Syl thought it was quite funny.

The police sergeant gave her a look and exclaimed: "Lady, in all of my years, this is the first time I've ever had someone come into the station house to report a theft and think that it was so funny."

The insurance paid for Sol's golf clubs, but because of the deductible, I didn't get paid for my clothes.

Years later we were eating with some friends in a famous restaurant that used to be a speakeasy in Manhattan called Frankie & Johnnies, which was upstairs on Forty-Fifth Street and Eighth Avenue. We were again parked on the street (we hadn't learned our lesson). We could see the car from our second-floor window. Syl was looking out the window, and she at first screamed and then started laughing as we saw two guys pop the trunk, grab the golf clubs, and then run down the street. They were nice enough to close the trunk.

BEN KELLNER STORIES

By now you should have a good idea of what kind of person BK was. When I became president of Kitty Kelly, I was determined not to fall into the trap that Irv Shirline had fallen into by catering to the boss's every whim. Some things could have been passed on to other people, while there were some things that I was obligated to endure.

BK would usually arrive anywhere between 11:00 a.m. and noon and stay on until at least past 7:00 p.m. If I was in town, he would call me around six o'clock to come across the hall to his office for a meeting. His first words would then be, "Sit down, fella. We are going to kill the bugs." That meant he was going to pull out a bottle of Scotch from his cabinet and pour both of us a full-size water glass. There was a tall plant on my side of the desk, and that was where most of my Scotch ended up. He would rant on about the old days and then tell me how his son Warren put him into Chapter 11 bankruptcy. He would then go on to tell me how much he respected me and that he was saddened that his son didn't have my genes.

As I have mentioned, he was a very astute real-estate man and ended up with prime locations in the large cities that we had stores in. His next idea was to have a Kitty Kelly store right in the Empire State Building even though we already had one in Grand Central Station, and one at Thirty-Fourth Street and Seventh Avenue. He said: "Fella, I'm going to teach you the real estate business."

The owners of the Chrysler Building at the time were Goldman-DiLorenzo, whom we proceeded to call, and we made an appointment for the following week. BK told me to listen and keep my mouth shut so that I could learn the procedure. Alex DiLorenzo's reputation was even tougher than Ben's, and his secretary told us that we had fifteen minutes and not a second longer to make our case.

We arrived a few minutes early, and Alex's secretary again reminded us of our time constraints. On the button we were ushered in. I could see that Mr. DiLorenzo was not a man of patience, and neither was he a man of too many niceties (the rumor was that he was involved with the Mafia). BK proceeded to babble on about how his store was going to help these two moguls with their reputation and again told the same old stories.

I noticed that the hourglass on Mr. D's desk was starting to wind down, and I tried to signal BK to get to the point. The sand was now at the bottom. Mr. D rose from his chair and loudly announced: "OK, THAT'S ENOUGH. UP! OUT!"

Kellner was stunned. "That dumb wop son of a bitch doesn't know the first thing about real estate," he mumbled as we left. My lesson was over.

BK was generous and paid his entertainment expenses in cash. One Friday morning, I got an early-morning (uncharacteristic) call from Mr. K. He needed my help. It seemed that his granddaughter Michelle was sick in Europe, and his son Warren needed to bring her back to the States. Warren didn't have a passport or the necessary cash, and I was amazed to find out that BK didn't have the ready cash either. I had contacts at the consulate and got Warren an emergency passport and an airline ticket from my friends at Merriway Travel, and I sent my own cash to help with his expenses. BK had suggested we take cash from the store, but I had to explain that that would set a terrible precedent, so we couldn't. I laid out the money, which BK gratefully returned to me very soon thereafter.

BK was also very innovative, and he was one of the first to start to import footwear. Just before I arrived on the scene, BK made a trip to Italy along with Sol Pollack, the buyer. They were going to hire agents to find factories and supervise production in both the Florence and Adriatic areas of Italy. Angelo Ristori had been recommended for the Florence area. It turned out that Angelo was one of the best.

Studio Scavo, who had arrived in Florence from Ancona, which is on the Adriatic Sea, was a different sort. In the Second World War, he was an Italian Air Force pilot. Unlike BK, he was quite polished, cultured, and apparently high bred. BK was obviously intimidated by Scavo, so he made a quick deal, which was against Sol's advice. BK agreed that he would give Scavo three percent of the value of whatever Kitty Kelly bought, not realizing that Scavo was already going to receive three percent from the factories. Naturally Scavo didn't say anything. Why should he?

Sol had already been drained because traveling with Kellner was a nightmare. It seemed that the train from Rome to Florence had been delayed, which was unusual. By the time they got to the Excelsior Hotel in Florence, their room had been sold from under them, and they were told that they didn't have a reservation. Knowing that BK would blame this on him, Sol pleaded for a room, any room. The hotel had one small suite left, but the problem was that there was only one bedroom and one bath (European hotel rooms are notoriously small).

OK, they would take it, as it was already close to midnight. Kellner got the bedroom, and Sol got the couch. Sol was trying to patiently wait for his turn in the shower. After a while, BK came bounding out screaming that the plumbing didn't work and for Sol to call the maid. Sol was mortified as he called down to the desk. "You need to send the maid up."

It seemed all of the maids had already gone home. "Well then, send anybody up!"

The downstairs clerk wanted to know why it was so important to send someone up to the room. "Is somebody sick?"

"No. Nobody is sick, dammit. Ben Kellner just shit in the bidet!"

Sol was dreaming of getting back to Clifton, New Jersey, where he lived, but he was going to have to endure another evening in Florence. BK wanted to go to the best restaurant in Florence. Cavillini Ristorante was a fine restaurant that had both an upstairs and a downstairs dining room. Sol was praying that he wouldn't order a Rob Roy, but as they got ready to leave for the restaurant, he saw that the minibar was open, and the empty bottles were lined up on top of the mini fridge. BK was already talking out of the side of his mouth, and that was a bad sign. The place was jammed, but they had a reservation, and they are seated upstairs at a table for two in the middle of some other parties.

Sol was hoping that nobody spoke English, especially when Mr. Kellner started screaming how smart he was because "WE F—ED SCAVO; WE F—ED SCAVO."

There was one small problem: Studio Scavo was sitting with a group of people just two tables away. Sol was panicky, wildly gesturing to BK, putting his fingers to his lips, but BK went on and on, slurring his words and cursing out of the side of his mouth.

Finally Sol spotted the Scavo party leaving and asked for the check. They paid, and as BK started to walk to the staircase, he rolled down the entire flight of stairs just like a jelly roll. He landed at the bottom completely unhurt and stood tall (all five feet five inches of him) and looked up into the face of Studio Scavo. "Mr. Scavo," he said, "I didn't know you were here. It's so nice to see you. It is going to be such a pleasure to work with you."

Mr. Scavo, looking stoic as ever, graciously shook his hand and left.

National shoe shows were normally held in New York, either at the coliseum or one of the major hotels. However, once a year there was a shoe show at the Palmer House in downtown Chicago on State Street. Directly across the street was one of our large Kitty Kelly stores. We of course attended all of the shows.

This year BK wanted to make the trip, and he wanted to meet some of his old manufacturing cronies. Sol, Irv Shirline, and I all dreaded what we knew was going to be a very trying few days.

Sure enough, his first stop was the State Street store. This was a very busy operation with a competent, old-time manager and crew. BK bawled out the manager over some nonsense, and when Tom, the manager, objected, BK fired him. Tom was devastated, but I rushed him to the rear stock room and explained to him to just stay out of sight until BK left and that Tom was definitely NOT fired.

While BK was fuming, we were getting ready to go across the street to the Palmer House Hotel, and Sol, Irv, and I hatched a plan that would slow him down and, hopefully, tire him out. Who knows; it might even kill him. If it did, when he was buried we would have him screwed into the ground so that he wouldn't pop up again. There were three mezzanines at the Palmer House. Each one had a bar. We would inform BK that the elevators were out of commission and that we would have to climb up the steps. We hoped that by the time we got to the third mezzanine, he would be too tired to continue.

We should have realized that this tough old coot was close to indestructible. As we walked up each floor, Mr. K stopped for a quick drink at the bar (Scotch, neat). By the time we reached the third mezzanine, we were pooped out, but there he was, twenty feet ahead of us. "Whatsomatter, guys, can't you keep up with me?" he slurred.

"Mr. Kellner," we said in unison, "we think they have fixed the elevator."

We endured the rest of the day with him as he told his war stories to his old cronies. Finally he was ready for dinner. Irv knew of a nice Polynesian place to eat, and off we went. This was going to be bad, as BK ordered the dreaded Rob Roy. Now, you couldn't expect them to know how to make a Rob Roy in a place like this. Sure enough, it was sweet and not dry, and BK went nuts. He was screaming, and the waiters were ignoring him.

BK spotted what looked like the manager on the balcony above us. "Hey, chink," he yelled.

We were dumbfounded but had nowhere to crawl. The manager yelled back that he was not Chinese, that he was Hawaiian.

BK responded that he looked like a "chink" to him and to "get down here."

I knew one thing, and that was I didn't need Irv to nudge me—we didn't even taste our food. We didn't want to imagine what they laced it with. I made sure to avoid traveling with him from then on.

KITTY KELLY TRAVELS

M r. K had a good friend who was a labor lawyer with all kinds of contacts. BK called me into the office one day and informed me that we may want to develop imports from Malta and Cyprus, as both of these places wanted to develop their industry. Since Sol was the merchandise manager, I suggested that he accompany me. According to the lawyer, all had been organized and arranged, and we would be met by government officials who would take care of our arrangements and introduce us to the factory and other business people.

We arrived first in Cyprus. It seemed that the Greeks and the Turks were fighting with each other more violently than usual. Nobody had time to spend with us, and we were advised to skedaddle, which we did. We left quickly but not before having a delicious charcoal-barbecued lamb.

Next we landed in Valletta, Malta, which is close to Sicily in the center of the Mediterranean Sea. Since they all spoke English there, it should be easier. There was only one problem: nobody was there to greet us. Nobody whom we asked knew anything. Worse, it was a national holiday, and we couldn't find anyone to talk to.

Finally we spotted this young fellow who looked like a clown. He was talking fast and making quick, nervous movements with his arms and body. When we explained our dilemma to him, he got serious and said that he could help us.

We gave him the names of the government contacts we had. He knew them all but again reminded us that it was a national holiday. He offered to take us for a tour of the "temples," but when we said that we wanted to take the next plane back to Rome, he offered to call the commerce secretary at home. The short of it is that we were offered a fine meal with their special Maltese bread at the secretary's home.

After seeing some interesting sites and temples, we went back to Rome without accomplishing any meaningful business. The Maltese were interested, and they depended on tourism, but they did not have the capacity for manufacturing.

Now that we had our agents set up in Italy, it was time for us to expand our overseas buying. Sol and the buying team had made excellent selections, and our business was growing nicely.

I decided to make the next trip with Sol. We were staying at the Villa Medici in Florence, and we had heard that Spain was making some exciting styles; however, our schedules were such that neither one of us had the time to go to Spain and visit the factories. Luckily, we had received word that there were some Spanish manufacturers staying at the hotel.

I could speak passable Italian but no Spanish. The owners of the factory spoke no English. I mentioned to Sol that we could solve that problem since wine stewards, due to the nature of their work, spoke numerous languages. We went downstairs to the restaurant to see if we could get a hold of Angelo, the wine steward at lunch, and asked him whether, instead of going home, he would spend a few hours doing some work as an interpreter.

Angelo was excited to do this, and he enthusiastically agreed. Angelo did a fine job, and the meeting went well. We purchased a number of styles from one of the manufacturers.

A couple of months later, the shoes were delivered, and they sold extremely well. The problem had developed that on one of the styles, the heel was coming off. So now we had a claim against the factory.

Sol had commitments in New England, so I decided to make the trip to southern Spain. There was a direct flight from Paris to Alicante, Spain, which I took. I arrived at the Carlton Hotel in Alicante, and I was given a nice, comfortable corner room. I had the address of the factory, but not speaking the language, I had to find a good interpreter. Since this was a manufacturing problem, a wine steward as the interpreter was not the solution. Therefore, I decided to go down to the desk to explain my predicament.

The manager was gracious, and he said that he had the perfect person for me. He made a call, and it was arranged that the interpreter, who had knowledge of shoe manufacturing, would arrive the next morning along with the factory owners from Elda, one of the nearby shoe-factory towns. The next morning they arrived, and Jacque Bentata introduced himself to me and said that he would solve the problem since he immediately saw the heels detached from the shoes.

I proceeded to explain the problem, the number involved, the costs to Kitty Kelly, and so on. However, I understood enough Spanish to know that Jacque was not interpreting what I was saying. I pointed this out, but his response was that he could either interpret what I was saying, or he could solve the claim.

Obviously, I wanted the claim solved, and sure enough, after some more discussion, he announced that we were proceeding to the factory to pick up the equivalent amount of money that was due us in the local currency, which were pesetas.

We went to the factory and collected the money for the claim. I then mentioned to Jacque that we were going to need an agent, as we wanted to start buying more shoes in Spain.

Jacque laughed and said that he had become our agent the moment we met back at the hotel. It turned out that he was from

Egypt, so we always stuck strictly to the business of factory production and shoe styling, with no discussions about politics or religion.

We worked well together except for the fact he always took me to restaurants that served crawfish. I was not a big fish eater, and I especially was not fond of shellfish that looked like large insects with bulging eyes and long feelers on their heads. One day I said that I wouldn't go to lunch with him unless he found a restaurant that served lamb.

He agreed, and as we were walking out of the Melia Hotel in Playa San Juan (right on the ocean where Northern Europeans gather every summer), a manufacturer who wanted to work with us stopped him. This happened to be a famous bullfighter who also owned a shoe factory. We couldn't turn him down. So, where did he take us but to his favorite haunt, where the specialty was crawfish. I scared Jacque by making believe I was walking out but then sat back down and suffered through the meal.

Now it was June of 1967, two years later. We were driving in the desert to a town called Elche. Jacque had the radio blasting, and by now I could understand at least some Spanish, and I heard the radio announcer shout in an excited voice, "The Israeli Air Force has just destroyed the Egyptian Air Force."

I was frightened and afraid to look over at Jacques, when all of a sudden he swerved the car to the side and shouted, "Did you hear that?"

"Hear what?" I said, trying to be innocent.

"The Israeli Air Force just destroyed the Egyptian Air Force. Isn't that wonderful?"

"Wonderful?" I ask. "Aren't you Egyptian?"

"Yes, I'm Egyptian, but I'm also a Jew!"

Sometime after that (when Franco was out of power), the Bentata family established one of the first Synagogues in Spain since 1492, which I happily contributed to. A note: When Franco ruled Spain, he was a very conservative and tough ruler. No single women were allowed to accompany a man to a hotel room.

No woman would even look you in the eye, and if you tried to bring a *Playboy*, or even a *Mad* magazine, for that matter, into the country, it was confiscated.

It took a while for Spain to change, but change it did. In later years, I would take buyers and friends to a restaurant on the top of a hill called the Castile. Dinner started just before 11:00 p.m. We became friendly with the flamenco dancers, who finished their act around 2:30 a.m. and then came to our table, where we were known to drink and dance on the tables until around 5:00 a.m., after which I would go back to the hotel, take a shower, and be ready for work by 8:00 a.m.

Back in Italy, I was scouting out various parts of the country for ideas and good resources, and on one trip, I took Syl to the Ancona area, which is on the Adriatic and in which Scavo was our agent. Italy, ironically, was not known for its white wines, but the Adriatic is where Santa Margherita Pinot grigio comes from. It was first introduced to the States at around three dollars a bottle and now goes for just under twenty bucks.

Anyway, we enjoyed our visit with Scavo, who, as I indicated, was very influential in the area. Since we were running late, he had the two-engine prop plane held up for us. It had eighteen seats, a pilot, a copilot, and a stewardess. As soon as we took off for Rome, it started to storm, and the turbulence got fierce. Syl was very, very scared. The stewardess stood up and was starting to make an announcement when she stopped in midsentence and started crying uncontrollably. Next, the curtain opened, and the copilot came out. And with a typical dramatic Italian gesture, he opened his palms and shrugged his shoulders and then retreated back into the pilot's cabin.

The ride was awful, gaining and losing altitude constantly, and there were sudden bumps and lightning flashes all the way to Rome. I appeared calm in an effort to try to ease my wife's hysteria, but when we finally landed, I swore to travel by train or car in Italy from then on.

Back at the office one day, I got a call from the receptionist. There was a fellow out front from Italy. He had no appointment. Our rule was that we saw everyone, appointment or not, especially if they came from afar. Sol had appointments with sales people all day, so I said to show him into my office. In came Aldo Finiziio. He was maybe all of twenty, with just a little command of English. He explained to me in Italian that he was from Naples and his father had a shoe factory, where his father had just invented a new process. It was an indestructible ceramic heel. He then proceeded to open his battered old sample case and pulled out these fine-looking women's sandals with ceramic heels. Then, from his back pocket, he pulled out a large hammer and started hammering the heels unmercifully. Bam, whack, bam.

OK, OK, enough already. I looked at the sandals, and they were the most magnificent things that I had ever seen. Sol was the buyer and I wasn't going to take his job away, but I wrote down the number of pairs that I thought he should buy and told him that he needed to get into my office, fast!

I had put down a very large number, and when I asked Sol what he thought, he also wrote the number of pairs that he thought we should buy. The numbers were almost exactly the same.

I then said to Aldo that we would place the order, but since we were unique, we had to have exclusivity. He was thrilled and said he would fly back to Italy immediately.

I asked him how he had come to us, and he said that his father had told him to go to Thirty-Fourth Street in Manhattan and, when he came to a shoe store, write down the name and look up their address at a pay phone.

The shoes were delivered to our warehouse on time, and they came in perfect. We placed them in some of our key stores, and they sold out to the pair in less than a week.

I placed an urgent call to the factory in Naples. "Aldo, we have a problem." He interrupted and said that the factory would make good on any damages. I said that there were no damages, but we need to double the order, and we needed the sandals flown to our warehouse within thirty days.

He then spoke to his father and called back and happily said that it would be done as we had requested. This was quite an accomplishment in the shoe industry, but they ended up doing just as they promised.

Everything was fine for a little over a year, and then we received a visitor from the Italian Leather Company. This was the newly married son-in-law who was an ex–Alitalia steward who had taken over from Aldo. We no longer had exclusivity, and our great run was over.

It was the sixties, and another fashion hot area was London, where their outlandish styling suited what we were after. I met with Leslie Fossey, who was a character also. He took a liking to me and promoted me in the English trade press. He got me into the Billy London Club and appointed me president, as well as the International Sporting Club (gambling), Crockford's Palm Beach Casino Club (London club), and others. I appointed him as our agent in France and England.

Syl and I had him and his fiancée, Lisa, put up in a room at the Meurice Hotel in Paris. Syl and I were returning to London, and Leslie and Lisa decided that they would show us the English countryside. They took us to a hotel in Kent called the Bickley Manor. When Syl saw the dump, she was beside herself. We were supposed to get the new wing (hate to see the old wing), and we walked up an open flight of stairs in the noisy lobby. We opened the door, and Syl screamed. The shower was in the middle of the living room, and it was leaking.

So I said to the bellman, "Take the luggage back down."

Leslie had to drive us almost two hours back to London, where we were lucky to get the last available room (London was always booked up) at the Dorchester Hotel.

When we were not visiting factories, Leslie took us on some fine tours, including old RAF bases and Chartwell, where Winston

Churchill lived. Starting down the staircase, I was enamored by the photographs on the walls, and I managed to go flying down the entire flight of stairs, embarrassing Sylvia. Syl got even in Paris, however, when she clumsily knocked over a statue. I was about a hundred feet away when an old woman looked at me and said: "Did you see what that American woman did?"

"No madam," I replied. "I didn't see a thing."

Back home at 4:00 a.m. one morning, the phone rang. It was Leslie. He had just made the most amazing find in a factory, and he couldn't wait to call me. It seemed that they were renovating a shoe factory outside of London, and when they tore a wall down, they discovered four thousand pair of shoes that were manufactured during or right after World War II. They were high wedge sandals, made out of plastic.

I said great, but these shoes would be as stiff as a six-inch sheet of ice and would surely fall apart. Leslie insisted that he had tested them (Leslie was prone to exaggerating sometimes). I said that we were not going to risk buying four thousand pair of antique plastic shoes (Sol was on vacation), but for publicity's sake, I would buy 360 pair.

The shoes came in. Kellner went nuts and said that I had lost my mind. We put them in just the Manhattan stores. Not only did they sell out in two days, but the fashion editor of the newly published *New York* magazine came by, photographed the wedges, and put an article in the magazine. The remainder was then shipped, and the antique shoes sold out in a week. We had started a fashion wedge craze.

One afternoon Leslie, who was always unpredictable, showed up at one of our barbecues. He was dressed in a tuxedo and top hat. It seemed that he had entered a race up to top of the Empire State building, but he had to stop by first to take his barbecue along for refreshment.

On another occasion, I met with Leslie in Paris so that we could shop the stores together in order to find new fashions and styles. It was May 1968, and we were in the Latin Quarter, near the Sorbonne. We were staring intently at a store window, not really paying too much attention to our surroundings, when we heard a large racket. Both of us were stunned when we looked up. On one side of us was a phalanx of police in riot gear. Facing them was a bunch of young students shouting and breaking up paving stones. They started to throw the slabs at the police.

We were in the middle of the ruckus, frightened for our lives. We scampered into the store, which was immediately shuttered, and when things quieted down, we made our escape.

At that point, we decided that France was not the place for us to be. If I remember, the protests did not last that long, but we weren't going to wait around to see the result.

KITTY KELLY NEARLY GOES PUBLIC AND THE BOSS'S SON RETURNS

K itty Kelly was doing well, extremely well, so now Mr. K's idea was for us to go public. Seymour Fields prepared the records, documents, and red herring, and we sat with the underwriters numerous times. Our figures were good, the company was growing, and we were showing an excellent net profit. The underwriters had extensively interviewed all of the key executives and board members. They were quite thorough in their approach. I was in the office when they asked Mr. Kellner why he had gone bankrupt almost five years ago. Mr. K said that his son (with the regressive genes) turned out to be an incompetent thief and that he was the cause of the problems and the bankruptcy but that there were no worries now since Warren had nothing at all to do with the business anymore.

In Mr. K's mind, we were already a public company, and he was ready to celebrate. He called a meeting of all of the executives and the board and related to us how we would all become rich since we were the ones responsible for the great success of the company. We all were naturally excited and lightheaded and were, in our own way, spending our newfound wealth in our minds.

Since we would probably be expanding our stores to more states and eventually nationwide, I was getting ready to go to Europe to solidify some production deals. A few days before I was scheduled to leave for Europe, Mr. K called me into his office. I thought maybe he was ill because it wasn't the usual bug-killing session. No Johnny Walker or water glasses were brought out. It was obvious that something was on his mind. "Bill," he said, "I have a problem, and I need your help." It seemed that he had again put his son Warren in business. This would be for the third or fourth time. BK had personally rented space for Warren in Grand Central Station and put up a kiosk to sell handbags. If you have any idea of the traffic that would pass this kiosk on any given day—or hour, for that matter—you know that it would be almost impossible for this kind of business to fail. It would take a rare screw-up to accomplish that. So I guess Warren was that rare screw-up. BK was almost in tears. He knew his son was an idiot, but after all, it was his child and his flesh and blood.

BK wanted to know what I would think if he brought Warren into the company in a minor role. I was shocked, and without getting excited as I felt my pulse racing and the anger welling up to my head, I explained that a week before, he had told the underwriters how bad his son was and also that it was his son who had caused the past problems. I then suggested that I would solve the situation for Warren and that I would have no trouble getting one of our good shoe or handbag suppliers to hire Warren in a sales capacity.

That seemed to calm him down somewhat—or at least that was what I thought at the time. When I related what had occurred to some of the key executives, they just couldn't conceive how someone as sharp as Ben Kellner could even suggest something so bizarre.

I now went off to Europe. Merriway Travel made the arrangements. They were travel wholesalers with exceptional contacts with the people who counted in both the airline and the hotel industries. Kurt Huebner was the president, and in years to come, I would drive him to absolute distraction with my constant changes and demands. He was a jewel of a person, though, and he would get me upgraded to first class on almost all of my flights. On my flight to Rome, I thought of my first flight to Europe and how, when I landed in Fiumicino Airport in Rome, I was met by a taxi driver who saw my shoe sample cases and said that he took care of Sam Liebowitz whenever he came to Italy. I knew Sam. Everyone did, as he was famous in the slipper business. As they say, the world shrinks when it comes to meeting people or hearing about them in strange places.

Anyway, on to Florence, and after a couple of days, between strikes and demonstrations, I was managing to accomplish a number of things. As beautiful as Florence is, many people forget that during the flood in 1966, much invaluable and irreplaceable art and many artifacts were destroyed. I came to Florence about a year after the flood, and they had painted marks on the buildings where the water had risen. Some of the markings were over two stories high. If you look at the Arno River, it is hard to conceive how it could possibly have risen to that height. Much could have been saved, but the government told everyone in the area to stay put and not to worry. No precautions were taken.

I had been eating dinner in Harry's Bar, which was on the Arno River, just up from the Excelsior Hotel, and I would eventually become known to Carl, who was the owner. The restaurant was always jammed, but he would always hold a small table for me in the rear. Untypically Italian, he would serve me tomato soup and the most delicious chicken curry. No pasta, but wine and grappa after the meal.

Anyway, when I got back to the hotel, there was an urgent message for me to call Sol at the office. What could be so urgent (unless BK had died or something)? I called Sol, and he was talking crazy and saying that I had to get back to the office immediately but that he couldn't tell me why.

After I blew up at him, he sheepishly told me that Warren was back!

Back? What do you mean back? Who hired him? What was his job?

It seemed that BK had hired him, but nobody knew what his job was. I had to cut my trip short, and on the flight back, my plan was to just play dumb and not say anything until BK let me know why he had overridden my authority and why in the world he hadn't waited for me to get back and obtain a job for Warren.

I was never one to suffer from jet lag, so I went directly to the office from JFK. I thought back to a trip that I had taken in the winter. I had landed at JFK with the worst cold and stuffed head that I had ever had in my life. I had even bought an overcoat in Paris, as it was rare for me to wear a coat. In those days, there weren't that many customs lines, and I knew many of the customs agents. Still I made a point of declaring everything I had bought so that I wouldn't be put on any of their lists, which would hold me up going through customs in the future. Also, strictly as a courtesy, goodwill gesture, and marketing tactic, really not expecting any favors whatsoever, I would give the agent a ten-dollar Kitty Kelly gift certificate.

Going through, I did this and told the agent, whom I knew, that I had a terrible cold and needed to get home. As usual, the customs agent quickly marked my list OK and wished me good luck.

Two men in dark suits suddenly approached me and said that they wanted to ask me some questions. I was in no mood for a survey, and I told them that I was tired and sick and didn't have time for surveys. They then pulled out badges and told me to follow them. I was bewildered and getting pissed, but I followed them to a small room. They said that they were going to give me a chance to declare anything that I had forgotten to declare. I told them that I had declared everything.

They then sternly said that they would give me a last chance to declare what I had purchased. I scanned my brain, but I just couldn't think of anything else. Now they ask me to strip to my shorts. This was wintertime, and I tried to remind them that I had a terrible cold. This did not make any impression. They continued to thoroughly go through all of my bags, feeling around— I guess for secret compartments—my clothes and my pockets. They double-checked my customs list.

I was standing there in my undershorts, and now these two jerks were laughing. They apologized, and when I asked them why they had picked me, they said that my overcoat pockets were bulging. Why were they bulging?

It seemed that I had stuffed all my tissues in the pockets because of my cold, and I had two smoking pipes and a tobacco pouch in the pockets also. I learned my lesson and never went through customs with bulging pockets ever again.

Anyway, back to the office, where I saw lots of nervous faces. I went right into BK's office. He asked about the trip, and I asked him if there was anything new in the office.

Not much, he answered.

This was all very strange. As I was going through the office greeting everyone I ran into, Warren was wandering around the hallways. I introduced myself and asked him what he was doing there. He replied that he was the new handbag buyer, also in charge of real estate, and that he reported directly to his dad.

Trying to hold my temper, I trotted back to BK's office and asked him what was going on. He sheepishly responded that he couldn't help himself. He was desperate, and he had to save his son.

"What about the underwriters?" I asked him.

His stupid answer was, "What they don't know can't hurt them."

When I asked about Warren reporting to him, he said that maybe he would report to BK on real estate, but with handbags, he reported to Bill Morgenstein.

After Warren's first week, he submitted an outrageous expense report. The controller was a stickler and was rightfully tough on what I spent, but this was impossible. I took the report to BK and said that if he thought it should be paid, he would have to countersign it. BK didn't like that.

Next I got a panic call from the Fourteenth Street store. It seemed that Warren was in the back room holding a meeting on a busy Saturday, and only one salesperson was on the floor trying to take care of customers.

I was steaming. I got in my car and arrived at the store, where I got everyone back out on the floor. I loudly and angrily berated Warren, questioning not only his common sense but his sanity. His lame excuse was that the sales people were not selling correctly. Fine, but you don't train on the busiest days during the peak hours!

I could see this was not going to work out, as Warren ran back to his dad, and the Lord knows what he was telling him.

Not two weeks later, Warren was wandering around the halls aimlessly as usual, and who walked in? It was the underwriting team returning on an unannounced visit. I ran to BK's office in order to warn him to get Warren out of the building, and the underwriters came right into BK's office without knocking. They wanted to know who that guy was wandering around the building.

BK responded that that was his son but that he had a very minor role in the company. You would really have had to be there to see the puzzled looks on the underwriters' faces as they reminded BK of what he had said about his son when they were last there. The underwriters gave one another other knowing looks and then stepped outside the building for no more than five or six minutes.

They returned to BK's office and announced that the underwriting was OFF and that they would not approve it! BK was devastated and incensed. I went home and told Sylvia, who couldn't believe what I was telling her.

The next morning, BK arrived earlier than usual with his attorney. He called me into his office and accused me of telling the underwriters about Warren, sabotaging the company, taking bribes from Angelo Ristori, and creating dissension all the way around.

I tried to explain that Angelo had the reputation of being the most honest agent in Italy and that since I had become president, we had shown record profits. This was all to no avail, as it was obviously preplanned, so in effect I was summarily fired.

Everyone was shocked, although I was not completely surprised. It had been a good two-and-a-half-year run. I ended up suing Ben Kellner for defamation and breach of contract, and through my excellent attorney, "Bulldog" Joe Reichbart, I won a nice settlement.

Not very long afterward, Ben Kellner passed away, and few people bothered to attend his funeral. Warren lost the business quickly again and ended up, I believe, selling handbags somewhere.

I remained friendly with the crew, especially Sol, who went to work for a Pennsylvania shoe manufacturer. One day he was telling me that corruption had increased in our industry and that more people were being paid off. I told him that I thought he was exaggerating. He said that he could prove it to me. He took out an envelope with cash in it, and we proceeded to S. Kresge's (one of the early five-and-dime stores) office. From the waiting area, we could see the buyer stalls. I watched when Sol was called to a buyer's open cubicle. Sol reached into his pocket, pulled out the envelope, and gave it to the buyer. The buyer immediately wrote out an order. I was totally shocked.

A. S. BECK

The shock of leaving Kitty Kelly was not so much leaving the company, as I knew that I couldn't fight a family situation and that I couldn't prevent their self-destruction, but it was the uncalled-for accusation and recriminations that hurt. There was shock in the industry, and all of the comments and letters were kind and supportive. Job offers started coming in, but I felt that I had to be careful and make the correct choice.

One evening at home, the phone rang at a little past midnight (throughout the years, I worked with people from all over the globe and would receive calls at ungodly hours). The call was from Jesse Wachtel. Jesse was well known in the shoe industry. He was known as having a very sharp mind and also as being a very talented merchandiser. For a couple of weeks after that, he would call me from Italy at least three times a week. It was six hours later in Italy, and he would talk for hours with Syl lying next to me in bed trying to get some sleep. Jesse had been recently hired as president of the conglomerate that owned A. S. Beck shoe stores, which was a long-standing shoe chain of a little over a hundred stores. They had once had almost two hundred stores before they fell on hard times. They were now trying to make a comeback.

Jesse said that he had just hired Vince Camuto to run their import division. I knew Vince and his partner Jackie Fisher quite well. When I was buying for Thom McAn, I used to buy from their factory in Maine. I had ordered shoes for an upcoming ad, and it was getting close to delivery time. I called Vince a number of times, and he said not to worry. I knew that when a manufacturer told me not to worry...it was time to worry. I got on a plane to Boston and rented a car to drive to Maine. I arrived at the factory door on a cold, bleak day and was greeted with a sheriff's notice pasted on the front door. "Factory closed due to creditors." I was naturally very highly agitated and got Vince on the phone at his home. He apologized profusely and promised one day to make it up to me.

After their factory closed, Jackie and Vince went to work for Washington Shoe Company in Japan, which was the largest shoe factory and one of the finest shoe companies in Japan. I was promised (as I imagine every other buyer was also promised) the first deliveries. The shoes came in and were some of the finest pearlized pumps that I had ever seen. The pumps sold out immediately. We wanted to but couldn't reorder, as the factory had no more production space for exports. Sadly for all, it was a short run. The Washington Shoe Company management saw to it that they were hired by Sumitomo Shoji, as Sumitomo was eager to export to the United States from various factories throughout the world. (I'll tell that story later on).

In the meantime, Jesse was assembling a top-flight crew for the various divisions of the company, and he was offering me the position of president of A. S. Beck. I wasn't giving him an answer because I was concerned about bringing back to life a company that had been in trouble. When I did finally make up my mind that I would give it a try, I called Jesse, who then informed that he had hired Fred Randolph for the job just two days before.

They still wanted me to join the company, however. Since Fred was strong on operations, they would make me executive vice-president in charge of merchandising and buying. Their old buying staff was just about decimated, including the dress-shoe buyer, Larry.

I was in part responsible for Larry's demise. When I was with Kitty Kelly, Ben Kellner discovered a shoe in their Fifth Avenue window that was supposed to be exclusively ours. It was embarrassing for me, and I called Harold Sterin, the sales rep at Evy Shoe, who claimed it was an oversight. Oversight my ass! Beck had the shoe marked at $6.99, so I reduced our price to $4.99.

Panic ensued. Harold called and said that Larry was going to get fired because they thought that he must have overpaid—or worse, that maybe he was taking bribes from Evy Shoe Company. The owners of Evy Footwear, who had some large factories in Pennsylvania, were afraid to lose Beck as a customer. I didn't want to hurt a fellow buyer, so I decided to compromise and marked the style up to $5.99. Larry followed suit.

Larry was no longer with the company when I decided to join it. A. S. Beck was located in Midtown Manhattan. I had a pleasant meeting with Fred Randolph, the president, and I could see by his demeanor that we would get along just fine. It turned out that we would remain friends for many years thereafter, until his recent passing in Florida. We both knew that this was going to take a lot of very hard work. The day I started, we had a meeting in the boardroom. As we entered the room, we were both struck with the same horror. There was a very large painting of a shipwreck with high waves and sailors falling off the ship after striking sail. No wonder the company had problems previously. We laughed and called in a crew to remove the painting forthwith.

I kept people whom I thought had promise and added buyers and merchandise people where I thought they were needed. In my training, I explained that importing would be the coming thing in the fashion business, as it was hard for the New England factories to maintain the production that would be needed. It took a couple hundred hand processes to make a shoe, and young people wanted higher pay and cleaner work.

The fashion was developing in Europe, so we planned a trip both to "shop the stores" and also to find sources in order to supplement our domestic resources. Except for me, it would be everyone's first trip to Europe. They were all excited. I had my assistant make the arrangements in detail through my friends at Merriway.

Throughout the years, I was always envied that I had the opportunity to travel so extensively. International travel, at least for me, was no fun. I liked to work on a tight schedule with as few surprises, delays, and disruptions as possible. That almost never worked out. Some connection would invariably be missed and some appointments not kept. There were riots and strikes, and in the seventies, bombs. It always confounded me when people would come up to me tell me how lucky I was to travel all over the world.

Not that there weren't good parts to traveling. I got to meet some very fascinating people and made some very good friends. I had a taste for good wine and fine food and where possible would seek out the finest and newest restaurant that had the excitement that the critics were writing about.

This trip seemed to be going rather smoothly, which made me happy, as the natural feeling was that you wanted to impress those you were responsible for. The glitches started when we went from Switzerland to Germany. For some reason, the customs agent at the Zurich airport forgot to slam his stamp down onto my passport (why do the civil servants just love to do that?). Since I wanted to make sure there was no problem with anyone, I was the last one to go through customs in Germany. I was absent-mindedly looking up at the large clock, since I was a little confused as to the time, when I realized that this large female customs agent was hollering at me. I came to my senses and realized that she was saying in that harsh Germanic tone, "YOU ARE NOT IN GERMANY; YOU ARE NOT IN GERMANY."

"What do you mean I am not in Germany?" I responded. "The sign above the clock says Dusseldorf and I've been here before, and unless something happened since my last trip, this IS in Germany."

She explained that my passport was not stamped.

I explained that the plane that I had come from had originated in Zurich and I hadn't paid any attention to the stamping. She then gave me a dirty look, slammed the customs stamp on her table loud enough to scare the pigeons on the rails above, and on we went.

The five of us arrived at the Intercontinental Hotel in Dusseldorf, and I immediately pulled out our confirmation. The desk clerk asked our names, ignoring the paper I had just shoved at him, and announced loudly (I swear he had to be the brother of the customs agent), "YOU HAVE NO RESERVATION!"

"What do you mean we have no reservation? It's here in black and white."

He went back to his card file, came back, and announced, "YOU HAVE NO RESERVATION."

I could see it was pointless to argue. I told him that we needed five rooms for the night, so would he be kind enough to get us rooms in another good hotel?

"Oh," he says, "we have rooms, and you can stay here, but: YOU HAVE NO RESERVATONS."

Germany was going to be our last stop, so it would be a relief to get home.

Back at Beck, things were starting to move. Vince Camuto, who today is of the best and most well-known shoe designers, was having a ball with the wholesale and import divisions. Happily, our A. S. Beck stores were showing excellent figures, with almost all of the stores showing dramatic increases in their sales.

Fred asked me to accompany him on a tour of the stores and attend a shoe show at the very same Palmer House where the BK stair incident took place. There was also a high-volume A. S. Beck store on State Street. The night before we were to leave for

Chicago, he invited us to a cocktail party at his penthouse apartment on the east side of Manhattan.

Syl and I perceived that the Randolphs did well. This was Fred's second wife, and the story going around was that she was loaded. It was a magnificent penthouse apartment overlooking the East River. Everything was fine except that my reputation of getting lost prevailed. With Syl in tow, I opened the door to go into the hallway, and we found ourselves in the middle of a walk-in closet. It was quite embarrassing walking out of a closet into a crowd of people who were exiting the apartment.

The next day, we left for Chicago, and when we arrived, we went to see some of our Midwest stores. This would be the first glimpse that the store managers were going to get of their new bosses. We were anxious to get to our State Street flagship store. You should know that Fred was tall and good looking, with very bright-blue eyes, and he was very sharply dressed. His manner was friendly, but those eyes sometimes intimidated people.

Upon entering the store, we asked for the manager. Tom, the manager, was a good six inches shorter than Fred, and when we told him who we were, the look of absolute fear could be seen in his face. You could see beads of sweat breaking out on his forehead.

Fred noticed this right away, so he tried to ask Tom what he considered some very softball questions. "Do you have enough stock in your store?" This was a nice, simple question.

Or so we thought. Poor Tom was stuttering: "I have, I have, I have...I don't have any," he finally blurted out.

I was about to break up, and I couldn't take it. So I ran out of the store, into the lobby, and I was actually doubled over from laughter. I couldn't control myself in order to go back inside. Every time I looked into the store, I saw poor Fred trying to control himself, so I went out into the street and laughed until the tears were streaming down my face.

Fred came out and said that we really hadn't acted the way top executives were supposed to act and that I shouldn't have left him alone with the manager. And then Fred burst out laughing himself. Neither one of us had the nerve to return to that store during the rest of the trip. On the flight home, we both laughed whenever we mentioned poor Tom's name.

Our total business was going along nicely, however—until I examined the books and saw that cash was being taken in large quantities from A. S. Beck to Baker Industries. I immediately called Jesse, who was the president of the controlling company, to complain, and he used a word that was unfamiliar to me at the time. It was called "upstreaming."

You could call it what you wanted, but to me it was called stealing! Against Jesse Wachtel's instructions, I made an appointment to see the chairman of Baker Industries at his apartment on Fifth Avenue to complain. Against all of my arguments on how he was going to ruin a good chain, he said that it was a necessary procedure and that all would be well.

I didn't like him, and in my mind, I perceived this clown to be a crook. There was no reasonable explanation as to why he was destroying the most profitable divisions in the company. It was obvious that we had to leave before our reputations became damaged. Both Fred and Vince fully agreed, and we all departed the company very soon afterward.

Sandia International: Lots of Travel

J esse, Fred, Vince Camuto, and I all realized that what was happening at Beck did not bode well for us. We probably should have hung the painting of the sea disaster back in the boardroom.

None of us was going to have any trouble getting placed in areas that fit our talents. Some very good offers were coming my way, but the one that I found the most interesting was from Eric Metzger, who owned a company called Sandia ("watermelon" in Spanish) International. Sandia was an importer and exporter of footwear. They also were associated with a company in Paterson, New Jersey, that manufactured rubber boots (Kaysam). My title would be executive vice-president. I would report to Eric, and I would be in charge of all sourcing and styling for Sandia only, along with selling of the major chains that Eric was not already handling.

Besides the broadening of my experience, the office was in Englewood Cliffs, New Jersey, which was less than fifteen minutes from our home in Teaneck. I would have to drive into the city every day as before, but I would be doing some extensive international traveling.

The other thing that I would have to overcome was jealousy in the office, as both Bob Cook and Don thought that they would get the job. Eric said that he would smooth things over and explain that they needed someone with my background. Eric did that, so the tensions were brought down.

Eric was considered one of the most astute salespeople in the entire industry. He was extremely shrewd and honest, and he was an incredibly hard worker. He was also a generous person with his help. He loved to throw parties and barbecues for his workers at his home.

On the commercial side, Eric was very careful and conservative in his approach to business, and that meant that he didn't like to take too many chances. Eric was a refugee from Germany, and when he arrived in America in the late thirties, he was penniless. The relatives he stayed with didn't have much either. He took his battered suitcase and went to a shoe wholesaler on Duane Street in Lower Manhattan and in his broken English asked if they had any territories open. Lester Pincus of Pincus Shoes was not one to turn down someone in need, so he gave Eric the New England territory while slipping a few bucks into his worn trousers.

Eric then got himself a battered used car and immediately made the trip north to Boston. He was in the stores from 8:00 in the morning until they closed at 10:00 or 11:00 at night. Through hard work and dedication, he became successful quickly and decided to strike out on his own. Only now the difference was that nobody was paying for his hotel room, so that meant that he would sleep in his car. He never forgot his struggles, and when he became extremely successful, he maintained his ability to negotiate with people and run a very tight business.

He also appreciated the good life, living well in a fine home and enjoying the theatre and the best restaurants, especially if they served lobster or crab. Eric always picked up the check when we ate together, although I made a point of picking up every third one so as not to feel embarrassed or have him think I was a *schnorer* (taker).

In the years that I was with Eric, I learned a great deal from him, and at times he would truly amaze me.

One day he called me into his office and said that he'd like me to drive with him up to Framingham, Massachusetts, which was just outside of Boston, to see a discount customer called Zayre. I asked him why in the world he would want to see that customer because of all of our customers, that buyer was the one we had the poorest luck with. Every order that we shipped to them was either late, or there was a quality problem. They had made it known that they had no intention of placing any more orders with us. So why waste our time? Another quality of Eric's was that he was very stubborn, and he insisted that we were going to see them and that he had just the right styles for them, and further, that he would walk out with an order. This was something that I was going to have to see because in my mind, we were just going to waste our time.

We arrived at Zayre, and feeling a little embarrassed, I followed Eric into the buyer's office. As soon as we entered, Eric laughed and said to Steve, the buyer: "You know something, Steve? If I were YOU, I would throw ME out!"

Steve howled, and we all laughed and relaxed. Sure enough, we walked out with the orders, and I learned another lesson as Eric gave that nervous, funny shrug of his as we were leaving.

Upon our return, I was preparing for my first overseas trip with the company, and that was going to be to Brazil. I had never been to Brazil before, and I was looking forward to it. Eric had made one trip there just prior to my coming to the company. He made one purchase. The factory had quoted a price of $2.45 for a style called the desert boot, but Eric said that the price was too cheap and that he would pay $2.51. The factory owner was impressed, not knowing that the duty at the time was 10 percent for a leather shoe over $2.51 but 15 percent for anything under that. Therefore, in effect, it was costing Sandia less, and in turn making the factory owner happier. That was the good part.

The bad part was that Eric had the chance to lock up the production in the finest factories in Brazil, but, he was fearful of their prices, however, which were much higher than anything that he was used to. Therefore, he passed up what was to become a multimillion-dollar opportunity, as these factories would go on to become the major suppliers of the famous Nine West women's brand.

If you remember, Jackie Fisher (he's fancy now and calls himself Jack) and Vince Camuto were selling and styling for Sumitomo after they left the large Japanese manufacturer. They were both doing exceptionally well, making close to a million dollars each per year. The president of Sumitomo called them in and said that they were making more than the president himself, so their commissions were going to be cut. They would have none of it, and they both quit.

Sumitomo had been developing footwear in Brazil, so both Vince and Jack decided to exploit it further. That was when they made a deal with the three best factories (the ones Eric passed on), with the idea of having the volume of J. C. Penney as their base. Since they took offices in 9 West Fifty-Seventh Street, they called their line Nine West. They had both told me that Brazil was going to be the place for a number of years, so I was prepared for a successful trip.

This was the era in South America of tough, really tough military governments. Many times I would see instances of what tough, repressive governments were like. The Brazilian government was export minded and subsidized their factories, so the prices and costs were incredibly low. Also, the Brazilians tended to like North Americans. In the early days, one factory didn't realize how much they made on exports until the end of the year when their accountants told them. They made a week-long party for the whole town, but a few days after that, the owner had a heart attack as he was climbing the stairs of his factory and died on the spot.

Upon landing in Rio de Janeiro, I was met by Roberto Goncalves. Roberto was one of these fun-loving characters who knew the factory owners, government people, and entertainers. Roberto was going to be our agent in the Rio area, where there were a couple of small factories that we were starting to do business with. In a couple of days, I would be leaving for Southern Brazil, taking the hour-and-a-half flight to Porto Alegre and then on to the small shoe-manufacturing towns surrounding Novo Hamburgo.

Roberto, in the meantime, gave me a quick tour of Rio and introduced me to the *baroa* (baron) of Ipanema, who was a famous ninety-year-old character who used to hang around the local bars. The highlight, however, was when he introduced me to Heloisa, who was just becoming famous as the "Girl from Ipanema." I can report that she was tall, young, and beautiful, just as the song says.

When I landed in the south, I met our agent, who was Paulo Kreuff. Many of the people from that southern state, Rio Grande do Sul, were descended from Hamburg area of Germany. The center of the shoe-making industry was a town called Novo Hamburgo, where Paulo was born. Paulo had come to the United States as an exchange student. He spoke perfect English, was very bright, and had excellent contacts with both the factory owners and the government. This was their incipient stages of exporting shoes to the United States, and any order placed was exciting for them. They had a club that met on Wednesday evenings, and it was appropriately called the Drunkard's Club. Since I had placed some orders early in the week, I was invited as an honored guest. Each factory would announce the quantity of business that they had received and then exaggerate it by at least ten times. It was all in fun.

Southern Brazil is Gaucho country, which is the equivalent of our Texas—cowboy country. Country dress, music, food, and rodeos were de rigueur. Each factory had a room where the men would drink matte tea in the mornings and look at the pictures of scantily clad women on the walls. The food was beef and chicken oriented because it was cattle country, with the mainstay being the *rodizio* (churrascaria) style of cooking. This was becoming very popular here in America, and Paulo had recently told me why. We used to have lunch (sometimes lunch and dinner, which would be impossible today) in a small town called Sapiranga, at a restaurant called Mateus. It was a very hearty meal, and the local cowboys would bring (except for the ample salads) everything out on skewers, starting with sausage, chicken wings, chicken hearts, and the progressively better cuts of beef, until the prime piece of sirloin, which they called *picanha*, was brought out. You ate until you told them to stop. The barbecue was grilled outdoors with a heavy coating of salt that was knocked off the meat just before serving.

Now how did this start? It seemed that many years before, a couple of tourist buses pulled up, and they were overwhelmed with people to serve. They brought out long tables and benches and quickly fired up as much of anything that they could find. They then had their cowhands place the food on skewers and go around to serve everyone. It was so successful that from then on, that was the way they served all of their customers.

This was as Paulo told it (some years later) one day when we were having lunch at Mateo's, which was the restaurant that originated the concept. I had a buyer from the States with me, and I started to explain to him that this concept would go over fantastically in the States; however, you could only do this with Southern Gauchos. There would be no way to teach these people English, get them visas, and even get them interested in emigrating.

Boy, was I wrong. At the next table, there was a group of Brazilian advertising executives who overheard my conversation. They went on to establish the first churrascaria in Miami, and through the years, this concept expanded to every large city all over the world, but especially here in America.

On one of my trips to Brazil, the owners of one of the factories that we worked with was also the lieutenant governor of the state. He said he would like Paulo to bring me to Brasilia, the capital, to speak about the economic situation in Brazil from an American standpoint. Brazil at this time was suffering from severe inflation and the usual corrupt government. The saying went that "Brazil is the country of the future and always will be." They had just banned a book called *Brazil for Brazilians* by a Hungarian author, detailing the corruption in the government. If they found him, they would shoot him.

So now I was in this long room with mostly military men. None of those sourpusses had a damn smile on his face. I started to explain my plan for improving the economy of Brazil: "You will need to lower your restrictions on imports, as the restrictions and high duties are causing inflation. You need to tie the cruziero (the currency at the time) in with the dollar, you need a modified gold stan—" And all of a sudden, I felt myself being lifted physically out of the chair by two large military policemen. I was thrown into the hallway, and the door slammed behind me.

Claudio Strassburger, the lieutenant governor, and Paulo were mortified. What the hell did they expect me to say? If they wanted my opinion on how to help the country, I had to tell the truth. Nobody was forcing them to listen to me!

I was put on the next plane back to Sao Paulo and then on to Porto Alegre, fearful that when I got back to the hotel, the militia would be waiting to cart me away. I couldn't wait to get home.

The next week, my friend Hank D'Girolamo sent word for me to get him bailed out of the local prison. It seemed that he was in a bar, and the MPs came in for a routine check of papers (routine for them, not for us). Hank gave them some lip, so they hauled him away and threw him in a cage.

There were other disadvantages in Brazil. Southern Brazil had the reputation of having the worst drivers. Fifty percent of the buses got into accidents each year.

Paulo was also a very fast driver, and there were no seat belts in those days. I tried to get him to slow down on numerous occasions without success. One day we were coming back from the factories, driving on the main road from Novo Hamburgo to

Porto Alegre, and Paul swerved toward a bus stop to pick up a young girl, who got into the backseat. Off he went, flying along, at the same time turning his head and talking to the girl. We were speedily approaching a line of cars that were stopped for a red light, which he didn't see because he was talking to the girl in the backseat. Smash, bang, as I was thrown through the front window. Paulo smashed his jaw into the steering wheel, and I was lying on the road, unconscious.

Just at that moment, by sheer coincidence, Paulo's brother-in-law approached the scene and stopped to assist us. Paulo exclaimed to his brother-in-law, "What am I supposed to do with a dead American?"

It turned out that I was not dead! The girl in the rear was not badly hurt, but they took her to the hospital for observation. Paulo went to another hospital, and I was rushed to a *pronto socorro*, which was a first-aid station where they treated traffic crash victims.

They treated me, took X-rays, and then released me in the care of Paulo's family. But I asked to go back to the hotel because I had an important negotiating meeting the following day. The doctors thought I was crazy, but they released me anyway.

I'm not sure how I attended the meeting the next day, but I did—drowsy, woozy, and looking like absolute hell. I wanted to make Eric proud.

The following week, I returned home with the whole right side of my face black and blue. I had never told Syl that I was in an accident, so when she met me, she was in absolute shock and didn't believe me when I said that it was a car accident. She was sure that I had gotten into a fight. She insisted that our first stop had to be our beloved Dr. Griffel. The doctor was the last of his breed. He was like three or four doctors in one and made sure that he spent ample time with his patients, no matter how long that took. The good doctor also made house calls when necessary. I can still picture him in my mind as I sit in the synagogue thinking, now there is one holy man. In Hebrew we call a holy man a *Tzadik*.

I explained to the good doctor what had happened and then told him that I had already had X-rays and that there were no cracks or concussions. He then gave me one of his looks, and I knew that I was going for more X-rays. Sure enough, they found a small concussion and also a small crack in the skull. I had back and neck pain, but that went quickly.

Some years later, the neck pain returned, so I went to a local chiropractor (for the first time in my life), and he discovered that I had been in an accident and made the usual adjustments with the usual twists and cracks. I never had any back pain again.

There would be many trips to Europe, Brazil, South America, Asia, and Africa.

FINDING NEW MARKETS

E ric's aim was to find new and exotic markets to develop or re-
fine their shoe-export capacity. That meant traveling to Asia,
Europe, South America, and Africa. It was not only important to
try to develop new markets, but it was also important to find both
fashionable and quaint styles at low prices.

Many of the foreign airlines were good, with Singapore
Airlines, BOAC, Varig, and others priding themselves on their
service. A couple of the exceptions were Alitalia, which could
very well go on strike just as you were ready to board the aircraft,
and Air France, which we renamed Air Chance because of their
attitude and poor service.

My favorite airline, however, was Pan Am because we were
always treated royally. The influence of Merriway Travel and being a member of the Clipper Club also helped. This was true
especially when changes had to be made because of delays or
uncertainties that often popped up. At JFK, Mary was in charge
of the Clipper Club, and we would exchange stories about our
days at the University of Alabama, where she was also a graduate.

One of the countries that we were serious about developing was Argentina. (More about Aerolineas Argentina later on).
This was now in the early seventies, and Argentina was ruled by a

tough, nasty, and brutal military junta. My first trip to Argentina was from Brazil with a Brazilian manufacturer (Nestor de Conto). Our goal was to buy leather from a tannery in Cordoba. Driving from the airport to the hotel was frightening, as these young soldiers would stop you every few kilometers in order to check your papers. You rolled down the windows, and they stuck tommy guns in your faces, sometimes ordering you out of the car as they looked at your ID. It seemed that Cordoba was a university town that was considered a hotbed of youth unrest. Many of the political dissidents would disappear throughout the country.

Finally we arrived, late and tired. We checked into our respective rooms. No matter how late it is, I have to take a walk around before I can fall asleep. We had, however, been warned not to leave the hotel at night under any circumstances. The room had two large windows facing the bed, and it looked like a good-sized balcony outside. After I took my shower, I opened the window, ready to step out onto the terrace, and there was a guy standing there with a rifle over his shoulder.

I quickly dashed to the nightstand and called Nestor's room (somewhat in a panic). "NESTOR!" I screamed into the phone. "There's a guy with a rifle just outside my room."

Nestor was calm, and he said, "Bill, do yourself a favor. Get into bed, pull the covers over your head, and go to sleep. I'll see you in the morning."

I did that, and not five minutes later, the phone rang. It was Nestor, who was in the next room. Now he was in a panic. "Bill, I just opened the window to the balcony, and there IS a guy out there with a gun."

I replied, "Nestor, do yourself a favor. Get into your bed, pull the covers over your head, and go to sleep. I'll see you in the morning."

We left the next day for Rosario. Although it was calmer, the room that I was given (after again arriving very late) was over the kitchen, and it was infested with hundreds if not thousands of cockroaches. Nestor found me the next morning sleeping on the couch in the lobby.

Of course, when I got back to New Jersey, Eric thought this was all very funny, and he told me that I now had to go back to Argentina to develop their factories for export. We had to find an agent in Argentina. My idea was to work from the top down, and through various government sources, including the Argentine consulate and the Argentine trade bureau, we would interview the various candidates they had recommended in Buenos Aires.

I decided to take my assistant, David Meltzer, on the trip in order to assist with the details and make recommendations where necessary. After we landed in Ezeiza, which was the international airport in Buenos Aires, Dave was relieved that the warning that I had given him did not turn out as bad as we expected. Although there were soldiers in military vehicles stationed in various spots on the way to the hotel, our taxi was not stopped.

We set up shop at the Sheraton Hotel and went on to start our interview process. The most impressive candidate was a dynamic fellow by the name of Jorge Engel, who, along with his assistant, Hector Padilla, had us convinced that they were the ones who could do the job for us. Jorge explained to us that the only way to get things accomplished was through the support of the government. He mentioned that the next day, we would meet with the various ministers and that he would bring two members of his staff with us. One was a retired general and the other a retired admiral, and both would come in uniform. That certainly sounded very exciting to us, as Jorge had indicated that this would ensure our success.

Dave and I celebrated our find with one of those fine Argentine steak dinners. Their beef is incredibly soft, flavorful, and tender. Early in the morning, you can see the trucks lined up from the countryside waiting to enter the city to deliver their beef to the stores and restaurants. They call Buenos Aires the Paris of South America, and it is well named, as it is a beautiful city that includes some very luxurious and fine areas.

The next morning, we had a hearty breakfast, and Jorge and his crew arrived promptly at 10:00 a.m. The days started late and ended late, with dinner not usually starting until 10:00 p.m.

Dave saw that I was upset when they entered. He was not sure why, but he counseled me not to lose my famous temper. When I was in Korea, we had UN units from various countries, and one of my jobs was billeting (finding sleeping accommodations) for foreign military visitors. Protocol said that it had to be prioritized by rank. This meant that I had to know the ranks of those from various countries. I knew immediately that the so-called general was a noncommissioned officer and that the "admiral" was a boatswain's mate. I was thinking that if this guy was going to lie about this, could you imagine what else he would lie about? Especially when it came to working with the factories.

I called Mr. Engel aside and told him that I was sorry, but we could not afford to work with liars. He was quite surprised that I knew the ranks of the two he had brought along, and he went on to explain that since I didn't know the culture, if he told us that he was bringing noncoms, we wouldn't go along with it. He then went on to say that noncoms in this country could get more done than officers, as they knew things on the "street level."

"You have nothing to lose," he said. "Come with me to the ministry, and if you are not satisfied with the results, we will part as friends."

Further, he gave his solemn promise that from here on in, he would be absolutely straight with us in every way.

I agreed, and off we went to the various ministries, which were all housed in the same building. We met with a number of ministers, including the ministers of defense and economics, neither of whom was impressive.

The last minister was His Excellency Sr. Hector Alvaro Fernandez Mendy, and he was as impressive as his name was long. His office was right next to that of Alejandro Lanusse, who was the military president of Argentina. He was frank, and I liked him and felt comfortable diplomatically telling him about my impressions of the other ministers. Jorge had mentioned that I might even get to meet the president, which would have been a big thrill for me. Sr. Mendy was the minister of agriculture, and he stated that his family had owned vast farms for many generations and that he would be very secure in his job, as he was not in it for the glory or the money as the others were.

When I asked to meet the president, he laughed and asked when I would be returning to his country. I said that it depended on what we accomplished, but it could be within three or four months. His response was, "Fine, because by then you will meet a real president. Juan Peron will be returning, and he will do a complete house cleaning except for me."

That sounded logical, and can you imagine that I was going to meet Juan Peron himself? I also could see by everyone's reactions that they respected Jorge Engel, and they promised to help with the factory introductions.

We went on to the factories, and the meetings went well, with one of them, called Triay, giving us a contract of exclusivity for their exports. (That entailed another trip to Cordoba, where Dave was scared out of his wits, as the unrest had seemingly gotten worse.)

I had also decided to keep Jorge Engel as our agent. About four months later, I scheduled a return trip to inspect the production, which although moderate was important for certain types of footwear, especially boots. The Triay factory had also been running late, and since that was our most important factory in Cordoba, I wanted to see what the holdup was.

I was excited to get back to Argentina because I was looking forward to meeting with Juan Peron, who, as Sr. Mendy had predicted, had triumphantly returned as president. Jorge met me at the airport, where I had landed from Porto Alegre, and I told him that the first thing that I want to do was have Sr. Mendy introduce me to the new president.

Jorge laughed. Unfortunately, I was not going to meet anybody in the government. It seemed that when Peron returned, the first person that he fired was the minister of agriculture, Sr. Mendy. So although disappointed, we went on to Cordoba.

It was relatively quiet and a bright, sunny day as we entered the Triay factory. I was greeted with the usual handshakes, hugs, and matte tea (which is drunk in all of the gaucho countries in South America). They apologized for the orders running late and gave us the usual factory excuses.

I then went into the production area to see our orders, only to be shocked to see my competition's shoes going through the factory. When I ranted that we had an exclusive contract, one of the Triay brothers explained that his half of the factory gave us the exclusivity, and he showed me a curtain between the two lines. I then told the brothers that that would be the last order they would get from us. At that point we stormed out of the factory. Such is life in the shoe industry.

When my mother heard that I was going to South America, she reminded me that we had relatives in both Brazil and Argentina and that they were relatives from my grandfather's side. When the brothers left Poland to emigrate, one came to the good old U.S. of A, and the other one settled in South America. They were separated not only by distance but by personality. Izzy and Anna, my grandparents, were straightlaced, honest, and very hardworking people. Before he came to America, Izzy worked as the head tailor at the famous Gallery Lafayette department store in Paris. He could make furniture, clothes, and pickles and fix an automobile. When Izzy ran his food business, he would buy only the very best.

As a kid, I knew that whenever we visited them, I would get a hearty kiss and hug, along with a five-dollar bill. I don't remember them ever smiling very much, however. His brother, on the other hand, was mysterious, and my mother was sure that he was some kind of thief or smuggler, and that may have been confirmed because every time I called them and tried to meet with them, I got very evasive answers. The last time I called, they wanted to know why I was calling. "Did somebody die?" I gave up after that.

There were many other trips to many other places, and I enjoyed the parties that Eric gave, learning the techniques of the import-export business and meeting some very nice and fascinating people. There had been talk of Kaysam buying out Eric's business. Although I did get along with the executives of this domestic manufacturing company, I felt that they were too structured and really didn't understand our business. I was now selling many of the major accounts, doing all of the styling and supervising much of the production overseas. I therefore felt that the timing was such that I should move on and form my own company. I knew Eric would want me to give him time to replace me and train the new person, so I sat down with him right away and explained what my plans were, including the fact that I would do nothing to hurt his business or work with any resource that he already had.

He said that he wasn't surprised by my decision, but he really didn't want to lose me. So he offered me the opportunity to both work on my own and continue to work for Sandia on a modified basis. That sounded very appealing to me.

I couldn't wait to tell Syl that evening. Sylvia is a very clear-headed person, and although cautious, she thinks things out very clearly. She asked me if I thought that I could make a success running my own business. When I said that the answer was yes, she said that I couldn't have a business and work for Eric. It should be one or the other, as you couldn't be successful having two masters. I should make up my mind accordingly.

I gave it some thought, and respecting her insight, I decided that I would go out on my own. I gave Sandia the notice that they requested and bade my farewells to everyone. We then decided that it would be best to cancel our vacation trip that we were going to take to Acapulco, Mexico, and rebooked the trip to Brazil.

Eric and I remained friends for many years thereafter, and I never lost my love and respect for him.

The next step was for me to go to the local National Community Bank and negotiate a line of credit with Charley

Strickler, who was the manager. Charley was always polite and friendly, but rightfully treated the bank's money just as if it were his own. The only debt that I had was the mortgage. I formed the corporation and put some of my own cash in, but I still needed the line of credit for letters of credit to buy merchandise and set up offices overseas.

I chose the name Marquesa because the mainstay of our business was going to be Italy, Spain, and South America, and the name Marquesa rang true in all those areas that spoke the romance languages. It would be relatively easy not to conflict with Sandia because I was much less price minded than Eric was, and I also was more into new ideas and advanced fashion trends. Whenever I did anything pricey or "fast" at Sandia, Eric would go into his nervous, head-shaking mode, running around the room crying doom. I had no such qualms.

Next was the excitement of forming my own company.

STARTING MARQUESA
INTERNATIONAL

O ur goal was to become an agent for the large shoe chains and the large name-brand footwear operations in various countries, specializing in women's footwear. I also had to be careful not to infringe on Eric's operation. This would be easy, as Eric concentrated on selling to the discount chains. Both the styling and the factories would be different.

To start, it meant finding agents in Spain, Italy, and Brazil, which would be our mainstay countries for starters. Roberto Goncalves no longer worked for Eric in Rio, so he readily agreed to come aboard. Roberto then accompanied me to the southern area to help me find a suitable candidate there. We found a nice chap by the name of Paulo di Lima. We had a sample line made up, and I bought a few shoes to get started and to dip my toes in the ocean, so to speak.

From there I flew to Italy, where I met a freight forwarder, Piero Albini. Our families would eventually become very close. Piero introduced me to various potential agents, and for the Tuscany area, I chose Maurizio Amoroso. Maurizio was knowledgeable and honest, although I suspected that he was a little pig headed and lazy.

I set up a small sample line and bought a few styles to sell when I returned to the States. Upon my return, I made the rounds to some of my friends who had smaller operations. My first was a thirty-store chain called Simco. If you had something hot or new, you went to them first. They were the fastest payers in the industry. If the shoes came in their warehouse on a Monday, they cut you a check on Friday. Also, if it was something new, they tested it, disregarding any budget considerations. After they left the scene, the fashion industry changed, and it became a business of accountants and numbers. That is why today you see that many styles of clothes, including footwear, don't really change that radically. Creativity has become somewhat stifled. Public companies have to answer to their quarterly results and to their shareholders.

In our day, in my opinion, we had sharper buyers with the guts to overcome budgets. The Bootery on Thirty-Fourth Street was similar and famous for its "fast" styles. Stanley, the owner, was as sharp as they come, and he bought with a small group of some very good operators. The vendors came from all over the country to "knock off" his styles. Stanley has eyes in the rear of his head. His spot was in the front of the store. One day I was talking to him, and without turning, he said, "One of my salesmen is taking shoes out in the back and putting them in the garbage to be picked up later. Excuse me for a minute while I call the cops."

Bennie Shafer had been my operations man at A. S. Beck, and after he left, he opened a shoe store in the Village on Eighth Street. If a style was wild and crazy, he carried it. He gave me my second order. Fred Braun Shoes and Strawberry Stores were other stores that gave us a shot. The exposure was terrific. The styles sold, and we were off and running.

My plan was always to keep a small inventory in our warehouse for testing, but the thrust of the business would be for the large companies to buy direct from the factories on a letter of credit basis. Once their goods were placed on a vessel or airplane, the factory was paid, and I then billed them our 10 percent commission. Most importers received commission from both the customer and also from the factory. I didn't believe in that. Besides the fact that I didn't think it was honest, I also felt that we would be more competitive, as the factories could now lower their prices.

My other practice was never to pay off a buyer. I would go as far as giving tickets to a show, a fancy dinner, or a Christmas gift (under fifty dollars), but that would be it. When I had been a buyer, I was actually offered a bribe only once. It was an old-timer selling shoes from Haiti. He was hinting around all during dinner, and I had no idea what he was talking about. He finally realized this and blurted out, "Dummy, don't you realize what I am doing? I am offering you a BRIBE!" I turned him down, and the next day I reported it to Fred Randolph, who thought it was extremely funny. I began to wonder: Was Fred taking bribes? Through the years, I realized that it cost me business and kept me out of some very large companies, who shall be nameless.

After I received my first orders, I was able to open an office in Englewood Cliffs, New Jersey, and I was able to start attending the shoe trade shows. I hired Sherwin Tunic as my first salesperson. His job was to sell the shoes that were in stock. The first large chain that I sold was Montgomery Ward. I had sold Joel Berlin before when I was with Eric, but in order to sell the better sport shoes, I had to sell Howard Malter (both are friends to this day). Howard had a great sense of humor, and you would rarely see him without a smile or not telling a joke. I was getting good-size orders from him, and whenever I went to his office, he made sure that it was around lunchtime, at which point he took great glee in inviting his entire staff and anyone he could find on his floor to join us for lunch. I knew Howard's routine, but I still got a kick out of it.

Bill Schutz was a crazy dude from Montreal who worked for a Canadian company called Phil-Penn, which I had started to sell. Before Bill joined Phil-Penn, Joe Kraut, the owner, invited me to go with him to a town called Batawa, where I was to meet the famous Thomas Bata. Tom's family was thrown out of Czechoslovakia by the communists. They had a very large shoe factory, and they even maintained a company village. When they came to Canada, they ended up establishing the largest shoe company in the world, including shoe stores and factories all over the world.

Joe and I were expected to meet Mr. Bata at 5:00 the next morning, at which time he would follow his routine of jogging. Jogging at 5:00 a.m.? It was a command performance, so we did it. Tom Bata was a fascinating person whom I was delighted to meet, as for years after that, Bata would be a good customer of ours. Mr. Bata told the story of how he had opened factories in Africa. He sent two people to Africa, and they spent a couple of weeks and then came back with their reports. The first one said that Africa would be a losing market because the population went around barefooted. The second one reported that Africa was a great opportunity because the people were not wearing shoes, but as the continent progressed, the market would be terrific. Mr. Bata went with the second fellow's report and established successful shoe stores on the entire continent.

On the next trip to Canada, I took Syl along, as we figured to do some sightseeing in Quebec and Montreal and also to spend some time with Joe's new hire, Bill Schutz. After we finished our work on McGill Street, Joe and his wife were driving us to a party at Bill Schutz's home, which they not seen before. We drove to this fabulous house in the best section of Montreal, got out of the car, and walked to the rear, where the party was already in progress at a very large pool. Joe looked at us in amazement and exclaimed, "This guy works for me?"

We changed into bathing suits, and Bill poured us brandy in a large brandy snifter glass. Syl gave me one of her looks, so I realized that I had to dump most of it because Bill was not taking no for an answer as he kept refilling the large glass. Next, Bill was on the roof of the house asking me to join him so that we could jump into the pool from the roof. Syl screamed as I finally coaxed Bill down.

I knew Bill from before, when I had worked with Eric. Whenever he came to town, we invariably had to pick up the check. I got word one day that Bill would be arriving late in the afternoon and that we should take him for drinks and dinner. I made it very clear to him that this time HE was picking up the check. "Sure," he laughed. We had one drink at the Regency, and he pulled out some cash and paid. From there we went to this "gangster" joint that he knew from previous visits. We had lots of drinks and fine food, and when the check came, Bill informed me that he had no money left and that he had forgotten his wallet in the hotel room. I wasn't falling for that shit, and I let him know that my wallet was also in my office.

Bill was amazing. He had incredible charm as he called over the waiter and signed his BUSINESS CARD! on the back and told the waiter to have the bill sent to his office. Next thing we knew, this big, ugly dude came to the table and wanted to know what seemed to be the problem. I don't know how Bill did it, but he persuaded this brute of a man to take his business card and send the bill to his Montreal office. For the record, the bill was sent, and Bill sent the check, paying it in full.

But now let me tell you how we lost the chance of a lifetime. It was a dreary Friday, and it was pouring outside when I received a phone call from Bill. "How would you like to be with me when I get an order for a hundred thousand pair of shoes?"

Of course I didn't want to miss this. I drove to Manhattan in the rain and arrived at their office on Fifty-Ninth Street just across the famous Plaza Hotel. I proceeded to the third floor, where there was a company called El Greco. This company used to manufacture shoes in Brooklyn, and they had some problems with sandals that they had made falling apart. Charley Cole, the owner, was there with his sons Neil and Kenny. Bill was already there and was showing a one-band sandal on a plastic unit that he called a Candy. Charley said that he liked the idea and if they could have the name "Candies" that, they would start with an order of a hundred thousand pair. Then, if they sold well, the next order would be one million pair.

The order was written, and they sold like crazy. Bill couldn't keep up with the orders and asked me to meet with Ken Cole and see if I could have more of the shoes made in Italy. I then called my illustrious agent and told him to meet Ken Cole in Milan and to get the orders placed. Ken flew to Milan. Maurizio was nowhere to be found. Ken Cole found another agent, who delivered millions of Candies. Ken Cole became very famous.

Naturally, when I asked Mauricio why he didn't show up in Milan, the idiot told me that he was busy and didn't believe the buyer was real. I immediately fired him over the phone. As Marlon Brando said in his famous film: "I could have been a contender!"

Italy became very important to us not only for obtaining certain types of footwear but because of the shoe fairs, fashion, and styling development. We went on to "Modelista's" in Tuscany and the village of Stra near Venice. These were designers who would develop styles and place the upper leather pattern on a wooden last (the form that gives a shoe body). They had small design studios, and they would inform the buyers and designers when their collections would be ready.

Invariably I would run into Vince Camuto, who was already known as a top designer. We were friendly competitors, and neither of us wanted the other to know what we were doing, so when we were there together, it was fun to watch us dance around, hiding which models we were selecting. Since either one of us would travel to any country for ideas, I once let him overhear my conversation to my group that I was leaving for Latvia, where the new "hot" fashion was developing. The joke was on me, however, as he had mentioned Helsinki, Finland. When I got there, I learned nothing and had a tough day with my interpreter, who was trying to teach me the toughest language that I had ever heard.

Italy is a complicated, varied, and marvelous place. Our agent in Milan was Enzo Caramaschi (Syl preferred the shoes on Via Spiga to the ones in the Marquesa showroom). Enzo and his wife were indefatigable workers, and we were good friends. Enzo met me at the airport one spring day and said that he had just moved into a new suburb of Milan, and he wanted to show me his home and wine cellar.

When we arrived at the gate of the development, Enzo explained that it was the first in Italy built like what today would be a condo development. Later on, the Caramaschis would take me on a tour of the fine furniture stores to buy a giant chandelier for their hallway entrance. In the meantime, I was fascinated by their extensive wine cellar. This cellar had not only fine modern Italian wines but large casks of generations-old wine from his family.

Time was passing, and for some reason, Enzo was now starting to panic. He had to take his caretaker home. I was puzzled at the urgency, and then Enzo explained to me that there was a rule in his building association contract that contained a "restrictive" clause.

"Restrictive to what?" I asked, fearing that maybe they didn't want Jews or dark-skinned people to live there. Enzo laughed. "No. The rule is that no southern Italian can remain on the grounds after dark. It seems that the builder is a nut job whose father was a noted industrialist and decided to give his son X number of lira to do what he wanted."

I didn't believe him until he showed me the actual clause in his contract. Northern Italy, especially Milan, is considered the business and fashion outpost. Anywhere north of Naples there was a deep distrust and scorn of the southern Italian, where the perception was that the boot of Italy was Mafia country. The Naples area, though famous for Vesuvius and the Isle of Capri, was also known for its tough criminal element.

When I would travel to nearby Avellino, I put my wallet and money in my sock if I went by train, and if I went by car, I took extra vigilance at the gas stations. Traveling on the Autostrade was always an experience. When you stopped for gas, you had to go through a maze of toys, food, clothes, and wine (I once found a good bottle of Rothschild wine, which I immediately grabbed) before you got to the cash register.

Once Syl and I stopped for lunch just outside of Bologna and ate in the Autostrade restaurant. We were shocked to see tuxedoed waiters serving incredibly fine food. Can you imagine having a four-course meal on the New Jersey turnpike?

Tuscany, where most of our factories were, was something special. Our new agent, Aldo Mangoni, came from a fine, well-known family. He used to joke about the fact that all Italians, if they are reincarnated, wanted to come back as agents, like him. He lived in a fine villa just outside of Florence with servants—the works.

Much time had to be spent with our freight forwarder, Piero, and his sidekick Julio (who would take Syl shopping and touring while I was in the factories). Piero gave me the facts about various aspects of Italy: the politics, strikes, number of Italian holidays, and the unique system of Italy. For example, in the early 1980s, Italy was ranked near the bottom of the European economic ladder based on their gross national product, yet they were second in cars, first in TV-set ownership, third in refrigerators, etc. When I asked Piero about this, he laughed and said that Italians don't pay taxes, and they pay for almost everything in cash, including homes, and that their sons lived with their mothers until their thirties. It was a shadow economy.

On another occasion, I arrived in Florence on a day that the Communist Party of Italy was having their national convention just outside the city. I mentioned to Piero that we should have dinner in a fine restaurant because the commies couldn't afford it. This amused him, and he explained that if the Italians ever really thought that the Communist Party would win, they would unanimously vote the Christian Democrats into office.

He also mentioned that the head of the Italian Communist Party owned the largest Mercedes Benz dealership in Milan. Sure enough, we sat through our dinner in the midst of all of the red banners and multitudes of empty wine bottles in a fine restaurant packed with those who had been marching and chanting during the day.

On another occasion, Piero and I were going for lunch, and Piero said that he was going to take me to a restaurant in Lucca called Il Vipore, which the tourists generally don't know about and whose owner did not encourage tourists. Lucca is located outside of Florence in an area where we had a number of factories that we worked with. He explained that the owner didn't like tourists because they thought that pasta was a main dish, but in Italy pasta was just a starter, with the main course coming afterward.

As we were having our lunch, an American couple somehow found their way in and was seated at a small table for two. Piero winked and said, "Watch this."

Sure enough, after a salad and pasta, they asked for the check. The owner happened to be on the balcony directly above them and was yelling in Italian, "How they get into my restaurant?" ("Come hai fatto a trovare il mio ristorante?") He then came down and berated the couple (in English), insisting that they order a main course, which they did.

Besides the many holidays, there were the strikes. These could disrupt my tight scheduling, and it was a particularly grueling adventure in Italy, which had the most and the worst strikes. The concierge at the Excelsior Hotel would call me early in the morning to give me a list of the day's strikes—gas stations, postal services, garbage pickup, etc.—so that I could plan my day accordingly.

One morning the phone rang, and it was Sr. Salvatore, the concierge (concierges in Italy do not work directly for the hotel, as they are independent contractors). "Io non c'entro. Pero…" It has nothing to do with me, but I cannot give you the strike report this morning, he went on to say. When I asked him why not, he went on to explain that HE was the one on strike.

The Italians were set in their ways. Except for business dealings, they did not readily accept foreigners into their midst, as they were clannish. They also had a lot of pride. If a poor person was invited to a restaurant or party, he or she would not dream of taking home any leftovers. I am sure that it has changed today, but there were no "doggie" bags then.

I remember once working in a factory in the Parma area. We were anxious to get to the Trieste area when we finished, but we were still working in the factory at lunchtime. Everyone who was working with us was nervous because in all of their lives, they had never missed their lunch and their afternoon nap afterward.

I suggested that they send someone to a local restaurant and bring a meal in. This was not possible, as this was something that they had never done before, and even the idea of eating lunch in the factory repelled them.

So I rushed through everything, and Gino and I left the factory around 2:30 p.m. Aldo was white, as apparently he had never missed a lunch either. He begged me to look out for a restaurant that might be open at this time. I saw one up the road, and I noticed a woman watering plants in copper-colored pottery. Although it was dark inside, the door was open.

Since Aldo was now mute, I asked her if it was at all possible to get something—salami, cheese, anything. "Va beni, pronto," she said as she graciously invited us into her cozy restaurant. She offered us the area special, which was boiled beef in a horseradish-type sauce.

As Aldo was gobbling it up like a hungry tiger, I asked for mustard. She returned with some kind of red sauce. By now he was able to speak, but when I asked him if *mostarda* wasn't Italian for mustard, his answer was that he didn't speak her dialect (when Italy was city-states, there were over two hundred dialects).

It turned out that it was this region's mustard, but it had beets added to give it the red color.

Piero's office was on the Arno River in Florence. You are not allowed to change any structures in Florence that would modify a structure that went back to the Renaissance. They needed a wall broken in order to put in a door connecting Piero's office with his assistant. Even with all of his family's influence, the city managers would not budge. The Albini family was told that if they attempted any renovations, they would immediately be put in prison. Piero's comment was that his family could get away with murder, but if they put a hole in a wall, Italian justice would move very swiftly.

One evening Piero took a suite at the Excelsior Hotel and brought his customers in for a large party. It was a wild party, and the champagne was flowing like the river Arno. They were shaking the bottles and squirting the contents up into the ceiling. I noticed that the ceilings had some very fine-looking artwork, and I wondered how they were going to get the stains off of the ceilings.

Not surprisingly, when Piero checked out, he was presented a bill for the equivalent of about $40,000 US dollars. I think he got out of paying that by promising to have a crew clean everything up.

For a while I worked with a factory outside of Palermo. I found the Sicilians quite unlike both what I had been told and what I had expected. The train ran from Rome to Reggio Calabria, where it was put on a barge, and then it reached the island. The train was again put on the track and continued on to Palermo.

The factory owners insisted that I stay with them, and they treated me as if I were part of the family. They were good, hardworking people, and if they had any Mafia connections, I never saw any sign of them. Actually, the subject rarely came up unless there was something in the local paper about an investigation of some Mafia figure.

They didn't want me to leave, but when I did, the whole clan accompanied me to the train station. Although I certainly liked the fine cuisine of the various areas, especially Bologna, Trieste, and Montecatini Terme (the best penne arrabbiata in all of Italy), I also loved the hearty southern cooking of Sicily and especially the home cooking of this fine factory family. The only *lupara* sawed-off shotgun that I ever saw was in the *Godfather* movies. They were unforgettable people.

Marquesa in Brazil

During the many years that we were in Brazil, we saw many changes. Although we started small, we grew quite rapidly. Vince Camuto and Jackie Fisher of Nine West were quite right. Brazil was the place to be. Just before the Nine West company exploded into the powerful organization that it was to become, Jack Fisher and I were sitting in a jazz joint in Paris called Le Bilboquette, where he told me that he would become fabulously rich and that one day he would become king of the shoe business. He certainly went on to become very wealthy, with a notable art collection, a yacht, and a large home in Palm Beach. Maybe not to the extent of Nine West, but in any case, we were growing.

Our first office was in Novo Hamburgo. Phone service was primitive. Phone lines were limited, with a wait of over a year for a phone that cost the equivalent of $1,400 (1970s). Worse, they were the old-fashioned, non-dial phones. That meant that we had to hire a person just to hold the phone waiting for an operator to come on the line. If we were lucky, the wait was fifteen to twenty minutes. Sometimes, however, it could be an hour before an operator came on the line. If you were calling someone in a nearby town, it was faster to send a messenger there. Once my wife was in a panic in Rio de Janeiro, waiting for me to call from Novo Hamburgo. It took me three days to get though to her.

The infrastructure at the time was crude, with poor highways. Going to a city like Criciúma, for example, which was in the next northern state, was a five-hour drive on a dusty, unpaved road. Brazil is almost the size of the United States, and at least their air travel was developed much better than their road infrastructure, where bus or auto travel was extremely dangerous. Varig was the major airline, and their service was excellent once you got on the plane (airport service was only so-so). Because the government was involved, there was a lot of waste and bureaucracy, which eventually caused Varig to go out of business.

When Varig was in its glory days, they gave us extraordinary service, both due to the airfreight that we generated and also because of Roberto Goncalves's contacts (he was our man in Rio).

When I arrived from overseas, whether on Pan Am or Varig, I was given VIP treatment. This meant that I disembarked the plane along with the crew, and then we were met by a special bus, where my passport was taken by one of the Varig staff to be stamped so that I didn't have to go through customs. If I was staying in Rio, I was brought to the terminal, where I was met by my driver. If I was going to Porto Alegre, I was taken to the VIP room to wait for my flight. Varig's flight from Rio to Porto Alegre was about one and a half hours, and they always put me in the second- or third-row aisle seat. All seating on this flight was like first class, with unbelievably good service that included drinks, champagne, and a choice of delicious entrées, which could run from lobster to shish kebab to sirloin steaks. Upon our return from the Porto Alegre airport, our freight forwarder put us in the VIP waiting room. Often there were celebrities in the VIP rooms; they would have to be pointed out to me, as unless they were sports figures, I had no idea who they were.

If I was departing Rio on Pan Am's flight 202 to JFK, I would stop at the H. Stern's Jewelry store in the duty-free area and pick up some costume jewelry for the gals in the office. There was one woman who took care of me, and not only would she find something different each time, but she would also give me a nice discount.

One day I was reading an article about Hans Stern, the owner. He had escaped from Germany just prior to World War II, and he started his precious-stone business in Brazil. I wrote him a congratulatory letter, praising his operation and thanking him for receiving a discount. Soon after that I received a curt letter from Mr. Stern saying that H. Stern never gave discounts. He also wanted to know name of the clerk who had provided me with the discounts. I wrote him back that I didn't know the name, but it was from their factory store in downtown Rio (where they had a pretty-good-sized staff), hoping to confuse him. When I told the woman at the airport, she became frightened that Hans Stern would track her down and fire her, so she understandably had to stop giving me discounts.

Rio's airport, Galeão, grew and modernized throughout the years. When I worked for Eric, Roberto would load up to twenty large sample cartons without paying any overweight, and then we would go to the only air-conditioned place in the airport in order to wait for the flight to be called. That happened to be a small corner of the airport coffee shop that had a small window air conditioner.

With the new, expanded airport came air conditioning, many nice shops, and a fine VIP room (Varig or the Clipper Club if you were flying Pan Am). While waiting for your flight, you could hear a beautiful, soft voice announcing the flights.

The flights to North America and Europe left late. One evening, Roberto and I were taking a late flight from Rio to Porto Alegre, and I mentioned to Roberto that the person announcing the flights had a magical voice and that I was curious to know whether she was as pretty as her voice. It turned out that Roberto knew her, and he brought me into her booth to meet her. It turned that she was every bit as beautiful as her voice.

We then settled in for out flight to Porto Alegre, where we would then travel by car to meet with factory owners in the wine country, after which we would fly to Belo Horizonte and then to Bahia in the northeast. It would be a long, tiring, and grueling trip. Roberto was anticipating this, so after some work in our office in Novo Hamburgo, we set out by car the next day to the wine area (Caxias do Sul and Bento Gonçalves).

Roberto was driving, and I noticed that he was stopping at gas stations every few miles, going to the bar, and ordering a *caipirinha*. This Brazilian drink is very popular today. It is made with *cachaça*, which is a powerful sugar-cane, alcohol-extract drink. The alcohol is poured over the limes, which are crushed along with sugar, so the sweet, powerful drink goes down quite easily. It seemed that it was too easy for Roberto, as he made four stops and ordered the drink each time.

By the time we arrived in Bento Goncalves, Roberto was barking like a dog. We checked in, and I was hoping for some rest. As luck would have it, they put Roberto next door to me, and I heard him loudly singing away. He called the room, and since I couldn't rest due to his racket, I agreed to get ready for dinner. As I was washing up, there was a loud pounding on the door.

When I opened the door, there was a large palm tree plant blocking it. It was so large that I couldn't move it, so I had to call down to the desk for help get it back to the center of the hallway, where it had come from.

While we were having dinner, Roberto staggered over to a woman and sat down at her table. I decided to finish my meal and took a cab back to the hotel.

In the middle of the night, I heard a racket in the hall, which I suspected was Mr. Goncalves. The next morning, we had breakfast as if nothing had happened while Roberto related with a broad smile that he met a fine young lawyer the evening before.

When we checked out, the manager came dashing from his office and angrily shouted that we were never to darken his door again, as we were not welcome to return to the hotel.

Roberto did have a serious side, however. Once he was driving me to a café that was on the top of the botanical gardens in Rio. As we were driving up the mountain, we stopped at a spot where a short time before there had been a "Macumba" ceremony, which is the everyday term used by Brazilians in Rio de Janeiro to describe two types of African spirit worship: Candomble' (followed in northern state of Bahia) and Umbanda (a newer form originating in the city of Niteroi). We stopped nearby and noticed the offerings made to the gods which included food and cigars.

I was about to grab the cigars when Roberto warned me that I would be desecrating their religion if I disturbed or took anything. Of course I respected that, and while we are discussing this, I noticed that a dog was chewing away at the food.

I then got a very solemn look from Roberto. "That dog will not survive until sunset," he exclaimed.

When I asked if he believed in Macumba, he responded that while he was not a believer, he WAS a respecter of their cult.

We then had our late-afternoon beers, after which we left as dusk was approaching. As we went down the winding road, we passed the dog on the side of the road. It had apparently been run over by a passing car. Roberto just gave me a knowing look, with no words being spoken.

Sylvia was arriving the next day, and our plans were to pick her up at the airport and drive out to Roberto and his wife Wilma's weekend-and-vacation home in a resort town called Cabo Frio. It was roughly a hundred-mile drive from Rio to Cabo Frio. Syl was in the backseat getting very nervous because we were driving through some very poor neighborhoods.

Then, as we turned a corner, a Swiss-style chalet appeared before us. There stood two uniformed guards, who opened the large, fancy wooden gate for us. As we drove in, we noticed the servants' quarters in the rear. The sea was on the side of the chalet, and there were two large swimming pools on the other side. We settled in quickly. Our accommodations were fine, even without air conditioning, the exception being some very unusual bugs and lizards on the walls, which we discovered when we went to bed.

We had a grand party with their friends. The food was great, with the shrimp being pulled from the inlet leading to the Atlantic Ocean, and they were barbecued in olive oil and garlic. Syl was continually asking me whether Roberto worked for us— or was it the other way around?

Brazil had the reputation of being a dangerous place. You were generally safe if you know where to go and what to wear and also what not to wear. You didn't wear expensive jewelry, and you never left money or your wallet on the beach. Roberto had a cousin, who was a police lieutenant, and one time when we were staying in Cabo Frio, his cousin drove up to the house and announced that they had just captured a "murderer," and as he was saying that, they opened the truck of the military vehicle, and there was this bloody body.

Another time I was staying at the Maksoud Hotel in Sao Paulo, and as I was walking out the door of the hotel, the police were popping the trunk of a Volkswagen. Directly in front of me, I saw this body full of bullet holes. When I asked what was going on, I was told that it was common for either drug dealers or the police to dump bodies in the trunks of cars.

Aside from the danger during that time, Sao Paulo was a city with many ethnic groups, including the largest Japanese population outside of Japan. There was no type of food that wasn't available, and they served some of the finest cooking in the world.

Luckily I was only robbed once. It was in Porto Alegre. I had gone to a soccer game between Gremio and an out-of-state team. Gremio was a powerhouse, and it was favored. I had been invited to the game by one of the factory owners, who was a *socio* (partner), so we sat in the special partners' section. There was only a small section for the opposing team. I felt sorry for them and told my factory friends that I wanted to root for the other team. They were horrified, and I realized that there was no way that

I could do that, and I soon found out why. The opposing team scored first, and their small group started to cheer for them. The Gremio fans were furious, and they started to beat up the little group. All of a sudden, about fifty military police came out of no-where and with their clubs beat them up and start to drag them away. It was shocking for me to watch this.

After the game, they dropped me off at the Everest Hotel in Porto Alegre, where I was staying. That evening, I was scheduled to have dinner with some of my people. After a shower and a rest, I went downstairs to wait for them in the front of the hotel. I had just come from Europe, and my pockets were stuffed with all kinds of currencies—dollars, cruzeiro, lira, marks, pounds, and pesetas. Just a few feet behind me stood the hotel security guard. In a flash, I felt someone brush up against my left side, and I realized quickly that this kid was running with my money in his hands.

I went chasing after him, but a large guy was in front of me blocking my way. All during this time, the so-called security guard was just standing there like a store mannequin. When I asked him why he hadn't come to my assistance, he mentioned that it was too dangerous a situation for him to get involved in.

I then went inside the hotel to complain about their so-called security (apparently only for show) and have them call the po-lice. When the police arrived, they explained that there would be no way to catch these guys and that besides, it was my fault for carrying so much money in my pockets.

I said that I could understand that they could the dollars and the local currency, but what were they going to do with the European money?

Their answer was that they were going to have a big party at night, get drunk, keep the cruzeiros and the dollars, and burn the rest in a bonfire.

Of course, thievery is not exclusive to Brazil. In some places, it takes a very sophisticated turn. I was on a short trip to buy leather in Cochabamba, Bolivia, which was a hellhole if I ever saw one. The telex name of the tannery was Alligator, so you can imagine the rest. I left there fast.

My next stop was Paraguay, which was known as "Smuggler H.Q." They could get you anything there, including some things that you wouldn't want to have. At the time, Paulo de Lima was my office manager in Novo Hamburgo, and he asked me to bring back some Jack Daniels for our crew. Import duties were extremely high in order to promote domestic liquor, which was not too drinkable. The duty on imported liquor was around 300 percent, but if you brought it in from a duty-free shop (limited quantities), you were fine.

Leaving Paraguay, I was amazed when I was told at the duty-free shop that I could bring four bottles of Scotch or American whisky into Brazil. I was happy to get to our office in Novo Hamburgo, and when I arrived, my crew was excited. They couldn't wait for me to open the first bottle. When I poured mine and tasted it, I immediately knew that there was something wrong. It was not bourbon. It was not Jack Daniels, and it was not even liquor. Something was wrong, and I immediately warned everyone not to drink another drop. At best it was tea, but at worst, who knew what they had poured into those bottles? None of us could believe that the bottles, with all the seals on the top caps, could have possibly been tampered with. That is, until I turned over the bottles and saw the drill holes in the bottom. And remember, they came from the government's duty-free shop in Paraguay!

Chronic inflation was endemic to Brazil. There were times when merchants had no idea what prices to mark their merchandise. Long lines at gas stations formed when a price increase was anticipated. On one trip, I was asked to bring back some Brazilian flags. I found a store selling general merchandise and found three flags. The clerk quoted a price that was the equivalent of about three dollars each. When I arrived at the counter, the owner said that the clerk had made a mistake and the price was thirty dollars per flag. By the counter there sat a bicycle, and I asked the price of the bike. It was thirty-six dollars. When I questioned the comparison, the owner said he knew that there was no logic to the pricing, but there was nothing that he could do. I ended up buying the flags at the airport for around six dollars apiece.

Marquesa was growing quickly. We had made a nice deal with the Felsway Corporation; we would be their exclusive agents in South America. Lionel, who was the flamboyant chairman of Felsway, set up a meeting for us in Rio, where we would meet with Petrobras, which was a large government monopoly that controlled the oil industry in Brazil. Petrobras was trying to promote exports at the time, so the thought was that with their backing, we would have an inside shot at working with the best factories. Felsway and Marquesa formed a partnership, but due to the obtuseness of the executives at Petrobras, things didn't work out.

My technical man at the time was George Svoboda. I had the highest respect for George, as he was technically very proficient. After he was discharged from the Russian army, he went back to his native Czechoslovakia, where he worked his way up in their shoe factories. When we spent time together, he would relate horrendous stories about the brutality and the sadistic nature of those in the Russian army.

I soon saw that George was overworked and that he needed relief, especially since we would be expanding to Uruguay, Argentina, and Chile. I had met with Phil Barack, who was chairman of US Shoe Corp, while I was still at Melville, and I had recently run into him at a shoe show in Dusseldorf. He mentioned to me that one of his top technical people who had worked for one of his divisions had recently departed his company due to a personality conflict. The man's name was Dave Pupps, and I contacted him immediately. I set up a meeting with George Svoboda, Dave, and me. We quickly reached an agreement where George would maintain production and quality in Italy and Spain, and Dave would handle the same thing in South America. The only proviso with Dave was that his wife Irene insisted that he spend at least five days out of the month in the United States. Since Dave was one of the best in the business, I readily agreed.

DAVE PUPPS OPENING NEW MARKETS

D ave was a great big guy, about six feet two inches and 250 pounds, with a deep, commanding voice, and he was used to getting his way. This was an important feature for a technical man who had to work with factory owners, who could be very difficult sometimes.

When Dave was working for US Shoe, he was expected to live in Brazil, and although he liked it, his wife Irene could never get used to the country or its people. When they first arrived in Brazil, they found an apartment, and Irene immediately went to the butcher shop to buy a supply of meat. The butcher was anxious to please the North American with limited Portuguese language skills, so he gave her the best cuts that he had. The beef turned out to be fine, especially since one of the factory owners' wives told them how to prepare the meat.

So Irene returned to the butcher shop, where the owner was anxiously awaiting her verdict on the meat. Here is where not understanding a culture comes in. Irene made a gesture with her thumb and forefinger, moving her hand forward and back. To us that means OK, but to a Brazilian, that gesture happens to mean "go screw yourself!"

The butcher was furious, and he threw poor Irene out of the butcher shop. When the poor thing found out what she had done, she went back with Dave, and they apologized.

Since Irene was not an easy person to get along with, they didn't make many Brazilian friends, and now she was happy that she wouldn't have to move back to Brazil.

Dave's first trip for Marquesa went off extremely well, as the factory people liked him, and they respected his technical acumen. Dave would return for his five- or six-day stay in the States, but since he was bored, he would come into the office every day.

One day he asked me to find something for him to do while he was in the States. My suggestion was that he go out and sell. His reply was "I am not a salesman, I am a technical person."

I said that I would prove him wrong, and we set out to Ohio to see some customers. Dave was a steak-and-potatoes man, but he knew that when he ate with me, it would almost always be at an exotic restaurant. We had dinner in Pennsylvania, and I had found a Mexican restaurant, so his question to me was: "Bill, don't you ever eat anything normal?"

When we sat with the customers, it was obvious that the buyers sensed and respected both his technical aura and his honesty. I pointed this out to him, and he got the point. The following month, when he came back from Brazil, I gave him a sample bag with some new styles. He left on a Monday and returned on a Thursday, at which time he stormed into my office with a stack of orders a foot high. "I told you that I was no damn salesman," he said. His multiple talents continued to pay off for us.

My sources were telling me that Uruguay was going to be the place to make boots. I would have to go through my usual routine, and that was to work through the Uruguayan government to make our factory contacts. I met with Jorge Sienra, who was the head of the Uruguayan Government Trade Bureau in

Montevideo, and he introduced me to Humberto Goyen Alves, who was the consul general. Humberto and I became great friends. When he became president of the Society of Foreign Consuls, he invited me to the reception at the UN.

The contact they gave me in Uruguay was Dr. Hector Di Biase, who in October 1975 took us to meet the owners of various factories. Some of them looked very promising, and one of them said that he would meet with me in my Englewood, New Jersey, office.

I left Dave with the assignment of establishing an office and hiring a capable person to supervise and run it. Dave wasted no time, and within days, he found a qualified person to run the office, Ruben Vitabar, and an Argentinean designer, Miguel Curti, both of whom were living in Uruguay at the time. They both turned out to be very talented people. Ruben had excellent technical and organizational skills, and Miguel was a superb footwear designer.

We had formidable competition in Uruguay; however, in time we would surpass them all, and we became the largest boot exporter from the country. The government was anxious to develop manufacturing exports. Their largest export was wool and beef, but besides the shoe factories, they didn't have much of a manufacturing base. There was no auto manufacturing, and most of the cars on the street were vintage pre–World War II autos.

I guess that since I always had a cigar in my mouth, they directed me to a cigar factory called La Republicana. Their brand was Jim Porter, which they had been making for over a hundred years. Ruben and I went to the factory and met with Juan, the owner. He gave me a bunch of boxes of half Corona and quarter Corona cigars to see if I could sell them. In order to augment my supply of Cuban cigars, I used to buy cigars at JR Cigars in Manhattan. Lew Rothman, the owner's son, took a few boxes and said that if he liked them, his first order would be one million cigars. I was to call him in a week, which I did. Lew said that the cigars were excellent for the price but that there was a problem with the tips. He said all the factory had to do was buy a special machine for around $8,000, and that would solve the problem.

I couldn't wait to get back to Uruguay and tell the factory the good news. When I arrived in Montevideo, Rubin said that they were very traditional, and he didn't know if he could persuade them to make a change in their factory. Sure enough, when we got to the factory, Juan told us that they had been making cigars for over a hundred years, and they were not about to change their methods or add any machinery. They didn't care how large the order was!

So that ended my chance to get into the cigar business.

Getting back to the incipient stages in our Uruguay project: A factory owner by the name of Raul Fernandez was one of the owners whom we had met under the auspices of the Uruguayan government. Raul arrived in our office one Sunday to discuss the idea of our being his exclusive distributor in North America. After a few minutes, I realized that my Spanish was not good enough to negotiate an agreement, so I called Amalia, who was our head bookkeeper and who had a Latin background herself. She was too busy with her own work to act as a translator, but she knew of someone who had been brought up in Puerto Rico and spoke the language fluently.

I called this fellow and put him on the phone with Raul. After a brief conversation, Raul gave me the phone, and I asked the translator if they could understand each other. Perfectly, he said, so I asked if he could come in the next day for an hour and a half and translate for us, and I would pay him fifty dollars for his work. He readily agreed, and he arrived promptly on Monday, which was a cold December day.

His name was Larry Laurentius, and he had just left his job in order to start classes at the University of North Carolina. All went very well, with an affinity developing between Raul and us, so we all agreed that Larry, Raul, and I would travel around the area to meet with customers. Our quick trip was successful, with both shoe orders and an order for ten thousand handbags in our hands. Raul immediately insisted that Larry accompany him back to Uruguay, where Raul and his family would teach Larry the shoe business from the ground up. This was in 1976, and when Larry returned to the States after learning the various aspects of the business, I immediately hired him.

Fernandez was making shoes for us; however, he was not a rational character. One night when I was in Montevideo, Uruguay, at the Plaza Hotel, I received a late-night call from Raul Fernandez. It seemed that he was in a club with a girl, and when he returned home, his wife locked him out of his house. The next morning, I received a call from Raul's wife asking whether I knew where Raul was. I responded that he was sleeping in my room. It was a Sunday, so I was not rushing to go to the factories.

Within thirty minutes, there was a loud banging on my door. I opened the door, and it was Raul's wife, who was screaming like a madwoman. She wanted to know where the women were. I tried to explain that Raul had been with me last night, and I hadn't seen any women (which was true). She then started on Raul, screaming at him, pulling his hair, and ripping his clothes. The next thing I knew, she opened the closet door and started ripping my clothes, so I had to push her out of the room and lock the door.

On Monday, the buyer from Morse Shoe was arriving to inspect the shoes from Raul's factory. The customers of that particular style were complaining that the first shoes delivered did not fit. Bob Eichen was the buyer, and Morse Shoe was one of our largest customers in Uruguay. Bob had been working in Brazil with Roberto Goncalves, and they would be traveling together en route to Montevideo.

Ruben picked me up early Monday morning, and we went to the airport to pick up Bob and Roberto. Our first stop would be the Fernandez factory. When we arrived, Raul looked somewhat nervous, and I attributed that to his weekend escapades and to his marital problems. Bob was concerned about his orders because he had placed them for an ad that Morse was running, so if they didn't fit, there would be big problems.

When Ruben was advised of the problem, he immediately went to the factory with a model to retest the fit, but Raul would not let him into the factory to inspect the shoes. We soon found out why. Bob and Ruben went down the factory line, and they returned to Raul's office as white as a plain sheet of paper. The model could not get her feet into the shoes.

Bob then informed Raul that he was canceling the order. Raul went into a fit of anger, saying that the orders couldn't be canceled. He then yelled to the guards (all factories have security guards) to bar the front door and not let anyone leave.

Bob was in a panic, but I told him to calm down and I would get us out of the factory. I then took Raul to his private office and said that the best way to handle the situation was for me to talk to Bob back at the hotel after he had some time to calm down. Raul finally agreed to release us from this hostage-type situation that he had us in.

Ruben dropped us off, and I told him to go home and get some rest. We returned to our rooms at the Plaza, where I broke out the two bottles of Scotch that I had brought from the airport. Roberto was making calls, so I asked Bob to join me for drinks. He readily accepted.

It wasn't too long before we both became roaring drunk. My fifth-floor room faced the beautiful plaza, which was surrounded by some government buildings. Every few minutes, a bus came by the front of the hotel. Bob and I were giddy, and we decided to have some fun. We had plenty of ice in the room and also an extra supply of plastic laundry bags. We opened the windows and tried to time the bags, which were filled with water and ice, to hit the bus as it passed in front of the hotel entrance. We were doing great. We would hit the roof of the bus, and it made a very load boom as it hit. The bus driver would stop, look around, and then get back into the bus and travel on. One of our shots missed the roof of the bus and splattered all over a guy whose head was hanging out of the bus.

The driver stopped the bus and called over some of the police who were on patrol nearby. We sobered up very fast when we saw a bunch of policemen looking up toward our window. We knew we had to clean things up fast, and when we thought the police had moved away, we had one more bag of ice and water. We decided just to drop it straight out of the window.

Five minutes later, there was a knock on the door. It was the hotel manager along with a member of the national police. I opened the door, and there was this guy in full uniform, soaking wet. It was hard not to laugh when we saw the water dripping from his cap into his eyes.

"Somebody has been throwing water out the windows," he shouted.

"We can't imagine who," we said.

At that point they walked over to the windowsill, where, with a dramatic sweep of a hand, the remains of the water, on the windowsill came splashing up in the air. The policeman made a gesture by signifying handcuffs and said that if any more water went out the window, we would be immediately locked up. The sight was unbelievable as this uniformed police officer was standing in front of us soaking wet.

When we told Ruben the story the next morning, he couldn't believe that we hadn't been put in jail.

At this point we decided that we needed a break. Since Bob was an avid fisherman, I took him north for a day to fish for dorado in the Rio Negro. The dorado is one of the fiercest fighting fish in the world. Attached to the lures that the guide gave us was a band of metal since the dorado is smart enough to bite through a regular line. We managed to catch a few fish but unfortunately no dorados.

Ruben had learned his lesson, and he would never again permit himself to be banned from any factory. He was doing a fine job with the other factories, and I made him a vice-president of

Marquesa. He was instrumental in getting us an exclusive commitment from the best boot factory in Uruguay, by the name of Reyles. The Keushkerian family, who owned Reyles, was prospering, and on one of my trips to Uruguay, Roberto Keushkerian, who was the president, insisted on picking me up at the airport. He had just imported a new Mercedes-Benz from Germany, paying an enormous duty. The day was very hot, so I asked Roberto to turn on the air conditioning.

He responded that the car had no air conditioning.

"What?" I exclaimed. "Why no air conditioning?"

His answer was that few cars had air conditioning in Uruguay, and the $500 extra made it too expensive. (Some logic?)

Aside from the Fernandez fiasco, we were doing very well with all of the other boot factories. The Uruguayan government was pleased with our efforts. The general consul of Uruguay, Humberto Goyen Alvez, would occasionally invite me to the UN to have lunch in the delegates' dining room.

I decided that I would reciprocate when Jorge Sienra and some other dignitaries were arriving in New York. I called Frank DiCola, who was the host of Patsy's, a fine Italian restaurant located on West Fifty-Sixth Street in Manhattan. I told him that I had some very prominent government guests arriving, so I expected to have their usual superb service.

When Ruben, Dave, Syl, and the six Uruguayan "dignitaries" arrived, we were seated immediately. We had a superb Neapolitan dinner, but before we finished, Frank DiCola, along with three waiters, came out with a flaming dessert, and the four of them were singing: "Congratulations! Congratulations! To the president of Uruguay."

The group laughed, and they took this with very good humor. Syl and I, however, were very embarrassed since the president was not there (nor was he expected).

On my next trip to Uruguay, Ruben decided to take me to Ponte Del Este. This was a very upscale resort that during the summer season catered to wealthy Argentineans. As we progressed toward the main area of the town, he was pointing out the million-dollar homes on the hillside facing the ocean. He then took a road up to one of the luxurious homes, and he mentioned that he wanted to introduce me to one of his friends.

It turned out that his friend was Nando Parrado. Nando was the famous survivor of the rugby team that crashed in the Andes. Relating the story facing the Atlantic Ocean through a large picture window in luxurious surroundings had an unbelievable impact on me. The emotion is hard to describe. After the rescue films were made, books were written, including one that I highly recommend: *"Miracle in the Andes: 72 Days on the Mountain and My Long Trek Home"*. .

Ruben and I then left to find a restaurant. We were planning to have a party for our office people and the key executives from the factories we were doing business with. We found a restaurant near the casino that could accommodate thirty-five of us, including Sylvia, who would be arriving by the end of the week. It turned out to be quite a party, and we thanked everyone for their fine efforts contributing to our success.

After the party, I felt lucky and was hoping to recoup at least some of the $600 plus that it had cost us. Since the casino did not have blackjack tables, I played the roulette wheel at first, playing the color black and reverting to the number four. It came in twice in a row, and I won back $550 of the $600 that we had spent. Syl and I left Uruguay very happy.

We didn't realize that our Uruguayan success would soon be ending.

We had been hearing a buzzing that the Commerce Department was going to file suit against the Uruguayan government because they were subsidizing their footwear factories. The problem was that the Uruguayan government did this openly and blatantly. Hearings were held, and sure enough, a CVD (countervailing duty) was imposed. This additional duty amounted to an additional 35 percent over the existing 10 percent duty. In effect, that closed down the market for us.

I was in Porto Alegre at the time, and I wanted to return to Uruguay in order to see whether there could be any way to solve the situation. At the airport, I met a man I knew who lived in Uruguay but worked for one of the tanneries in Brazil. He mentioned that his dad was sick, and he urgently had to get back to Montevideo. It was a short flight with a stop in Buenos Aires. The weather was stormy, and after landing in Buenos Aires, we took off for the short flight to Montevideo. We then flew over the city but couldn't land, as there was a big black rain cloud over the city. It was a Pam Am flight, which the airline decided to cancel.

We were stuck in Ezeiza International, and I suggested to my friend that we should go to the domestic area and catch a local flight. Aerolineas Argentina was the airline run by the Argentine government, and this meant that they were not at all efficient. We went to the desk and asked to buy a ticket to Montevideo. I gave the clerk some fancy Marquesa pens, and she pulled out a sheet that had the stickers indicating that there were two seats left. She also mentioned that she was not positive what equipment would be coming in.

I then said that since so many passengers were trying to get on the flight, why didn't she put them on standby? Her answer was that when she gave out the stickers, her job was done, and she could go home.

She then left, and sure enough, when the flight arrived and we boarded, it was less than half full. For me, it was a good lesson in how governments and mercantilist systems are run.

When we arrived in Uruguay, Ruben informed me that there was no solution and that the countervailing duty would remain. None of our customers was about to accept a 35 percent increase in price. That was the end of our lucrative Uruguayan venture.

WILL YUGOSLAVIA REPLACE URUGUAY?

Although we already had some leather-boot production in Italy and Brazil, we needed a replacement for the styling, material, and price of the boots that we had been manufacturing in Uruguay. We purchased a nice-looking boot in one of the stores that we normally bought new styles from, and we saw that the boot was from Yugoslavia. It wasn't difficult to discover that the Yugoslavian government had opened up a company called Impex in the Empire State Building.

When I called, the company the operator put me in touch with Mr. Mihailovic, who was the director. He mentioned that he had heard about our company, and he was eager to meet with us. I arrived at their small office, and I brought samples of the boots that we had been making in Uruguay. Mr. Mihailovic was pleased with the samples. He said that he had factories that could produce them in equal quality and that they could come close to the prices that our customers had been paying.

I further explained that our customers would open up letters of credit to pay the factories, and the bank would pay the factories as soon as they placed the boots on a vessel. Our commissions would be paid from our customers.

If I approved the factories after visiting them, I would place an initial order of ten thousand pair. If those orders were delivered on time, and if their quality was satisfactory, the next order would be one hundred thousand pair.

There were two obstacles that we had to overcome. One was that since this was a communist country, their procedures did not permit us to have a quality-control person supervise their factories' production. The other obstacle was a man I knew: Chris Papadopoulos already had a foothold in the country. Regarding the first issue, I decided that we would try to address that after the first orders were shipped. On the second issue, I explained that by expanding the country's production capacity, we would help both the country and Chris, since we were better known in the States. I also emphasized that I would not interfere in any way with Chris's operation, hurt his production, or even want to see what styles he was working on.

This seemed to make sense to Mihailovic, and he stated that he was ready for me to travel to Belgrade. I made the trip to Belgrade, and I received my first taste of a communist country and the communist system. Their group picked me up at the airport in their battered Russian auto, which I think they called an Izhmash. I called it a mishmash.

They then dropped me off at the Hotel Moscow and told me that they would pick me up in the morning and take me to the office. Hotels overseas always hold your passport when you check in, so I always either carried an extra old one or a duplicate passport. The next morning, they picked me up and took me to the Impex office.

The fellow running the office was Blagojovic. They called him Blagoya, and every time they called him or mentioned his name, they accented the first syllable, and it sounded as if they were spitting out his name. They liked the samples that I had brought with me, and they said that we would travel to various factories in order to decide whom we would place the orders with and also who would make the samples we needed. We would require samples to sell from and confirmation samples for the orders placed.

The next step was to visit the factories. They were located in various parts of the country. There were numerous ethnic divisions, which, for the most part, were not discernible to me. For example, although I had no idea of the difference between a Croat and a Serb, they said that they knew immediately, even before they heard them speak.

There were also all kinds of special rules, such as our driver being allowed to work only so many hours a day. He was obliged to eat and sit with us in any restaurant that we went to, and he was to be addressed as Comrade.

The roads were generally good, and the forest scenery was breathtaking at times. I liked the factories that I visited, as their Italian machinery was up to date and their technique and quality were excellent. Two of the factories were chosen by Blagoya to make the orders, and since we were in the far north of Serbia on the Hungarian border, the group decided to celebrate our current and future success.

The restaurant was called Restoran Pescara, and it was good to see them finally warming up. Being government functionaries, they were excited by the booze and food. They were also obviously trying to get me drunk by plying me with vodka and wine. They were consuming some large quantities, and by faking it, I looked as if I were keeping up with them. The wine was quite good, incidentally, and the food was excellent.

When we finished the meal, they decided that since we were close to Hungary, they would give me a quick tour of the Hungarian farmland area. That would have been fine except I did not happen to have a visa for Hungary. They assured me that there was nothing to be concerned about since they were very friendly with both the customs people and with the border guards. The customs agent would hold my passport until I returned in a couple of hours.

It was an interesting tour, which I can only compare to *Fiddler on the Roof.* That was because I saw horses and carts and old farmhouses, but no cars.

Upon our return to the Hungarian customs area, my Yugoslavian friends had disappeared. A couple of customs agents started to question me in Hungarian, and I had no idea what they were saying. I just wanted my passport back so I could get back to Yugoslavia. A soldier joined them, and I had visions of being held hostage until Gary Powers's attorney came to rescue me (maybe if he could rescue the U-2 pilot in Russia, he could also rescue me). The three of them were babbling away and gesturing at me; I believed they wanted me to empty my pockets. That was not a good sign, and I really became frightened.

Then, from behind a screen, out popped my Yugoslavian friends, with my passport in their hands. They were laughing wildly, as they had really put one over on the "Yankee".

On the way back to Belgrade, the driver wanted to stop and camp out because he had put in his allotted time. When I offered him some US dollars, he relented, but only if I would let him pick up his family before he dropped us off. I had no choice, so we ended up with six people in the rear seat and three people up front.

It was Friday, and since I was not leaving for Italy until the following Monday afternoon, they left me to fend for myself over the weekend. I tried going out. I found a restaurant where they spoke Italian, and I enjoyed a hearty meal. Belgrade was a dreary town with few restaurants and no entertainment, so I ended up in the room watching films in Swedish with Yugoslavian subtitles. (Quite boring)

We had received small test orders from some of our key customers, including Sears, Felsway, and Montgomery Ward totaling ten thousand pair, which was our commitment to the Yugoslavs. They were all eager to receive the boots so that they could place large orders for both their stores and their catalogs.

The next step was for us to receive the samples, which had to be approved before the boots were put into production. Mihailovic kept telling me that everything was progressing smoothly. I had to try to persuade him to allow our technical person to go to the factories and make sure that everything was indeed OK. Mihailovic insisted that the government had not yet changed its policy, especially with the unrest in the country. That made me very suspicious, and I kept insisting that I wanted to see the samples.

I then took him to lunch at Brook's Cafeteria, which was on the first floor of the Empire State Building, figuring that perhaps he could not speak in the office. It turned out that I was completely correct. He apologized profusely and told me that Chris Papadopoulos had told the government officials that if any factory made even one pair of shoes or boots for Marquesa, he would cancel all of his orders and he would never place another one in that country.

My explaining the stupidity and shortsightedness on both sides did not change anything. It was out of Mihailovic's hands. This was a blow because not only had we lost a good source, but we had lost face with some of our key customers. Ironically, some years later, Chris Papadopoulos tragically lost his life on Pan Am Flight 103, which was bombed over Scotland. I always shuddered when I thought of that because I had taken Flight 103 from London to JFK a number of times myself.

When I left our meeting, I immediately went to my attorneys, Reichbart and Reichbart, whose offices were nearby on East Forty-Second Street. Robert Reichbart was the attorney who had obtained my settlement from Kitty Kelly. His firm was known to be very tough, and they had an excellent record of success.

After my meeting with Robert, I returned to my office and forwarded him all of the paperwork that I had. After he received it, he called and told me that we had an excellent case and that we were going to sue the government of Yugoslavia not only to recover damages but also to make sure that we received proper publicity in both *Woman's Wear Daily* and our main trade paper, the *Footwear News.*

We got a court date, and the trial was to be before a judge in the state court, which was located in Manhattan's Chinatown. I found it difficult to sit through the trial, with the only relief being that we ate lunch in Chinatown every day. Apparently I wasn't the only one who was bored.

On the fourth day of the trial, we saw that there was a new court reporter. When we asked what had happened to the previous one, we were told that he was so bored with the content of the testimony that he couldn't keep up with it, and he had asked to be excused.

On the fifth and last day of the trial, Mihailovic was called to the stand. Reichbart asked him whether he had personally agreed to make the samples.

Answer: Yes.

Did he agree to make the orders?

Answer: Yes.

At some point, did the factories accept the orders?

Answer: Yes.

Robert Reichbart returned to his seat flabbergasted. In sotto voce, he asked me why Mihailovic was telling the truth. I responded that maybe he was just honest. Outside the courtroom, Reichbart laughed and said that he might be honest, but he might also get shot when he returned to Belgrade. In any case, Bob said that our case was locked up, and it looked like a sure winner.

This was taking place in December, and the judge would not render his final decision until the beginning of April.

When April the first came, which was well named April Fool's day, I received a call from Mr. Reichbart. He started to say that he was not going to charge me for his preparation time or his time at the trial but only for their out-of-pocket expenses.

My response was that I didn't understand what he was referring to. "Just take everything out of the proceeds of our winnings."

His shocking response was that there were no winnings since the judge had ruled against us.

Completely shocked, I asked why we had lost.

It turned out that we lost the case on a technicality. Because the suit was over a certain amount and because it was an international suit, it had to be rightfully tried in a federal and not a state court. Robert said that we did have the option to appeal the case and that he thought we would prevail.

My immediate answer was that I was not prepared to sit in a federal courtroom for another week, and therefore he should just drop the case.

We paid Reichbart and Reichbart their expenses, and Yugoslavia ended up with a pass. Although we made some boots in other countries, we were never able to fully replace the production that we had lost in Uruguay. Both Ruben and Miguel then moved to southern Brazil.

Marquesa Continues to Grow

Back on the home front, I was hoping to have better contact with my two sons. Barry was the younger, and we were frustrated because he did not seem to have any direction for the future. One Sunday morning, I went upstairs to his room, where he was lying in bed, and announced: "Barry, they ain't coming to you. You will have to go to them." I then asked him what he wanted to become since he had no interest in our business.

Out of nowhere, he replied that he wanted to become a photographer. That was something that no one in our family had any aptitude for. It turned out that Barry was to become a world-class head-shot photographer, winning many awards along the way (barrymorgenstein.com).

My older son, Lee, on the other hand, did show some interest in the shoe business, so I put him in a slot helping to service our key accounts. He took to it immediately and was well liked, and he garnered the respect of all he came in contact with.

Of course, at times his father was tough on him, which he may or may not have appreciated. On our first trip to Los Angeles, both to meet with customers and find new styling, I

237

was continually getting lost. The rented cars did not have GPS in those days. I was taking Lee to the Brown Derby for dinner, and I got annoyed that he didn't know the way. His reply was that it was his first trip to California, so how did I expect him to know the way?

On a subsequent trip combining business and pleasure, we took the whole family. The itinerary included Los Angeles, San Francisco, and Tigard, Oregon, where we had just opened a small distribution center. It was a fun trip except that in LA, in my rush, I went through a red light, and we were sideswiped by a pickup truck. Luckily, no one was hurt, but the left side was wrinkled like an old man's skin.

When we drove up to the Beverly Hills Hotel, the doorman gave us a quizzical look, so I said to him that we needed a smashed-up car for our "set." He then ran to alert the bell staff. After that, we were treated with the utmost courtesy.

After a pleasant stay in the San Francisco area, we left for Oregon. A quick story about the relaxed people of Oregon: We were stopped at a light, and I was speaking with our new manager in the front seat. I had not realized that the light had changed from red to green. When I looked up and saw the line of cars behind me waiting patiently without anyone blowing their horn, I commented that if this happened in New York, the horns would have been blasting, along with people screaming at us.

In the meantime, we had established offices in Chile, which, along with our Argentina and Brazil production, helped fill what we had lost in Uruguay. Our shoe and sandal production in Brazil was booming in our multiple offices there. The largest one was in Novo Hamburgo, in a large rented house where we had a sample factory, a large sample room, a design salon, and offices. Ruben was the manager of over a hundred workers, and Miguel Curti was our designer.

I took Miguel on a trip to Taiwan and Japan to look at factories and footwear styling. Miguel had never been to Japan before,

so I explained that their culture was such that they expected per-
fection in all of their manufactured products. We were waiting
for the famous Tokyo Takashimaya Department Store to open.
While we were waiting, we could see the employees doing cal-
isthenics, singing, and cheering. The door opened promptly at
10:00 a.m., and as we entered, the girls at the door bowed, and
when we proceeded to the shoe department (which I knew was
at the rear of the store), young women were bowing all along the
aisle as we passed.

As we approached the footwear display, I defied Miguel to
find a single blemish on any shoe that was on display. He said
that in the shoe manufacturing process there had to be some
defects, even if minor. He was astounded that he could not find
a defect in any of the shoes. I explained to Miguel that when a
shipment arrived in a Japanese store, they opened it, and if there
was a blemish on any item, they would send the item back to the
manufacturer.

In Taiwan, we were just sampling the upper part of the canvas
shoes. These were sent to a factory in Miami, who finished the
upper and attached them to the sole of the shoe. This qualified
them to stamp "Made in USA" on the bottom of the shoe.

We had met a large Argentine company called Alpargatas
when we were exhibiting at the shoe show in Dusseldorf. When
we went to Buenos Aires, we signed an agreement to become
their agents, shipping them footwear for their Topper line
from both Miami and Brazil. Lee was instrumental in main-
taining our good relations with Alpargatas. On one of Lee's
trips to Argentina, in March of 1992, he heard a loud blast in
his hotel, and it turned out to be a bomb going off in front of
the Israeli embassy. But by then we were used to being where
the action was.

In October 1972, I was warned not to stay at the Sheraton in
Buenos Aires, and I heeded the warning and stayed in the Plaza
(which was nicer anyway). They had told me that they put all of
the foreigners on the twelfth floor of the Sheraton Hotel, which

was a bad sign. Sure enough, a bomb went off on that floor, killing a couple of Canadians.

In September 1975, I was in London with Leslie Fossey when a bomb went off at the Hilton. Leslie told me it was the IRA who had planted the bomb. We weren't near it. Sadly, there were a number of innocent deaths in all of these bombings.

If there was no existing excitement, Leslie would find a way to create some. When I landed in London on that trip, I was on the same flight as the popular singer Andy Williams. After leaving customs, you would pass through a glass-like tube to get to the baggage area. As I was walking through the narrow, plastic-covered passageway, there was a frantic crowd banging on the clear plastic shouting at me. I couldn't hear what they were shouting until I emerged from the tube. It seemed that Leslie had pointed me out as Andy Williams. I don't really look like Andy, but I did sign a few autographs anyway (my handwriting is terrible, so some poor schlub may be still holding on to it, thinking that it is valuable).

In June of 1985, I was at the Frankfurt airport when a bomb went off in the departure area. Luckily I was not in that area, but I was able to smell the cordite from the blast.

Aside from riots, military governments, and bombs, things were going well. Marquesa was importing, exporting, and growing quickly. In Brazil, even our Volkswagen Gol was air-conditioned.

There was an automobile called the Miura, which was manufactured in Porto Alegre. It was a two-door with a Passat engine, with the appearance of a Ferrari. The problem was that they only made twelve per day. I had forgotten about it when one day I was having dinner with Ruben, Miguel, and one of our manufacturers in a small town. A group of ten people came in, and they were seated not far from our table. I heard someone speaking English, and it sounded as if he said that he wanted to export ten Miuras.

Since he now had my attention, I looked up to see who was at that table because it was unusual to see Americans in this area. I nudged my guys and asked them whether the man in the center of the table was familiar to them. Nobody recognized him.

I knew who it was: Mohammed Ali. I was a big fan of his, but I knew that he was not completely well, and I didn't want to impose on him, his wife, and his group, so we left the restaurant without approaching him. To this day, I regret not going over and shaking his hand. I was brazen at times but at other times very shy, I guess.

Dave Pupps was arriving the next day, and since it was the start of the weekend, we decided that after picking him up at the Porto Alegre airport, we would stay in Porto Alegre and play golf at the Porto Alegre Country Club. One of the factory owners was a member.

Our group teed off around noon that Sunday. It was an extremely hot summer day in December (the seasons are the opposite in the Southern Hemisphere). Even though we were in the south of Brazil, where winter temperatures could dip to forty degrees, in the summer it was sometimes the hottest in all of the country. Dave was a very large person, and by the sixteenth hole, he could no longer take the heat. I barely finished the round, and I immediately went to the clubhouse, where the group was having their cold *chopps*, which was excellent Brazilian draft beer. They asked me if I knew what the temperature was. I didn't, and then they informed me that it was the equivalent of 116 degrees and that the caddies had been praying that we would stop our round sooner.

Our business in Spain was not large, but we had a factory, that we did business with, there. Although their specialty was espadrilles, they were also producing an article called the huarache. The factory was on the expensive side, so the plan was to move the production to Brazil.

While I was at the factory, I met one of their other customers, who was importing their slippers. His name was Carlos Musso, and we became friends. He indicated that he wanted to both open stores and start to wholesale shoes. He was very much interested in the idea of importing shoes from Brazil.

After he went to Brazil to inspect our office with his team and met with Ruben and Miguel, he made us his official agent in Brazil. We also represented other branded companies, but none on an exclusive basis.

The mainstay of his line became the huarache. The sales were terrific, and because it was a hot item and because we had exclusive rights to the best factories making this item, we ended up also selling it in large quantities to all of our major customers.

After we had sold our three millionth pair of huaraches, the Footwear News wrote a nice article with photos showing us presenting awards to such companies as Sears Roebuck, Genesco, Montgomery Ward, Unisa, and others.

We had the best quality and the best-priced factories making the shoes for us, which meant we could sell whoever we wanted. Actually, the only one we had approached who turned us down was Sylvia's cousin Irv Greenwald, whom, as I mentioned before, I worked for when I got out of college. Irv had both a wholesale company and a chain of stores out of Dallas. His reasoning was that he could get faster delivery from another factory. I knew the factory, and I also knew that their quality was inferior. Sure enough, when the shoes were delivered, they not only came in late, but they fell apart, causing him big problems. So much for trying to deal with relatives.

In other cases, we could use the huaraches to get a foothold with companies that we wanted to do business with, such as Edison Brothers, who had such brands as Chandler's, Wild Pair, and Bakers. Along with Edison, we had a number of other customers in Saint Louis, so I would travel there often.

I had a standing arrangement with a bell cap. I would call him in advance, and he would take my luggage and sample cases and drive me to the Hilton Hotel in downtown Saint Louis. I hadn't been to Saint Louis for a while, and when I arrived, we stopped to chat in front of the baggage claim. I pointed out my suitcase and one sample bag on the luggage belt. That meant that one of the sample bags was missing.

Then, in the rear, I saw this tall, shabbily dressed man wheeling my bag toward the parking lot, which was in the rear of the baggage claim area. I ran to intercept him, and when I caught up with him, I shouted, "What the hell do you think you are doing with my bag?"

He looked up, smiled, and said, "Oh, is this your bag?" And at the same time he reached into his jacket pocket. I thought surely he was going to pull out a pistol, but it was a pamphlet with some kind of a Buddhist prayer.

By this time, my driver had called the police. The police came and asked me if I would press charges. I replied that I would and that I would be willing to return to Saint Louis to testify if I wasn't out of the country. We went to the TWA offices in the basement, and I requested to see the airport manager. When he arrived, I explained that the lack of security at the airport was unacceptable and that they needed a system where the passengers' luggage tags were checked upon leaving the baggage area.

He agreed and he said that he would take care of it. TWA put gates around the area, and within a month, they were checking the luggage tags.

There was a regional shoe show in Saint Louis at the time, which I attended. One of the exhibitors was a friendly competitor. We were chatting in their suite when one of his salesmen was gesturing wildly to the owner. The salesman had spotted Simon Edison coming down the hall. Simon Edison was the chairman of Edison Brothers, and my friendly competitors were a major supplier of their largest division (Bakers). I didn't want to embarrass the supplier, so I darted out to what I thought was the hallway, but it turned out to be a large clothes closet. Now I was going to be stuck in this closet until Simon Edison left. Luckily, it had a light in the ceiling.

I could hear Mr. Edison making his polite pleasantries to the occupants of the next room. "Are my boys treating you right? Is there anything we can do for you?" Etc. Mr. Edison then bade his good-bye to his supplier.

He then walked into the closet where I was standing, and when he saw me, he said, "Bill, so nice to see you. Are my boys treating you OK? Is there anything we can do for you?" After that we both left, and we headed for the hall, but not before I saw the stunned look on the people in the showroom.

My traveling was constant, and I was constantly making itinerary changes, which drove Kurt, who was the owner of Merriway Travel, crazy. At one point Kurt said to the people in my office that he couldn't take it anymore and that if I continued to make so many changes, he was going to commit suicide. The problem was that we had a lot going on, not only with multiple offices but also with shoe shows in the States and in Europe.

Ruud Bresson was our export agent. Once he was driving me back from Dusseldorf to his home and office in Maastricht, Holland. It wasn't a long ride, but Ruud cautioned me that when we got to customs at the border, they always gave him a hard time because he was driving a Rolls Royce.

I laughed, but sure enough, while customs officers waved the cars in front of the Netherlands' border through, they pulled us to the side. Ruud was fuming and cursing. He explained to me that in Holland, everything was unionized, even the customs agents, police, and army. I said that I would hate to see an army go on strike in the middle of a battle.

Ruud was flipping one cigarette after another on the ground, and one of the agents came and ordered him to pick up the butts. Ruud then blew up and started to holler, trying to explain that there were cigarette butts all over the ground.

Seeing trouble, I ran into the kiosk and asked for the person in charge. After some pleading, I got him to compromise. He said that he had to save face in front of his men, but if Ruud would apologize, he would let us go.

I was in for another surprise because when we got to his home and office, it was palatial. At that time, Ruud was married to the daughter of the heir to the Bayer Aspirin fortune. She was quite snobby, and it was little wonder that when they came to our house in Teaneck, she turned up her nose at it. The marriage didn't last long after that.

Ruben Vitabar was at our home at that time, and when introduced to Ruud's wife, got her confused with another woman whom Ruud had been with at a show in Germany. Ruben had assumed that the woman at the show was Ruud's wife. "Wasn't your hair darker when we last met? Oh! Excuse me, please. Me no speaky d English."

We were having one of our "famous" barbecues in Teaneck, where I did all the cooking by smoke and basted it with my special sauce, which I made from scratch. There was a good-sized crowd, which included buyers, friends, and manufacturers from various countries.

I was in the corner of our deck cooking away when I heard some loud splashing and confusion in our pool. It seemed that one of the Brazilians had jumped off the diving board into the deepest part of the pool. Since he couldn't swim, he was gurgling away. Luckily one of our friends quickly surmised what was happening, and she jumped into the pool, saved him, and saved us some real aggravation.

Sylvia was in the kitchen at the time, and when we told her what had happened, she didn't know whether to laugh or faint.

We had many barbecues for friends, family, workers, buyers, and factory people.

MOM IN THE OFFICE

My mom was managing a store in downtown Brooklyn. One morning on the way to work, she was robbed at gunpoint as she was getting out of the elevator. With the pistol to her head, she calmly asked the robbers if they could do her a favor and leave enough change in her purse to catch the subway to work. Amazingly, they did just that.

At the police station, the detectives pulled out a book of mug shots, and they wanted to know whether she was able to recognize any of them. She looked at the detectives and laughed, saying that she recognized almost all of them, as they came into the G & A store where she worked.

In any case, it was time to move her to an apartment in Teaneck. We needed a head bookkeeper to assist Amalia, who was our controller. Mom was a much-needed addition to our company. Ellen, our office manager, took care of the nonaccounting matters. We were getting ready for a trade show at the Javits Center in New York, and Ellen said that she would have one of her assistants prepare the checklist that we had for each show. This was part of a whole production, as we used a design team to come up with a theme for each show, and they prepared the background and the sets as if it were a stage production.

In the meantime, I noticed that there was something wrong with the young man preparing the checklist. If not illiterate, he was obviously very close to it. I asked Ellen, and she sheepishly admitted that his language skills were less than perfect. I immediately called him into my office and confronted this situation. Terry was embarrassed, but he readily admitted that he had problems with reading and writing.

"But didn't you graduate Dwight Morrow High School?" I asked.

Yes, he replied. He said that he was graduated, but because he was an excellent athlete, they overlooked his academics. This so-called top school had pushed him along academically so that he could stay on the teams.

I was of course appalled, and I explained that the school had not done him any favors since he was probably not among the few who would make it big in professional sports. Terry understood and agreed. Feeling bad, I offered to send him to any intensive English-language school or course of his choosing, at our expense. Terry asked for a day to make up his mind.

The next morning, he informed me that although he appreciated my offer, he was going to join the army since they had agreed to educate him and even have him obtain credit for a college degree. We were all sorry to see him go, as we all felt that he had potential.

Some months later, he returned to the office to say hello. He again thanked us for our concern and laughingly said that he could now make the check-off list for us with no problem. The army had trained him well. He had already made corporal and was considering going to Officer Candidate School, as he was going to make the army his career.

Jeanne (my mom) was a no-nonsense person. One day I was going through the day's mail, and I noticed a check from Ohrbach's Department Stores for $40,000. That was fine except it was a duplicate of a check that we had received ten days before.

Mom was looking over my shoulder, and I said that I would return the check to them in a week or so, but in the meantime, it would help our cash flow. She immediately snatched the check from my hands, placed it in an envelope, and addressed it back to them. At the same time she glared at me and made the following strong comment: "I did not bring up my son to be a thief."

That was my mom.

Just a few days later, we received another duplicate check (an even larger amount) from a wholesaler we represented in Brazil—Consolidated Shoe Company of Lynchburg, Virginia. I called the president of the company immediately and not only informed him of the duplication but also offered to travel to Lynchburg to show them how to avoid the problem in the future. This is the response that we received from Richard A. Carrington III:

Dear Bill,

After your call yesterday, I discussed the duplication of our check with our Accounting Department. It seems that you are correct in our sending two checks because we have copies of both. One was dated in February and the other in March. Needless to say, we are taking extensive measures to eliminate this problem.

By calling us about receiving two checks for the same commission, it says a lot for you, Bill. There are not many people who would do this, and it shows that you and your company have a great deal of credibility. I am very appreciative of your advising us of this matter and am glad to see we are doing business with such fine people. I will do everything in my power to continue this relationship.

Sincerely, Dick

Richard Carrington III

Now, that letter turned out to be truly ironic. Within ninety days, Consolidated Shoe decided to open up their own office in Brazil, spending a good sum of money on a building, local staff, and offices. I knew their manager in Brazil, and because he was being paid by both the factories and Consolidated, they were paying more for their shoes than they were when we were their agents. When I questioned the Carringtons why they were no longer giving us any business, their response was that they had too much invested in their office and that they had to justify the expense. I felt that they could at least give us **some** business since our prices were lower than what they were paying.

Mom was tough on me and watched me like a panther ready to pounce. We had hired a rather attractive young lady by the name of Litza to help out with styling. Litza and I went store shopping to buy some styles to be "knocked off" for chain selling. I would take a half pair to South America, and she was going to take a half pair to Europe.

Mom saw the shoes on Litza's desk and got my expense report on Friday with the shoe purchases on it. She immediately called Syl to ask why I was buying shoes for Litza.

Syl laughed and explained that Litza could not wear a half pair of shoes, and when they were brought to a factory, they were usually torn apart anyway.

On another occasion, I was taking a trip overseas, and when I called Kurt at Merriway, he mentioned that the leg of the trip from Rio to Paris should be made on this new fast plane called the Concorde. I explained that the timing was a day off and that I had planned a very tight schedule.

When I got to Rio for the Paris flight, we boarded late due to some mechanical problem. After we boarded, we sat and we sat and we sat. It was after 2:00 a.m. when the pilot announced that due to noise restrictions, we could not take off and we would have to spend the night in Rio, and further, Varig (the Brazilian airline) couldn't unload the luggage.

By the time I got to the Sheraton Hotel and showered, I could no longer fall asleep, so I had an early breakfast. The Concorde was leaving in the morning, but there was no chance to get on it at that late juncture. Besides, my luggage was on the Varig plane.

Landing in Paris, I was tired and feeling cruddy and sticky. The schedule was all bollixed up, and instead of spending the night in Paris, I would be flying to London. After washing up at Charles de Gaulle Airport, I proceeded to the Rue de Rivoli, where there was a Brooks Brothers store. I bought a silk shirt and charged it to my Diners Club card. In my mind, which was a little fuzzy from the trip, I had calculated the cost in cruzeiros instead of francs.

Next store was Catherine Perfumes, where I always bought a supply of perfumes. Catherine was a fine woman, and she would load me up with samples and then mail me the invoice in order to save time.

Upon my return to the office in Englewood, New Jersey, I submitted my expense account. Mom called me into her office, and she was quite upset. Why did I put a ninety-five-dollar shirt on a business expense account, and who in the world spends ninety-five dollars for a shirt? (That shirt, incidentally, fell apart after being worn less than a half dozen times.)

In the meantime, I felt that I had earned the shirt after not having a change of clothes for more than two days; however, I was shocked at the price, as I had calculated the cost as being less than one-half of that.

Speaking of Paris, I loved the wine country; the rural areas of France; the fine Parisian restaurants; and especially the restaurants in the French countryside and other parts of France, including the French Riviera, Marseilles, and other areas. However, I thought the food in Belgium was slightly better, and whenever I heard of a fine or new restaurant opening in Europe, I would try to make it my business to go there and if possible, take buyers to savor the experience of fine food.

One day I read about a new restaurant that was the new in place to go, but it was very hard to get a reservation. Since I was meeting some important buyers in Paris, I called the restaurant's owner and begged for a reservation. He finally agreed and told me to give him a call to confirm when I arrived in Paris in the morning, which I did. It was a damp, rainy fall day, and the restaurant was in an industrial area outside of Paris. Since the taxis in Paris do not accept more than two or three passengers, we had to take multiple cabs.

We arrived on time for our reservation and entered the sparsely decorated restaurant. They took our coats and flung them on racks that were similar to the airplane racks on planes and then seated us by the door. Every time the door opened, we were greeted by a waft of cold, wet air. I called the maître d' over to our windy table and told him that I had a cold and that the cold draft was not good for my cold.

He snootily said that there was nothing that he could do, as they were completely booked with their regular customers.

At the next table was a group with a very large dog. The dog had an odor, we guessed from being wet. Spotting the owner of the restaurant in the rear, I called him over and claimed that since I was allergic to dogs (not really true, as I love animals), could he be so kind as to move us to another table?

His reply was quick. "Sorry, monsieur, but we are completely booked with REGULARS!"

Not long after that conversation, the owner returned with a slab of beef and plopped it down for the large dog with a splatter. The dog was slurping away, and since there were not any other restaurants in the area, we were trapped. We were in the middle of our meal when I looked over to the dog's table, and I couldn't believe what I was seeing. The hound was taking a large dump right there in the middle of the restaurant. We couldn't wait to leave, and we ordered three taxis.

At this point I was mortified to have subjected my guests to this torture, and while I was in the cab, I could still smell a wet dog. It wasn't my imagination, as next to the driver was a large, smelly, hairy, wet dog. Apparently this was her protection for unruly passengers or worse.

When we finally arrived at the Meurice Hotel, where I was staying, the cab driver did not stop under the canopy in front of the hotel but instead let us off less than one block away. As I was walking toward the entrance of the hotel, I stepped in something very soft and smelly. You guessed it. It was dog crap. So ended an evening that was "for the dogs."

In the Paris area, I had an aunt from my mother's side who was a Moroccan Jew, and during World War II, she met and married a man while they were in the French Resistance during the war. They used to take me to their country home outside of Paris, where the people were much more courteous and the food was excellent.

Sometimes they would have me stay in their apartment, which was in a suburb called Montreuil. They had a gift shop not far from the apartment, and one day I was waiting for them to come back for their lunch break. There was a knock on the door, and it was a young fellow delivering their newspaper. I was a little shocked to see that it was *La Humanite*, which was the communist newspaper.

When I questioned them, they said that they were brought up as communists, but that they were not really political.

A few months later, I received word that sadly, my aunt had died. It seemed that the doctor who was treating her for allergies and diabetes gave her the wrong medicine. When Albert, her husband, returned from their store to check on her, he found her in a state of shock from which she never recovered. He couldn't prove it, but they suspected that her doctor was a Nazi who knew of her being in the Resistance, and that was his final revenge.

In London, I preferred staying in the fine and famous hotels. Once at the Dorchester Hotel, I was standing in line to go to my safe deposit box, and in front of me was an Arab sheik, and on the side was an entourage that I assumed was his family. Everyone in the line stood in shock as he emptied two large drawers with pound sterling and dollars and place them in large paper bags (the safe deposit boxes were in sight of those on the line).

When I left the hotel, I was chatting with the doorman, and I related what had happened. He wasn't at all surprised, and he told me that a month before, a sheik who had been staying at the hotel for a number of months, upon checking out, gave the keys to his Rolls Royce to the previous doorman.

After that, I decided to move to a less prominent hotel called the Executive Suites. There weren't really any suites, but I had made an arrangement in which the hotel would give me two adjoining rooms for the price of one. It was a very informal place, and they made you feel at home. The manager would come out and sit with me in the lobby and have a glass of English beer.

This went on for a few years, and then there came a time when I called for a reservation and there was a strange voice on the phone. When I arrived, they had the reservation, but they didn't seem to know anything about our arrangement. So I explained that I was to have two rooms for the price of one.

This unfamiliar person escorted me to the room, and when I asked to open the door to the second room, he said that the other room was on another floor. It took some explaining, but I finally got through to him that I wanted adjoining rooms. I then asked the new manager what had happened to my friend.

He said he had been fired because he was caught drinking with the guests. I tried to explain that it was good public relations for the hotel and that the reason I always returned was that he was so friendly. I could see that this was going completely over his head and that he was a jerk.

When I was checking out, he looked at me and said, "I know where you are going."

I responded that I was heading to Spain (not that it was any of his business).

He then said, 'No you're not. You are going to Cypress."

Cypress? What the hell would I be going to Cypress for?

He then said that I was with the "company."

I said that my company was Marquesa International.

His response was that I was with THE Company. At that point, some men in dark suits were walking down the stairs, looking mighty somber. The new manager looked in their direction and said that I was with them. He was obviously a nut case.

"Who is them?"

"Them is with the CIA," he said.

At that point I left the hotel, never to return to the Executive Suites in London.

Janine was our controller (who had taken over for Amalia, who had passed away), and in the course of interviewing a bookkeeping candidate, she turned down a gal who was obviously not qualified for office work. This person contacted her attorney, and we were taken to the county court. She claimed that Janine had discriminated against her because she was Yugoslavian. When Janine was called to testify, she was asked if she had discriminated against this person.

Janine said that it was impossible since she was born in Belgrade and was Yugoslavian by birth. The judge looked up, smiled, and said that the case was dismissed.

On another occasion, a woman came for an interview, and she was accompanied by her husband. He looked around the office, and when he saw a bunch of men, he then exclaimed that he was not going to let his attractive wife work around a bunch of handsome young men.

Janine laughed and said that he should have no worries, as these men only looked down at their feet to see what kind of shoes the women were wearing.

We had a few other strange incidents in our office. We had an additional office, store, and showroom in another building in Englewood. One day I caught one of our warehouse workers selling our shoes in the street in downtown Englewood. Another time, one of our female workers stopped a police car in front of our office, and when the officer rolled down the window, she slapped him. Once, another one of our workers got into a screaming match with her husband, also in front of our office. We called the police, and when the Englewood policeman arrived, her husband fainted dead away.

I wasn't completely innocent either, as sometimes when I flicked my cigar ashes into the wastepaper basket, it would catch on fire. I never burned down the office, however (I just stank it up a bit).

I had bought a new Maserati Biturbo 425 from a local dealer in Englewood and had been thoroughly enjoying it for over a year. The problem was that there was nowhere to drive it at full throttle. Luckily, I was only pulled over one time on the Massachusetts Turnpike going 180 miles an hour. It turned out to be quite a coincidence, as the state trooper who pulled me over recognized me from Korea. He laughingly issued me a warning for going "twenty miles over the speed limit."

A few months later, I was returning to Teaneck, New Jersey, from a late-evening meeting in Manhattan. The Harlem River Drive was rain slicked, and suddenly, ahead of me, a drunk driver caused a pileup of about eight cars. I tried to swerve so as not to hit the car in front of me, but unfortunately I hit the car on the front left side.

The tow truck came and took me to a garage in Harlem, where they said that they were expert at fixing foreign cars. The owner asked if I wanted the estimate to include the deductible. I replied, "Absolutely not. I just want a perfect car."

He said that nobody has said that to him before.

I should have realized that it would have been best to have had the car towed to my local Maserati dealership. It took almost a month to repair it. When I got a call that it was ready, I reminded them that I wanted a perfect repair job and that they should recheck everything.

When they called back, they had some bad news. When they took it for a test drive, the transmission was shot, and since they had to order the transmission from Italy, it would be another three to four weeks before I could get the car back. The additional cost would be $14,000, and due to some technicality, the insurance company would only cover part of it. (Aren't insurance companies great at finding technicalities?)

When the car was finally ready, I just didn't like the feel of the drive, so I put an ad in the local paper. A young man called and he said he was interested in the car and would like to come out and see it. When he arrived, he asked me if the car had ever been in a wreck, so I had to tell him the story. He asked to drive it anyway.

He went only a few blocks and said that if I would take $500 less than I was asking, he would buy the car.

I was stunned and asked him why he was so determined to buy the car.

He said that his grandfather was seventy-three years old and that all of his life, he had wanted a Maserati. He wouldn't drive it much anyway, so this was going to be his gift to his beloved grandfather. I was always lucky when it came to selling cars.

MISCELLANEOUS TRAVELS

In my earlier years, I visited a factory in Monterrey, Mexico. Our first stop was in McAllen, Texas. From there we took an airline by the name of Trans Texas Airways. The trip turned out to be a first and a one and only. It was a short flight from McAllen to Monterrey. It turned out that I was lucky because I had a seat. TTA, as it was called, allowed standees on the flight. That meant you actually had people standing next to your seat holding on to overhead straps. Neither that system, nor the airline, for that matter, lasted very long.

Marquesa International represented a large, well-known athletic shoe company that bought sandals and sport shoes from us in South America. During one of our shoe shows, Bob, the owner, proudly informed me that they had just built a new office and warehouse in Los Angeles. He also invited me to come out and drive his new Jaguar convertible. I promised Bob that the next time I came west, I would take him up on his offer.

It wasn't long after that meeting that I was informed that their company owed us over $40,000 in commissions. The amount was past due, and it looked as if we were getting the run-around from their accounts payable department. I then found out surreptitiously that Bob would be in his office the remainder of the week.

I decided to catch the next available flight to LA. Upon my arrival, I went directly to their office. It certainly looked impressive, and sure enough, the Jaguar was parked in plain view, right in front of the building. I entered and asked the receptionist for Bob, announcing my name and company.

After a pause, she said, "Mr. G doesn't seem to be in his office."

I responded that it was not a concern and that I was a friend, and Bob had promised to let me use his car when I came to town. "I see the car out front, so may I have the keys, please?"

She had a startled look on her face and moved to the rear of the reception area where I couldn't hear her conversation. Not even two minutes later, Bob bounded into the reception area saying that he was surprised to see me and that he didn't know I had been expected.

He then proudly took me on a tour of the warehouse and offices. We ended up in front of his large office, and I immediately sat in his chair and pulled out a cigar. He said that he had to run to a meeting in his conference room, and I said that was fine, and I would wait in his office until he returned.

After about forty minutes, Bob passed the office a couple of times and looked in as if he were confounded that I was still sitting in his chair (quite luxurious and comfortable). Finally, he came in and asked if he could do anything for me. I mentioned that I was quite comfortable, and since his bathroom was right there, all I needed was some water every once in a while, since I was prepared to wait until I received the money that he owed us.

"What? We owe you money? I didn't know that we owed Marquesa any money."

At that point he called in his bookkeeper, who sheepishly admitted that they in fact did owe us money.

"Prepare them a check," he said.

After about twenty minutes, Bob returned with a sealed envelope. He then stuffed the envelope, with the check inside of it, into my pocket. I immediately opened the envelope in front of him, and sure enough, the amount was about $15,000 short.

Bob then apologized and made the excuse that this had come on short notice but that he would mail us the balance the following week. My thoughts were that I had the choice to sit back down and hope that I could wear him down, or I could get to the bank and deposit it quickly. I chose the latter option.

Although we eventually received some of the amount still due, a balance remained that we never collected. It was ironic that some years later, I received a call from Bob's attorney. It seemed that the company was involved in a lawsuit, and they needed our records in order to help them with their case. My response to their attorney was simple: before I gave them any help, they would have to pay what was owed, with interest, and further, they would have to pay us a fee for our assistance. That was the last that I ever heard from either their attorney or from Bob.

When you fly internationally, you sometimes meet interesting people. Once on a flight from Buenos Aires, the person who was in the seat next to me was a tall, quiet man. I didn't want to intrude on him, but I was very curious since he was scribbling words in no particular order on a large pad. I surmised that he was either a scientist or that he was writing some kind of code. I didn't say a word to him until the meal came, at which time I wished him bon appétit.

He smiled, and we began to chat. He told me that he was on his way to Australia to play a tennis match and that he would not have much time to rest, as the match would start shortly after he landed. I wasn't a tennis fan, so when he told me his name, Guillermo Vilas, it did not register that he was a famous tennis star from Argentina.

When I asked him what the scribbling was all about, he told me that between matches, he wrote books of poetry and music for his guitar and that at some point, he put the words in a sequence that made some sense for his poem.

On another flight to Paris, there was a man and his son across the aisle from me. At one point the father got up to go to the lavatory, and from the back, he somehow gave the appearance of a very large fish swimming down the aisle. When he was returning to his seat, a couple of people asked him for his autograph, so I knew he was someone famous. I asked the stewardess (sorry, that's what we called them in those days) who it was, and she laughed and said, "Oh, that's Jacques Cousteau."

On another flight, I heard a commotion a few rows behind me. It seemed that John Derek, the movie actor, was about to get into a fistfight with one of the passengers, whom he accused of making a pass at his wife, who happened to be Bo Derek. Bo, who was very attractive, sat calmly while John was making a complete ass out of himself.

Then there was a flight from Rio to London on which a very pleasant Arab from Kuwait sat next to me. He was chairman of Kuwait Petroleum Company, and we discussed many topics and became friendly. I was staying in the Knightsbridge area near where he had an apartment, and he invited me to see it and enjoy a drink together. He also invited me to come to Kuwait, at which point I explained that that would not be possible.

When he asked why, I told him that I was Jewish, and I would not go anywhere where I was not welcome. He chuckled and said that would be no problem since I would be coming as his guest and under his auspices. He didn't say that some of his best friends were Jews, but he did jokingly say that no self-respecting Kuwaiti would only go to a Jewish doctor, if possible. When I asked him about the trade embargo against Israel, he claimed that behind the scenes, Kuwait and Israel did trade with each other.

When we arrived at his magnificent apartment, he unlocked a large cabinet fully stocked with liquor. "I thought that you were a Muslim," I intoned.

He said that he didn't personally drink, and besides, he was not Saudi or Salafi, and apparently he was not dogmatic or extreme in his beliefs.

Soon after I returned from that trip, I received a call from someone I knew at USAid, which had been organized in the early sixties to help poor and developing countries increase their commercial footprint. I wondered if my Kuwaiti friend had anything to do with it since the country that requested aid was Morocco.

We would also have brief stops in Tunisia and Algeria, with Morocco being our main focus. The idea was to develop the manufacturing industry in Morocco, and since I was considered the "expert" on shoes, they thought that I could help them develop footwear and related items for export.

We left on Air Maroc. I was paired with a partner who was Lebanese, but he also had stores and a wholesale footwear company in Miami. We hit it off immediately (I still have the prayer beads that he gave me). Samir would be a great help since he was fluent in English, French, and Arabic.

We were greeted by government officials at the Casablanca airport and from there whisked to the Hotel Monsour, which was in the center of Casablanca.

Samir and I were picked up early the next day and driven to the tanneries. Moroccan leather is probably the best in the world, but there was one problem: Moroccan law prohibits the export of leather in order to "protect" the leather industry. We knew it would be useless to try to get them to change any of their laws.

Government officials and the business people were particularly gracious to me. They made sure that I was shown a synagogue, a kosher butcher, and a Jewish neighborhood. They also explained that King Mohammed V in their tradition protected the Jewish populace. Under his rule, it was against the law to harm a Jew. This was not true in other parts of North Africa, and it was certainly not true of the other Arab countries.

The tour ended just in time for lunch, where I met with Samir. We were taken to one of the manufacturers' homes. He was extremely gracious and hospitable, even the more unusual since he manufactured products other than shoes.

In North Africa, you eat with your hands using the pita-type bread to scoop up the food. The beverage is tea, which is poured from high above into a long, narrow glass. I never saw anyone ever spill a drop of tea, and that always amazed me.

The next couple of days, we went on to Fez and Marrakesh, where the process of making shoes by hand was interesting but crude. Another interesting aspect was that when I asked where the camels were, they said that we would have to go to Agadir to see any camels.

Upon our return, we were going to be honored with a grand dinner, a show, and a military parade. Further, we would get to meet with King Mohammed V. This thrilled me because I had had so many near misses meeting a president or a king that I felt the time was finally arriving when I would meet the leader of a country.

The dinner turned out to be hosted by the gracious manufacturer who had previously provided the fine lunch for us. It was spectacular, with all of the traditional North African dishes, including couscous. The ceremony afterward was spectacular. Think of the Moroccan pomp in the movie *Patton*. Of course, the king never showed up, and I was again disappointed.

I thought of the story that the assistant manager of the first Thom McAn store that I worked in told me. He had spent some time in Casablanca when he was in the army as an MP. Out of respect, they gave him a tour of the local prison, where he spotted a young girl behind the heavy prison bars.

He asked the superintendent, who was taking him around, as to the reason the young girl was locked up. "Debt!" was the response.

"How much does she owe?" he asked.

"About twenty-five dollars in US currency" was the answer. "And if someone comes up with the money, she goes free."

He promptly paid the debt, and girl was immediately set free. She later showed up at his hotel room and offered to become his slave. (That's against army regulations!)

It was something sad to see how some countries' laws and ethics worked. Child labor was rampant. I don't know how many times I complained to factory owners about young people in their factories.

There was usually one of two responses. Either they were old enough under the law, or if they didn't work, their families would starve.

After Morocco, we left for our short stops in Tunisia and Algeria. Both were interesting. What I remembered most in Tunisia besides their friendliness, was their couscous, which was very spicy, which I liked.

While we were in Tunisia, we met a couple of Libyans who were in the shoe business. They asked us to come to their office in Benghazi. The mint tea was good, but the few hours that we spent there was more than enough. It seemed that the populace thought that we were Italians, whom they had no great love for.

Nobody in their office wore shoes—and that included the salespeople, whose job we thought was to sell shoes. There was no business to do there.

It was good to be home. Samir and Marquesa remained friends and continued to do business together. I enjoyed visiting his office in Miami, where I would eat some of my favorite Lebanese food.

One day we got a call from one of our customers, who asked us if we could make a large number of T-shirts in China. Mr. Wu, our agent in Hong Kong, indicated that he didn't have a factory that could make it at our target price.

At one of our shows, we had met a man from China who said that he had the best connections in Taiwan and Hong Kong. Professor Wan came to our office with a portfolio of pictures, which included photos of his immediate family, his parents, and his grandparents. There were also pictures of various government officials, including Chiang Kai-shek, communist leaders, and various businesspeople, along with copies of his various degrees and awards. He claimed that he had an excellent factory that would make the T-shirts and that he was ready to leave for the Orient immediately.

In less than two weeks, we received word that the order was ready. We responded that we wanted the name of the factory so that we could send someone to inspect the goods. A telex response came with the name and address of the factory. Fax machines (on oily paper) were just coming into vogue.

Mr. Wu was tied up with a project in Hong Kong, and everyone else in production was busy with his or her own projects, so I called my friend and salesman, Steve, to take the trip. Steve proceeded to make the long, tiring trip to China. There was no response at the number that the good professor had given to us.

Somehow Steve located the factory. They had the facilities to make the T-shirts; however, they had no government quota to export.

This became a very embarrassing situation, as we had been fooled either by a complete idiot or by someone with ulterior motives. We weren't able to find a factory that could make the order at the price needed. We not only lost a good order but certainly lost a good potential customer.

Although I blew up and lost my temper, Steve, with his kind nature, took the whole situation with uncommon calm. He returned home and continued his selling.

Changes, and Then a Little Embarrassment

On one of my trips to Brazil, I had a series of marvelous experiences. It was during Carnival, where the atmosphere and the pulse of the *cariocas* was a thrill in itself to experience. The Carnival clubs prepare for a year for the four days before Lent, although the Carnival season starts weeks before.

One of the families that I was friendly with invited me to attend the grand procession, which would make its way past the grandstands that were specifically built for the purpose.

They had choice seats, and they asked me to arrive around 6:00 p.m. When I asked how long the shows and marches would last, they said until around ten. I replied that I didn't know whether I could sit for four hours in one spot. They laughed because they were talking about 10:00 a.m. the next morning, but they said I could leave anytime I got tired.

My arrival was promptly at 6:00 p.m., and when the marches started, I was absolutely transfixed. I'm not sure how I did it, but I stayed through the night and only left when the last band marched through.

After a couple of hours' sleep, I met the family again. We decided to stroll and watch the craziness that surrounded us. All of us were getting hungry and thirsty, and we came upon a long line of people trying to get into Regine's Disco. We started to pass the disco, but Regine was standing out front. She suddenly rushed toward me, gave me a hug, and invited us all into her disco.

I had never seen or met Regine before, and all I knew was the she was a famous singer who owned a bunch of discotheques in London, Paris, and New York. She obviously had me mixed up with someone else. All I could remember was her flaming red hair and her grabbing my arm, guiding us into the disco, and seating us at a long table along with some of the Carnival school performers. They were scantily clad in these long white head-dresses and spectacular costumes.

The group of girls was seated across from us, and I guess I was staring at them because at first I didn't recognize whom she had seated me next to. When I finally looked over, I immediately recognized that she had seated me next to Pelé. Being a big soccer fan, I felt truly privileged to have the most famous soccer player in the world seated next to me. He was very friendly as we spoke about the new soccer club in New York, which was going to be called the Cosmos.

Next he invited me to attend the Formula One auto race that was coming in a few days. On the appointed day, he had his driver pick me up at the Sheraton, where I was staying. We sat in the special box and thoroughly enjoyed the race. He took my card, but unfortunately I never heard from him after that and never did get to see a Cosmos match.

Marquesa's business was booming, and we were getting almost weekly write-ups in the *Footwear News*. There were, of course, some skid marks.

We had hired Al Brief, who was still considered both a super salesperson and a top line builder. Al built a leather fashion boot line for us that was so hot that during a shoe show at the Javits

Center in New York, we were writing orders on the spot until around 8:00 p.m. After the show closed, the guards discovered us and threw us out of the convention hall.

The problem was he could be very stubborn, contentious, and hotheaded. We were in Europe together shopping for styles and ideas. We found a shoe in a high-priced shoe store called Prange on the Konigsallee, which is Dusseldorf's answer to Worth Avenue in Palm Beach. The shoe was very expensive, so I asked Al not to cut it up, thinking that maybe we could salvage the shoe. No sooner were the words out of my mouth than Al took out his trusty little sharp scissor and started chopping away.

Al then flew to South America to work with Ruben Vitabar, and I flew back to the office. It turned out that due to a clash in two very stubborn personalities, Al and Ruben were both bitterly and constantly fighting. Even though each recognized the other's talents, the sparks still flew. I received a call from Ruben saying that if I didn't call Al home immediately, he would leave the company, and that Al was impossible to work with.

Immediately after that, I received a call from Al telling me that Ruben didn't know what he was doing. Dave Pupps was very close to Ruben, and even Dave couldn't persuade Ruben to work with Al anymore.

It was quite a dilemma. Do I lose my top salesman and line builder, or do I lose my top man in South America? I made the sad choice: Al had to go.

So now we had to find a replacement. I knew Eddie A from back in the Thom McAn days. He had the reputation of being a top salesperson and a good line builder, though he did not have extensive overseas experience. At our interview meeting, he claimed that he could bring us some top clients that we didn't have, such as J. C. Penney. Eddie was demanding the same salary we were paying to Al Brief, which was well over $200,000 per year plus expenses. We ended up offering him close to that, along with a car.

Eddie wanted me to accompany him on his first trip to Europe. My work habits are nonstop, and when I told him that we would hit the ground running when we got off of the plane, I detected kind of a glazed look in his eye. That should have been a signal of things to come.

We were going to go first to the *Modelistas* (designers) in Stra, just outside of Venice. We had rented a Fiat and arrived quite late. You cannot drive into Venice proper, so you park in a large multistory parking lot. There was no one around to take our luggage, so we had to carry it to the boat that was take us across to Venice.

Eddie started whining that he couldn't take another step, which meant that I had to drag some of his bags along with mine.

We were both happy to get to the hotel. I told Eddie that we would have breakfast at 7:00 a.m., check out, and drive to Stra. Eddie was stunned, and he claimed that he needed some rest. I told him that he would rest when he got back to the States. I knew then that I had made a mistake by hiring him.

This was reinforced during the rest of the trip, as he didn't show much originality or promise. My only hope was that when he went out to sell, he would bring us some new customers. Upon our return, he went out on the road (or so he said), and for six weeks, he did not make a sale of any kind. Not even a shoelace. We terminated his contract for cause, and not unexpectedly, he sued us for the balance of his year's contract. I believe we settled for five or six months' pay. He also returned the car in very poor condition, which we didn't understand, considering that he had a pilot's license.

In the meantime, I received a call from a new organization called the International Footwear Association (IFA). This was a group of American importers whose basic aim was to lobby Washington regarding trade laws and restrictions. I had often made comments in the trade press about this subject, and they felt that I was somewhat an authority on the subject.

After attending their first meeting, I saw that most of the top footwear importers in the country had already joined the organization. We signed up immediately, and in less than a month, they had made me president of the IFA, which made me quite proud, as I was among some very big hitters.

In less than a year, we realized that we had some really big issues, not only with the government, duties, and trade policies, but also with the large retailers and retail chains. The retailers were squeezing the importers and wholesalers very badly in a number of areas. They were trying to go direct to our factories. They were squeezing us on price and our commissions. They were finding all kinds of excuses to return goods or issue chargebacks.

My idea was to form a cabal, and as a group, we would blackball any retailer who violated our standards. The group, because of their fear of losing business, roundly rejected that idea. The group's solution, if only partial, was to combine with the organization that also included the retailers. It was called the Footwear Distributors & Retailers Association (FDRA). Peter Mangione was an attorney and their dynamic director. I was put on the board and made a vice-president of the new organization. This was quite an honor for me, as the largest retailers and distributors in the country belonged. Names like Nike, Reebok, J. C. Penney, Nine West, and many others were members. We had many productive sessions and meetings.

At one of these meetings, I became friendly with Murray Weidenbaum, who had been chairman of the Council of Economic Advisors in the early eighties. Murray had written many interesting and fascinating books on economics, which I've always felt should have been more popular. We agreed that there was not only too much corruption in government but too much government generally. One of his themes was that every economic law that was passed ended up having the opposite of the effect that the law was intended for.

His stories and writing were humorous. Murray related the time in 1981 when then President Reagan asked his cabinet to come up with a plan to reduce the budget in each of their respective departments. Each one would make his or her submission and retire to an adjoining room. It turned out that none of them had lowered his or her budget, and when each of them would leave the room, President Reagan would find an excuse to defend that person.

Murray was very fond of the president, but he resigned in 1982 because although the president cut taxes substantially, he made no effort to trim the budget.

The outings were always fun except for one embarrassing moment. We had a meeting in Ponte Vedra, Florida, and we were scheduled to play golf at the famous TPC Sawgrass Country Club. The problem was that I was put in the group with Larry McVey, who was the president of Thom McAn; Lester Cohen, who was the president of Grand Imports; and another executive who was a scratch golfer. All were excellent golfers with the exception of me. I was not holding up my end of the tournament when we approached the par-three seventeenth hole. I was happy that we were getting to the end of the round. Happy, that is, until I saw this very intimidating hole. This was an "island" green, which meant the hole was surrounded by water (you crossed a narrow bridge to get to it). After hitting eleven balls into the water, I finally got my twelfth shot across and onto the green.

Everyone was very gracious to me, but I felt terribly humiliated. Although I never have, I have always wanted to return to Sawgrass and see whether I could play the seventeenth hole without losing eleven golf balls.

Success Goes to My Head

Marquesa was going full speed on all cylinders. Both our import and export divisions were doing fine. We had made contacts in Russia, and we were shipping boots from factories in Macedonia and Chile to Russia. We were soon invited to Russia, both to see what products could be exported and which could be imported. The plan was that I would make the first trip, and if it looked as if this was a viable situation, my son Lee would make the second trip.

It was 1992, and the Soviet Union had just collapsed. There was poverty all around. A doctor, for example, made the equivalent of about ten bucks a week. Fresh vegetables were almost nonexistent. There were no credit-card systems except for foreigners. There was not much in the way of currency, and the average person existed by trading and bartering. Parts from factories were being traded on the streets for food.

Sure enough, we were taken to a shoe factory that had the most modern Italian equipment. The problem was that no shoes could be manufactured because the workers had stripped all of the parts away. The subway, however, was spotless and exquisitely designed. The Kremlin was impressive, and Saint Petersburg was fine, except we spent very little time there.

We traveled first to Vologda, which is northwest of Moscow. My guides took me on a tour, and I asked to see the farmland. On a virtually barren plot, I met a very old woman who spoke some English. She said that I should look around and that in this area alone, there were some of the finest farms outside of the Ukraine. When Stalin came, the farms disappeared, and there were close to one million people buried there. They had died either of starvation or the brutality of the regime. With tears in her eyes, she said: "Socialism hasn't and can't ever work." (Unfortunately some countries are still trying it)

The government people I was with asked if there was anything that they could export. How could they export if they were stripping the factories of equipment?

The group decided to take me to an area where I would be the first Westerner to visit, and in fact, until recently, few Russians were allowed in. It was a sensitive military area, so we were met by a Soviet army colonel. They wanted me to see an optics factory. Even after mentioning that I didn't know the first thing about optics, they insisted that I meet with the colonel.

We met, and he started to interrogate me. Was I with the FBI, the CIA, or the State Department?

My answer was simple. "If I were with any of these groups, do you think that I would admit it?"

He thought that comment was quite funny, and he gave me a tour of the factory. When we finished, he asked whether I wanted any samples of microscopes or lenses, to which I answered negatively and just asked for a catalog to take back to the States.

I noticed that he had a Russian army officer's watch with a tank imprinted on the face. I asked him whether I could buy one at the duty-free shop when I left the country. With a flourish, he loosened the leather strap and tried to hand me the watch, which I of course refused to accept.

He then said that he would pick one up for me at their special store, which was comparable to our PX. He would then meet me at the hotel, and we would have breakfast in the morning. The colonel was cautioned by me that I would not accept it without payment. So the next morning at breakfast, he accepted ninety-five dollars for the windup watch.

Some months later, I was at the Paramus Mall in New Jersey, and there was a kiosk selling Russian trinkets. The owner noticed that I was wearing the army watch, and he asked where I got it. He gave out a guffaw and took me around to the other side of the kiosk, where he was selling the same watch at retail for thirty-five dollars. That thirty-five dollars included his cost, shipping, duties, and profit. He told me that his cost was a little over ten dollars per watch.

We did have our ups and downs in Russia. Lee made a trip to Russia and met with the people who were running our office. One night he was awakened to a noise in his hotel room. When he got up to investigate, he noticed that his jacket, which had been hanging on a coat hook, was missing.

In his jacket were his wallet, passport, and cash. Lee then alerted the police, who asked a lot of questions as to why he was in Russia, and who were the people we were working with? The police returned the next morning with his jacket and passport; however, the cash and his visa were gone. They also told Lee that the culprits were people from our office and that they "beat the hell" out of all of the occupants (that was Russian justice).

Since our office was in Vologda, Lee would have to go to Moscow and spend a day getting a new visa issued to him.

In the meantime, back in New Jersey, we were receiving large transfers of cash from Russia. The transfers would appear in our account. Our bookkeeper would call me frantically asking who was depositing these large sums of money. It would not be until some days later that they would inform us of what they wanted us to buy. Usually it was discounted footwear. This procedure went well until we made a fairly large shipment of shoes that the customers claimed did not fit properly. Our business with Russia slowed after that except that we were still shipping boots from Macedonia to various stores and wholesalers in Russia.

One day I received a call from one of our customers in the Midwest. They were wholesalers who were a division of a larger company. Steve was the son of the original owner, whom I knew and respected. He started to explain to me that their corporate headquarters wanted to start a countrywide chain of one-price shoe stores and that the principals were not only impressed with the way that we handled the wholesale account but had also heard about the tremendous job that Marquesa International was doing.

I, of course, was quite pleased to receive a series of complimentary phone calls, and of course I was curious as to what they wanted from us, as, although there were various hints, nothing concrete was ever explained to us.

Steve said that the president of the company would be flying into JFK en route to Europe and that if I could spend an hour with him at the TWA Club, he would explain in detail what he expected from our company.

The excitement was building, and I couldn't wait for the day of the meeting. At that time you didn't need a boarding pass to go to the airline clubs as long as you were a member, which I was.

The meeting went extremely well. After I answered detailed questions about myself and my companies, the president told me that because of our record, they would like us to represent their companies, including an old-time, branded shoe company that they had just bought. All the details would be finalized in their Midwest offices.

I was elated and couldn't wait to get back to my office to inform everyone of the exciting news. One of the problems was that our overseas offices were going at full capacity. Coincidently, we had been approached in Brazil by a large Brazilian department store chain that wanted to get involved with exporting to form an association. Since Steve's company only wanted to use us as their Brazilian agent, this seemed like a perfect situation.

When I arrived at the headquarters of Steve's company, where they offered to make us their Brazilian representative for their wholesale, retail, and branded companies. Further, we would be partners in the branded company.

But there were some catches, as it turned out. First, I was to make a nonrefundable deposit of $100,000 in order to enter the negotiations for the final contract. Second, we were to use their current Brazilian agent to manage the new office in Brazil. Third, I had to be willing to sign personally in the event that the new operation took any losses.

I spoke to my attorney, and he cautioned me that I could be liable if things went wrong. I signed the agreement anyway.

I was a damned fool!

On the positive side, the brand that we had was a famous name from the past, and the designer and sales manager were pleasant. I took a liking to Mike Maisel, the designer, right away, and I felt that I would have his full cooperation. Our first trade show under the newly formed company was very successful.

The Brazilian operation was more complicated. The new directors of the company insisted that since my existing staff was tied up with our ongoing operations, we use their person to run the new office. Roberto was his name, and he did not have the best reputation. As much as I liked our new designer, that was how much I took an immediate distrust to our Brazilian manager. The managers of the other Brazilian company that we were associated with also did not fully trust him. Ruben, who was in charge of our South American operation, also warned me to be very careful.

The orders that we received from the show had to be given to Roberto, who claimed that he had good factories to place them in. The first orders were placed, and since I was tied up in Chile and Europe, I did not get a chance to see them. When the orders were delivered, the quality of the shoes was terrible, and there was a poor-fit problem. For the most part, they were unsalable, and I came back from my trips to a real disaster.

I immediately fired Roberto, and at the same time I wanted to remake the shoes in our regular factories. Our partners were furious, and they placed the blame directly on Marquesa and me. The fact that they had forced Roberto on us apparently meant nothing to them. Their main thought and concern was developing a new nationwide retail chain. They took a very tough stand, and there was no reasoning with them. With astounding rapidity, they filed a $22 million lawsuit against us and the Brazilian partner company. We had to hire a top New York law firm to defend us. The costs were staggering. And because of the international nature of the suit, part of it was sent to The Hague Center for International Legal Arbitration.

The Brazilian partners settled. We fought on, however, as we and our attorneys felt that we were absolutely in the right. After some months, however, it was just taking too much of a toll, both financially and physically, from both Sylvia and me. We had already spent close to $400,000 in legal fees, and when I told the attorneys that we were running out of cash to pay any more of their fees, their response was that we had better settle since they would not continue without their high hourly charges.

So, much to our sorrow, we signed a settlement agreement and mutual release for a six-figure amount. Our period of rapid growth was now ended.

There were also jealousies in our Brazilian offices. That and the perception that we were now in a much weaker position would foreshadow future trouble. They made demands on us. Either we make them direct partners in Marquesa, or they wanted the ability to add their own customers. One day we learned that our largest Canadian customer had made a deal with our largest Brazilian office in order to work directly with them. This was not only treacherous on both the office's and the customer's sides, but the Canadian customer owed us substantial commissions on footwear previously shipped. They refused to pay us. We never got paid.

In fact, I sent Jerry, who did local collections for me, to Canada to collect the debt, but the owner refused. When Jerry called me from Toronto and asked what he should do, I said to him: "Come home, Jerry. We are not gangsters." I knew that my friend Jerry could get very tough, but I was not going to have anyone getting hurt on my conscience.

Although we still had our Russian business, losing our key office in Brazil was quite a blow to us. Our key customers were leaving us. We would have to build up a new Brazilian operation, and by this time many companies had fully established themselves. Uruguay was gone. Yugoslavia was gone. Spain and Italy had pretty much priced themselves out. Chile was still good, and the only thing that we did in the Orient was to ship uppers (the top part of the shoe, minus the sole) to domestic factories in Miami. The Miami factories then attached the soles and shipped them both domestically and to overseas markets.

Because of a change of management, our sales from the Orient to Argentina (Alpargatas) were slowing down drastically.

Since neither of my children was really interested in the shoe business, I saw little reason to keep the operation going. Barry would become a world-class head-shot photographer, and Lee would become an IT director for a medium-size accounting firm. Sylvia had opened a shoe store in Teaneck, New Jersey, but she was not getting along with her partner, so she gave that up. We had a small shoe store in Englewood, New Jersey, but that was more for getting ideas than doing a large volume. Most of the shoes and handbags that we marketed were presold, so there was not much inventory.

Therefore, we made the decision to liquidate what we had and close the business. We brought in a company that specialized in store liquidation sales. They did a fine job, and in less than a week, Marquesa International's small inventory was sold off in the store along with the furniture, computer, and equipment. Now I could go into retirement.

In less than two weeks, I was completely beside myself, and I had to find something to do.

MY NEW CAREERS

A fter two weeks of retirement, I was getting mighty itchy. Sitting around the house was not for me. Fortunately, I received a call from an old fraternity brother whom I hadn't spoken to in a number of years. Paul and his partner Jerry had formed a trading company. Paul was a nonpracticing attorney, and Jerry was a businessman who had lost money due to illness and a previous divorce. Supposedly he had extraordinary contacts with manufacturers and other businesses overseas.

They needed a financial partner, so I decided to meet with them. This was the start of what I characterize as "When smart people do stupid things." Their presentation seemed credible, so I agreed to invest $25,000 plus pick up part of the overseas travel expenses. We were trying to broker wheat, cement, sugar, and other commodities and an idiotic product called prime bank notes. I didn't realize it at the time, but prime bank notes are a scam and do not exist.

These ventures took us to Switzerland, Spain, France, Belgium, and England. I guess if we were going to get fleeced, at least we got to see some nice places in Europe. We were so sure that the tranches (deposits) were coming that we opened up accounts at the Swiss Bank Corporation.

Geneva, incidentally, was where I saw my first ATM. We were having coffee in front of the train station, and I saw this woman walk up to what looked like a mailbox and slide a card into it. The next thing I knew, Swiss francs seemed to come out of the wall. I thought she was playing a slot machine game on the street.

The next day at the bank, we went up to the top floor and met Otto Wyss, the vice-president of Swiss Bank, who was cordial and mentioned that he would see us in his private office on the first floor. As we were descending in the elevator, an argument broke out between another banker and a customer. Otto smiled and in an aside to me said that Swiss bankers were like kings in this country. He was right. When we left the building, we saw riot police jumping out of a van right in front of the building. They proceeded to beat the hell out of the guy who had been yelling in the elevator, as they dragged him into the van.

Our next stops were Marbella and Gibraltar, although no money had yet arrived. Although I was getting quite skeptical, my two partners were all fired up. They got a hold of a local real-estate agent, Joe Murphy. He was a very pleasant fellow. They thought that they would buy vacation spots, and I only went along to waste some time, as without any friends there, Sylvia was not going to spend her summers in Spain.

He took us first to a large apartment building, where on one of the upper floors an Iraqi wanted to sell his four-bedroom apartment. It was filthy, and the place reeked of a terrible odor. They asked him for something better. He had just the thing. It was a private villa on the beach. I was able to sneak in some pictures although I had been told that photos were not permitted. The grounds were large, and they had security, a guardhouse, servants' quarters, the works. It was gaudy inside, and when they asked for the price, without hesitation Joe said $46 million dollars.

I asked what the owner did. He had chemical plants in France and spent no more than six weeks in the house during the summer. Jerry and Paul said it was a bit expensive, so Joe took us next door.

That one was only $42 million. I was told that it was bought by the Frenchman next store for the prime minister of an African country (I forgot which country it was), and he only spent two weeks a year there with some of his wives.

All this travel turned out to be a complete waste. We never earned a penny. Besides losing the $25,000 investment, it cost me $30,000 in travel expenses. The closest that we came to selling anything was sugar out of Brazil. I gave a contract to the mill that I knew about, but they couldn't secure an export permit from the government.

My friend Lester was on the board of directors with me at the Footwear Distributors & Retailers of America. When I mentioned to him that I had closed my company, he suggested that I join his company as a consultant. His company had recently been appointed by a very large backpack company to be their agent for a line of Spanish hiking boots. Lester was also looking to sell chukka boots in both genders. He knew that I knew the important factories in all areas of Spain, including the Alicante and Zaragoza regions, and that I was friendly with their best local agents. We agreed to a figure of $1,500 per week plus expenses, and I would work out of his office in New Jersey.

Julia Moran was Spain's top agent and a good friend who had worked for me previously. Her office had been working with both Nine West and Donna Karan, but she was excited about both the project and the opportunity to work with me again. She said that when I came to Spain, she would personally devote her time to me and to the project. This made Lester quite happy, and he asked me to get started immediately.

I spent a few days in their office getting oriented, meeting with his staff, and preparing for my trip to Spain. Lester ran a very tight office, and he was a perfectionist, controlling every aspect of his business along with his wife. We had been out with both of them socially, including all of the FDRA and footwear conventions in various parts of the country.

They were known as a strange, secretive, and obsessive couple. One example was that before we went out to dinner at a convention, Lester inspected her clothes very carefully so that she would make a good impression on those we met. All the wives thought that this was quite humorous. On her part, she ran the office with a steel fist, making sure everything was in perfect order.

Upon leaving for Spain, I had the distinct feeling that for some reason there was some resentment of me as an interloper into their structured world. My interest was not in their petty politics, as I wanted to bring back a superb line of boots that would both give them access to a new country and fulfill their needs.

When I arrived in Alicante, Spain, I was given an unbelievably warm welcome not only from Julia but from the factory owners. The Spanish factory owners are an unusual group of people, as they are very loyal. Considering the fact that I hadn't been to Spain for over a year, I couldn't get over the graceful and cooperative treatment that I received. Even though the good factories were full and had commitments with well-known customers, they promised to execute my very difficult plan, and that was to have a line of perfect, extraordinary samples for me to take back in a little over a week.

They accomplished this, which meant that they worked long extra hours, sometimes working through their siesta, which is unheard of in Latin countries.

I was extremely pleased with the result and suggested to Julia that we celebrate at my favorite restaurant in the area. For many years, I was frequented to a restaurant called Pizzeria Romano. In all the years that I had gone there, I never had a pizza, but I would order their French onion soup. This was to me the best onion soup in the world, and it was a complete meal for me.

The owner was from France and had escaped to the Alicante area after trying to assassinate Charles de Gaulle during the

Algerian uprising. He was a big, red-faced guy, and whenever I arrived at his restaurant, he ran to the table and brought me my soup and a bottle of Rioja wine.

Julia laughed and said that the old restaurant was gone, but they had opened a new gourmet restaurant. When we arrived, I couldn't find onion soup on the menu, and I asked the waiter if they could prepare it for me. He shrugged and went to the back, where Jean, the owner, was peering down at me. Suddenly he flung off his white apron and came running to our table with tears streaming down his face. I stood up, and he was hugging and kissing me. Of course I got the onion soup—and a signed copy of the recipe book that he had just published.

Julia and the factories had done an incredible job, so I couldn't wait to get back to New Jersey in order to show the results of the trip. My enthusiasm was overflowing when I arrived at the office. I could see the look of satisfaction and surprise in everyone's eyes. Lester congratulated me on the samples, and he immediately sent a telex to Julia with the company's compliments.

There was a hitch, however, as the factories had quoted the costs in pesetas, which was the local Spanish currency at the time. Since I was one of the first to arrive in the office every morning, Lester instructed me to have a peseta quote ready for him when he arrived. The thought was that the company may buy futures in pesetas to protect against currency changes causing price increases.

When I arrived early the next day, I took the *Wall Street Journal* from Lester's desk in order to look up the currency rates, made a note of them, placed the note on Lester's desk, and replaced the paper where I had found it because I had been told that when his wife arrived, she would cut out articles that she felt were important to him, underlining in yellow marker the pertinent paragraphs.

Well, she arrived all right, and she started screaming: "Who wrinkled Lester's *Wall Street Journal*?"

I thought this was quite funny, and I suggested that maybe she should order an extra paper so that I could provide them with the information that they needed.

The next thing I knew, she was cutting up the paper, after which she pulled out a heating iron and proceeded to iron out the wrinkles.

I realized that with this kind of atmosphere and the air of coldness and jealousy, I was not going to stay long. My job had basically been done, so after getting more corrected samples and attending the upcoming shoe show, we mutually agreed for me to go my cheery way.

I knew that I couldn't sit around the house, so I perused the want ads in our local newspaper, the *Bergen Record*. Although I still had excellent contacts and friends in the shoe business, I wanted something different and less demanding and challenging. There was an interesting ad for a sales position, so I called the number listed and reached Joe Finga, who was the sales manager. After a brief conversation, he said that I would fit and that he wanted to meet with me.

When I arrived at the hotel at the appointed time, I was immediately skeptical, as there were about twelve people in a meeting room, and I wasn't in the mood for a group interview.

Joe was a super salesperson, and he persuaded me to hear him out. His presentation was exceptional, as he made it sound as if the company were almost giving away money. Of course it wasn't. The company was called Dining à la Card Division of Signature Group, which was affiliated with Montgomery Ward. I liked the fact that it was connected to Montgomery Ward, where I knew many of the top executives. Their concept was simple in that Dining à la Card would advance funds to a restaurant, and when the DALC members paid with their card, deductions would be made in order to pay off the advance, plus DALC's profit. This was an easy sale because nonchain restaurants were invariably short of funds.

After Joe's presentation, he asked me what I thought of it. My answer was that it was fine, but I thought that he was full of crap. This cracked him up. The job covered two adjacent counties in New Jersey, Bergen and Passaic, so my question was, How would there be enough restaurants to sell with twelve people covering two counties?

His laughing response was that within two months, there would only be two of us left.

As I mentioned, this was an easy sale, and I was fast becoming one of their top sales people. I got along extremely well with Joe, although he had a crazy side with a very bad temper, especially with customers, because in his mind he was doing them a big favor.

The company was throwing money around like crazy, as they were interested in growth. Profits would come later. Once Joe had a $50,000 check for a customer and made an appointment with the owner in Miami. The owner arrived late and started to question Joe about the program. Joe pulled out the check and said, "You see this check for fifty grand? Look at it closely because you can go screw yourself." Joe proceeded to rip up the check in small pieces and stormed out of the restaurant.

Before long I was offered a promotion to an area manager. They gave me a choice of areas, and since we had a winter condo in South Florida and since we also wanted to sell our house in New Jersey, we opted for the South Florida area.

South Florida became the top area in the country, and I was having a ball. I reported to Bob Castranova, whom I got along with famously (undoubted our sales figures helped).

Although I was conservative with my expense account, Bob wasn't. He would come to town and take my entire crew out to the finest restaurant. One evening he took us all out to a new steakhouse in Boca Raton called New York Prime. Besides the T-bone steaks, he ordered $600 bottles of wine. At the end of the dinner, he ordered Louis XIV Cognac at $125 a shot (I still have the Baccarat Crystal bottle, as you get to keep it if you finish the bottle). Then, as we were leaving, he presented me with a $700.00 Atlas briefcase as a gift (I still have it, but it is pretty beaten up).

As we were departing for the evening, Bob mentioned to me that DALC was going to collaborate on a big promotion with TWA airlines. TWA was headquartered in Miami, and they wanted us to sign up as many restaurants as possible in a short period of time. I would be in charge of a crew that would be sent from different parts of the country.

When they arrived, I gave them an orientation and detailed the best way to accomplish our goal. Patrick Lu was from Phoenix. He was a crackerjack salesperson who spoke Spanish, Japanese, Mandarin, Korean, and some Portuguese. Patrick assured me that he would sign up more restaurants than the rest of the crew together.

I laughed and I said to Patrick, "Go to it."

I was in contact with the crew on a daily basis, and I was also doing my part on the sales end. Patrick was on the phone to inform me every time he made a sale (and that was four or five times a day). That was incredible, and on the third day I told him we would go out together because I wanted to learn his technique.

The next morning, right after breakfast, we started making our way down South Beach. I had mentioned to everyone that TWA wanted us to sign up better restaurants when possible. Patrick called me "boss" (and does so to this day), and he said, "Whatever you say, boss."

As we were meeting with the owner of the restaurant, Patrick pulled out a card and announced that he was vice-president of TWA and that he would see to it that the restaurant would be featured in the TWA onboard magazine. The restaurant owner was filling out the paperwork as the blood drained from my face.

As soon as we got outside the restaurant, I asked Patrick to show me one of the cards that he was giving out. I blinked when I saw the TWA Airline logo, and in the lower left hand corner of the card: Patrick Lu, Vice-President.

"Are you crazy?" I screamed at him.

He laughed and said: "OK, boss, I'll stop using the card, but I have already sold fifteen restaurants."

Back at headquarters in Schaumburg, Illinois, they were ecstatic over the fact that we had made so many sales so fast.

All good things must come to an end, however. Not long after the Miami adventure, I received a call from Les Falk, who was the president of DALC. It seemed that the company was being sold to a company called Transmedia, which was headquartered in Miami. He said on the phone that I would have two choices: I could either go with Transmedia, or I could go with a new company called Advanceme. Les would be joining Advanceme as a consultant and temporary president until they got themselves fully established.

My response was that I would meet with the Transmedia people in Miami, after which I would make my decision. They had been our direct competitors, so I was quite familiar with them. I was not particularly enamored with them or the way they operated.

After meeting with their executives in Miami, I was even less impressed with them, so I decided to visit the Advanceme Corporation, which was headquartered in Kennesaw, Georgia. Les was already there. When I arrived at their offices, he introduced me to John Konop, who was the national sales manager. John was a bright, talkative character, and we hit it off immediately. John said that I could have virtually any area that I wanted. My reply was that since I lived in Florida and had my children in New Jersey, I would like to have both the Southeast and the Northeast areas.

I was amazed that he readily agreed—except that they would not give me New York City.

Advanceme marketed a unique product in that they would advance funds to businesses who took credit cards, based on their past credit-card history. The customer would then pay this back whenever he or she charged something. It was an expensive way to fund a business, but it was quick, and the businesses often could not borrow from the banks. It worked out as long as their profit margin was sufficient.

Like DALC, the Advanceme sale was an easy one to make. It was simple for me to bring the team that I had at DALC along with me to the new company. Whereas before we had sold only to restaurants and entertainment facilities, we were now able to sell to anyone who took credit cards as a form of payment. Between the two companies, I had personally put on hundreds of accounts, but now my responsibility was strictly training and sales supervision. This was lots of fun, and it was gratifying that some of my unusual techniques were used throughout both companies. (Since this is not a sales training manual per se, I won't go into detail here.)

Domestic travel was a lot easier than making those long overseas trips. In addition to our training sessions, we would attend various trade shows, with my favorite being the restaurant shows. Besides meeting restaurant owners who needed money, we sampled plenty of good food.

One day during the food show in Orlando, I spotted a delicious-looking loaf of French bread. As I was tearing off a piece of the bread, I spotted a woman who was apparently the owner of the stand talking to one of her customers in the aisle. I could see right away that there was something wrong. There was! I had torn off a piece of their display. I couldn't get back to our booth fast enough. Syl knew by the look on my face that something was horribly wrong. We must have laughed for twenty minutes after I told her what had happened. Of course, I never went near the bakery aisle again for the duration of the show.

It did not take long until I was promoted to a regional vice-president. There were two other regional VPs, and although we were very competitive, we became close and firm friends. The company was growing extremely fast, and although we had issues with top management at times, we felt that we could overcome them.

John Konop had a brilliant mind. While John was on our training conference calls, he couldn't shut up, and at times he tended to annoy some of his executives. I would try to interrupt with some humor, including blowing a loud train whistle; however, he just kept talking.

One early spring day he called me to take a trip with him to Cleveland, Ohio, to meet an important group in order to persuade them to join our sales force. When we met at the airport, I noticed that John was in his typical outfit: one blue and one brown sock, dirty long-sleeve shirt, and no jacket. There was one thing about John, and that was he was rarely insulted by anything that you said to him. I told him that there was no way he would impress anyone with the outfit that he was wearing.

John laughed and agreed and said it would be up to me to make him presentable. We rented a car and found Kohl's Department Store on the way to the location where we were headed. His pants were fine, so I got him a matching pair of socks, a nice shirt, and a fitting jacket. Our trip was successful, and we had dinner in downtown Cleveland, overlooking Lake Erie, with John's father, who was an attorney in town.

Advanceme had a satellite office on Route 4 in northern New Jersey. The office was on the top floor, partially overlooking New York City, and on an early fall day, I decided to have a sales training meeting there with a group of key salespeople from the Northeast. The meeting was scheduled for September 11, 2001, at 9:30 a.m. I had flown in from Florida the night before. I remember that it was a bumpy ride, and the pilot had a little trouble landing, hitting the tarmac with a thud. The next morning I arrived in the office around 8:00 a.m., and before long, the salespeople started to arrive. Fran and, of course, Patrick Lu were always early.

We were setting up the meeting room, and a new fellow who was driving in from Washington, DC, started to tell us that he saw a plane hit a building in Manhattan. I shook my head and gave Patrick a look as if to ask, "Where do we get these crazies from?"

At that moment, our comptroller came running in and announced that he just heard on the radio that a second plane had hit the Twin Towers. We were all completely stunned. I didn't know what to do except to cancel the meeting and tell everyone to go home in case there were further attacks. Patrick stayed by my side, in too much shock to speak many words.

Nobody really knew when flights would commence, as civilian flights had been suspended for few days. I was able to book a seat, and I returned on one of the first flights out of Newark. That was on the very next Saturday after the attack. Besides the crew, there were only four other passengers on the flight. I felt perfectly safe, but I was delighted to get back to my wife and my home.

STERLING FUNDING

S teve Norell had a credit-card ISO (Independent Sales Organization) out of Martin County, Florida. Along with setting
up merchant processing for his clients, he also gave us funding
deals at Advanceme. Steve was an excellent salesperson, and he
would travel anywhere, at any time, to meet with a merchant and
potential customer. In addition, he prided himself on servicing
his accounts. He could be loquacious and brash, but he knew
how to get things done. We developed a mutual respect for each
other, and we became quite friendly.

One day in the spring of 2005, I received a call from Steve
inviting to me to have lunch with him because he had something
serious to discuss with me. I figured that he wanted advice about
something pertaining to his company; therefore, I confirmed
the date the same week.

Our lunches usually consisted of stories, gossip, and business
tactics. This time, however, he mentioned that the credit card
company that he was doing business with was looking to go into
the merchant cash-advance business. They had heard about me,
and since Steve said that I was the best around, they wanted very
much to meet with me.

I explained to Steve that I had a very secure position with Advanceme, but we both agreed that there would be no harm in meeting the owner of the company, which was headquartered in Tampa, Florida. Sterling Payment Technologies was a successful credit-card processing company, with agents all over the United States. At its head was Paul Hunter. Paul was a country boy who had grown up on a farm in Plains, Georgia. After Paul received his master's degree, he became a stockbroker for Smith Barney. Like many of us, he was hit with the entrepreneurship bug and opened up a very successful chain of full-service car washes in Tampa. While running the car washes, he became familiar with and interested in the credit-card processing business, and he opened up Sterling in the late 1990s.

It was a quick flight from West Palm Beach Airport to Tampa, where I was picked up and driven to their headquarters on Westshore Boulevard. Both airports, incidentally, are a pleasure to fly in and out of.

Paul, who is tall, well dressed, and distinguished looking, was waiting for me. He immediately got up and gave me a welcoming smile and proceeded to give me a tour of the entire office complex. After the tour, he had me sit with some of his board members and top executives, who asked for some insight on how the cash advance business worked.

I then sat again with Paul, who explained that he wanted to start a merchant cash-advance business and that he felt that I would be the person to do this and make it a successful venture.

I told him that Advanceme was growing rapidly and that I had a bright future with them.

"What will it take to get you to come onboard?" he asked.

Since I had already taken a liking to him, I felt that the best thing was to be diplomatic and throw out terms and an amount that he couldn't accept. So without hesitation, I said that my starting salary would have to be $200,000 per year plus an automobile of my choice, plus all benefits including 401(k), profit sharing, and an acceptable health plan, along with a severance package.

Paul swallowed hard and said that they would need a few days for him to present it to his board, after which they would make up their minds.

I was relieved when I left their office, and in my mind I didn't think that there was any way that they were going to accept it because another thing that I had told them was that I couldn't take any customers or employees with me who were already with Advanceme. I figured that by the end of the week, I would receive a call from Paul with an offer that I could gracefully turn down.

The very next day, after I had returned from Tampa, Paul called and said that all of my terms were accepted, and they were anxious for me to start as the executive vice-president of Sterling Funding.

Sylvia couldn't believe it. The package was so attractive that there was no way I couldn't accept it. I immediately called Tom Burnside, the president of Advanceme, to inform him. Up until this point, we had been quite friendly with each other, but when I told him that I was going with a new company called Sterling Funding, he became decidedly unfriendly. In the next few weeks, Advanceme would try to accuse me of giving business to a company that in fact I had never even heard of and also of taking their existing systems.

I had given Sterling permission to check me out completely, and when I arrived in Tampa, I met with John H, who had been hired as the operations manager (at a much lower salary). We went together to take our required drug test, which we both passed.

John had a quick mind, took a lot of notes, and appeared methodical and somewhat distant. I explained to him that we would have to come up with our own forms and systems since I had agreed not to use any of the Advanceme systems. I also said that we would have to move fast, as I wanted to have business coming in immediately. Since in this type of business much of the selling was done by independent contractors, it was perfectly OK for us to contact and use nonemployees I had worked with previously.

Without exception, everyone I spoke to was ready to start sending us business. The deals started to come in on provisional forms and contracts that I had to set up until John could prepare those that he wanted to use. Frankly I was a little frustrated at the pace that he worked at, but I kept my focus on being in business. Eventually he got the forms and systems in place.

Another great perk was that I did most of my work from my home office on the east coast of Florida, coming to Tampa no more than two days each week. Paul was a licensed pilot, and on occasion he would have the company pilot fly me on the company plane or even pilot the plane himself.

He was a real Southern gentleman. Once we were having a fishing party for our better sales performers in the Bahamas, and Sylvia drove me to Lantana Airport, where Paul was waiting. He grabbed my bags and gave Sylvia a tour of the plane, giving her comfort that it was perfectly safe.

I didn't realize it at the time, but John was apparently jealous of my position and my salary. Even though we were adding ICs (independent contractors), we did full background checks on them. We had some key producers with whom John found had some moral or credit issues that he questioned. In hindsight, I should have dug much deeper into John's criticisms. During this period, I didn't really delve into the issues as much as I should have, and I reluctantly agreed with John that we had to let them go.

John would take copious notes at meetings or whenever we sat together and discussed policy or sales strategy. After a while, I suspected that he had built up a more serious resentment to me than I had previously suspected, especially after I squelched the idea of his to hire a sales manager who had no sales experience.

Worse, he was in charge of collections, and it turned out that during the downturn in the economy, starting in 2007, he was woefully neglectful in this function, causing us some big losses. Paul let him go when he discovered this.

Up until this point, we were doing fine. The independent contractors I brought on were producing, but those from the credit-card sales side were not. Even with my training, the sales techniques in each of the two divisions were entirely different.

Paul did his best to incentivize everyone with fun meetings, parties, cruises, and trips. Besides the company plane, Paul had a good-size fishing boat. In the summer of 2007, we flew in to Marsh Harbour Airport in the Bahamas, where Paul picked us up in his boat and took us to the large beach house that he had rented in Hope Town.

I learned to scuba dive, but I hated it, as I was scared to death. Besides drinking and eating (we had a Brazilian chef who met us dockside every afternoon when we returned from fishing with large glasses of Sex on the Beach), the fishing was great. I caught the most fish, including a near-record yellow-mouth grouper, which I estimated to be over eight pounds (the record for grouper is thirteen pounds).

Our last big outing was in the summer of 2008. Paul had rented a cottage ranch in the woods outside of Tampa, almost five miles of dirt road from the main highway. Here again it was carousing, eating, and drinking. The other diversions were racing around the fields on four-wheelers and target practice. I preferred the target practice, which I was more proficient at, especially using the Colt AR-15.

The bright, fun summer of 2008 then turned into the panic and stock market crash of September of that year. The era of subprime loans, cheap money, low interest rates, and global poisoned debt was suddenly having its effect. The signs of trouble had been there in 2007, when the value of homes started to fall drastically.

We at Sterling hadn't yet recovered from the losses that we took in 2007, and we were now getting hit with drastic punches to the gut. Our two regional managers had already left. My friend Bill Eng was not comfortable in a corporate environment, so he went back on his own, where he was always comfortable. Joe Pino had let his success go to his head and was demanding a dramatic increase in pay. We did not accede to his ultimatum, and we let him go.

Even with the two of them no longer with us and other cost savings being made, I realized that my staying on would only burden the company more. Paul was very understanding, and he kept his word and gave me my full severance pay. It would turn out to be the worst recession the world had seen since the Great Depression of the 1930s. The recovery was slow in coming, and the traditional big bounce back just did not happen.

COMMERCIAL LOAN BROKER

I love the kids. I love the grandkids. I enjoy my friends. I enjoy my wife (I have to say this because she is going to read the book). I'll play an occasional round of golf, although my complete lack of patience makes me a lousy player, and playing for four hours bores me to distraction. The hassle and cost of travel, except to some of our favorite spots, can only be an occasional thing. Reading about history and politics and blogging on the Internet can occupy only so much of a given day.

I therefore had to do something to occupy my mind. Since I did not want to get involved with something that would compete with my old company, I called one of my old reps from Birmingham, Alabama. We were friends, and although I appreciated his ex-military background and his Christian ethics, he was always a bit of a kvetch. Because he was an ex-banker and worked with commercial loans besides the cash advances that he did when he worked for me, I decided to reach out to him and see what I could learn about acting as a business loan broker.

Howard spent a lot of time detailing and explaining the procedures, forms, and pitfalls, both from the borrower's and the lender's side. He explained that for every fifteen applications that you receive, you will be lucky to have one come to fruition and end up being funded. Banks and lenders were very much risk adverse, especially during the recession that we were currently going through. Many were low on funds and were having financial problems of their own, and those that were lending wanted to take the cherry on top of the sundae. The borrowers oftentimes were overly optimistic as to their assets and the value of their businesses. Others tried to hide their shortcomings, lied on the application, or just didn't divulge negative information. This was discovered in the due diligence process that the lender performed, but in the meantime, effort and credibility suffered.

We decided that I would furnish the potential borrowers, and Howard would place the deals with a lender and after the funding, we would split the fees fifty-fifty. Our fees would vary, but they could range from one to three percent of the loan. I had previously set up my office in one of our upstairs bedrooms. Since there was about 150 square feet of space, there was ample room for desks, files, phones, a copy machine, a fax machine, and computers.

I then resurrected my old company name, Marquesa, and obtained an 800 number, and I was ready to go. The next step was to contact my old independent reps, most of whom were ready to join me in the new venture.

To start with, at least most of the deals would go through Howard, which meant a three-way split in the fees that we received. Howard was being very helpful and open about teaching me the lending process, and I had confidence in his ability and honesty, enabling me to put his quirky nature aside. We both realized that these were difficult times for small-business owners, so finding both qualified borrowers and lenders who were willing to lend would be a tough task.

It was therefore gratifying to receive a call from Howard telling me that he now had access to a new restaurant, hotel, and health-care TARP plan, supposedly backed by the government. In order to receive a ten-year, 4.75 percent loan, the requirements were as follows:

A. The borrower must have 10 percent to put down.

B. With the loan the borrower must add twelve new employees or more.

C. The minimum loan would be $500,000.

D. The owner must have a minimum average FICO score of 675.

This all sounded very exciting, so I called an associate, Ed Connor from Sterling, who was an independent contractor with some great contacts with restaurants and franchisees. He loved the idea, and before long, we had over forty franchisees. He had some of the best up-and-coming franchisers that they were looking to expand on. In addition, my other reps were bringing in these so-called TARP deals. Howard claimed that he had a funder for these but that he would have to call each one in order to make sure that they were truly qualified for the program. This seemed to make sense, and in our minds we were all calculating the commissions that we would be earning.

We were starting to sense a problem, however. I kept asking Howard for updates, and all l received were vague answers. My reps and their customers were bombarding me for answers, and I finally got Howard to admit that he hadn't been completely forthright with us. Not only that, but it turned out that he had been quite rude in some of his conversations with the customers. If their English wasn't letter perfect, he became insulting and demanded that they learn better English. This, of course, embarrassed and infuriated me.

I then found out that his so-called lender was not a lender at all but another broker. This was also shocking and mortifying. We all lost time (over three months), effort, and reputation with our customers. Many of my reps were willing to stay with me, and I was determined to make the commercial lending brokerage business a success. I seemed to be learning it the hard way. Experience teaches.

One day I received a call from one of my newer reps. He said that he had contact with a structured-finance hedge fund. They were looking for new projects, and if the company was solid and willing to put up a 5 percent capital contribution, their project could be funded within sixty days of the receipt of all the necessary documentation.

This sounded good, but before we proceeded, I wanted to investigate the principals, check out their website, speak with someone whose project had been funded, and send my man Brian, who operated out of Atlanta, to their main office. They also had a small office in Manhattan.

Brian visited the Atlanta office. Their name, Alliance, was on the door of a two-thousand-foot office with inner offices and people running around. Steve, the principal, was in Europe, but two of his associates were there. Jim and Chris were helpful in answering questions, and they stated that they were excited about the idea of working with us. Their website looked very impressive, and when Brian gave me his findings, I called both Jim and Chris. Chris was in the construction business, and he said that Alliance had funded his latest project, which included a golf course, and that Steve had asked him to come to help with the administrative functions.

All seemed fine, so I put the information into the monthly bulletin that I sent both for education and encouragement. The responses came quickly. Most of them were known franchises with owners who were looking to expand. A few of them did their own checking on Alliance and apparently were satisfied that they were legitimate.

Term sheets were sent out, funding agreements were signed, and the 5 percent deposits were made to Alliance. Now all we had to do was to wait for the borrowers to receive their funds, and our fees would be sent to us forthwith.

Nothing was arriving, however. Frantic calls were being made. Steve was overseas, supposedly rounding up the funds. Jim and Chris were desperately trying to get answers. We were told that everything was going to be straightened out, and then Jim called, saying the money had been transferred from a bank in Germany.

Still nothing arrived. We were receiving and making constant calls. We were then told that the bank had fouled up. They even gave us CUSIP wire numbers, and we still received no money.

This made no sense, and I realized that Steve was stalling for time and that nothing was going to happen. Panic calls, both incoming and outgoing, were constantly being made. A total of almost $300,000 in deposits was going to be lost. Ironically, we were able to recover $35,000 for one of the borrowers. He was desperate and said that he was going bankrupt and his wife was going to leave him. Luckily he got his money back, yet he was the only one who tried to hold us responsible for the fiasco.

Steve was no longer answering calls or messages. He was arrested at some point trying to enter the Atlanta airport from overseas, and because he couldn't post bond, he spent many months in jail. Jim told me recently that at some point some fool put up a $100,000 cash bond until his trial came up. The word is that he never showed up for trial and that there is a bench warrant out for his arrest.

When I questioned Jim about how he was getting paid, he said that he was not going to get paid until the deals were funded, so he was also out in the freezing weather. When I questioned Chris about how he was funded, his answer was that he was basically funded in both company stock and future commissions and that he would now lose his project and go broke. This was now the second blow to my credibility. Ed Connor, my vice-president of franchising, had now been burned twice.

We remain friends to this day, but naturally he does not send me any more business. Other reps also lost confidence in the company and in me. Sylvia was urging me to retire. We were already spending four months up north with our children and grandchildren. I am just not the type who gives up because of adversity, and I was determined that I could make a go at obtaining loans for small- and medium-size businesses and reclaim my reputation.

First, however, we decided to go to the one country that in all my travels I hadn't been to but always longed to go to, and that country was Israel.

Our Dream Trip

The trip to Israel was truly amazing. We landed in Tel-Aviv after a plane ride that was too long due to some missed connections. I felt a little ashamed that it had taken so long to make the trip, especially having visited some Arab lands in the past.

It is a sacred land, with Jerusalem a focal point whether you are Jewish, Christian, or Muslim. To set foot on the soil where David defeated Goliath, Saul was killed by the Philistines (after the Bar Kokhba revolt, the Romans gave the area the name Palestine in retribution and to wipe away any Jewish presence). Seeing the Valley of the "Dry Bones" that is written about in Ezekiel 37 is truly inspiring. We stood overlooking Mount Nebo where Moses is buried but hidden from view. The Israelites intoned that we should worship G-d and not a man. The spot under the Southern Temple Wall (tunnel excavation) near where Abraham was going to sacrifice Isaac, and most amazingly, not far from the location where it was said that G-d created humankind, and the spot where Jesus was baptized, tried, etc., filled me with awe.

We toured the Tel-Aviv neighborhoods and had dinner in an excellent fish restaurant at the Tel Aviv port overlooking the Mediterranean (which locals call the ocean). This is a relatively rich cultural center. Because Israel has an influx of so many immigrants (many now coming from Sudan and other oppressed areas), there are many, many poor. Charities raising money for food are everywhere.

The next day, we went to Rothschild Boulevard, Rabin Square (where Yitzhak Rabin was shot), Neve Tzedek (built in 1909), Tel Aviv University, and other interesting sites. Then on to eight-thousand-year-old Old Jaffa (clock tower, Saint Peter's Church), and then back to the Hilton for another restful evening.

We woke up early and drove north along the Western Coastal (Mediterranean) Road to Caesarea, which was the Roman regional capital. The Crusaders' city has been excavated, revealing an aqueduct, an amphitheater, and a horse-race track.

There was little privacy in those days, and even Pilate's stone bathrooms were open and outdoors. The amount of work in the building and the engineering of the aqueducts was and is astounding. Going east is one of the first Jewish settlements created by Baron Rothschild's vision. Now it is the Napa Valley of Israel. We toured a winery (I wasn't driving); had a light Mediterranean lunch (homemade bread); and tasted some good wine, fresh cheese, and fresh vegetables at the Amphorae Winery. The excellent wine was not exportable because of the special techniques the owner used to make the wines, including hand sorting of the grapes on tables.

From there we went to the Atlit Illegal Immigration Camp. The British had virtually stopped any immigration, and when they caught Jews arriving after being in Nazi concentration camps, they were again stripped and deloused. (Can you imagine the utter fear of going through the trauma of being imprisoned again?)

Then we went north to Haifa, which is Israel's third-largest city. It is 90 percent Jewish and 10 percent Arab, and the relations between them are very good. Mount Carmel goes back to biblical times (fourteenth century BCE). Mount Carmel is home to the beautiful Hanging Gardens, the spectacular World Baha'i Center (Baha'is accept all religions), and UNESCO's World Heritage site. The University of Haifa and the world-famous Teknion are located there.

We drove east to the Tiberius and Sea of Galilee area. (Rosh Pina). Wherever we drove, we saw very dry land and the use of excellent Israeli agriculture techniques. There were lush vegetables everywhere.

We then visited the Donna Gracia Museum. Donna Gracia Mendez Nassi was a Marrano whose story is both spectacular and incredible. She lived in the sixteenth century. She built synagogues and libraries, and resettled hundreds of Jews, returning them to their faith. After visiting a number of holy Jewish and Christian sites, we spent two nights at a lovely spa, where we had two excellent meals (I'm going to run out of superlatives). The next day we went to the Golan Heights. Strategically, the Israelis would be nuts to give this up. We went through the bunkers of a former Syrian base where some very harsh battles were fought in the 1967 war. Syrian troops were chained to the wall openings so that they could not run from the Israelis.

On to the "Valley of the Tears and the Oz 77 Memorial. This is where the Seventy-Seventh Brigade made a miraculous stand during the '73 Yom Kippur War, with many on both sides giving their lives. The Israeli tanks were greatly outnumbered by the Syrian tanks, which the Russians had secretly equipped with infra ray sights, which the Israelis did not have. The Syrians were defeated, and they retreated.

We then went back to the hotel for a spa treatment.

We left early in the morning for Beit She'an (fourth century BCE), the home of many kibbutzim and a large archeological park with excavations from the Roman and Byzantine eras. This was an important caravan stop. The excavations have uncovered a series of Egyptian temples. Later it became a Canaanite city, and in the time of Solomon, an Israelite city.

Earthquakes destroyed much of this area in the eighth century. Among the remains still being uncovered are a huge Byzantine bathhouse, a Roman temple, colonnaded streets, and a Roman theatre that had a stone stage and seated eight thousand people. Nearby Mount Gilboa (Gan HaShlosha) is where King Saul fell to the Philistines. He fell on his sword and then was beheaded along with his two sons. The heads were displayed for all to see.

This is a beautiful area with hot springs, a waterfall (very few in Israel), and ibex roaming. Beit Alpha has Beit Alpha Synagogue National Park, with its ancient mosaic floor. This mosaic has the twelve signs of the zodiac, which is quite unusual. Next to kibbutz Nir David is a replica of the first stockade and tower settlement, which was built in December 1936 in order to defend against marauding Arabs.

The next stop was Jerusalem. We checked in at the King David Hotel, which, although in "Old Jerusalem", is just a few blocks from the new Mamilla Outdoor Pedestrian Mall (fine shopping), overlooking the Old City and the Jaffa Gate. The King David was built in 1931 and it has quite a history. After a bombing attempt was foiled when the budding Israeli army (Haganah) warned the British that the Irgun was going to attack the hotel, the Irgun succeeded (July 1946) on their next attempt. Much went awry, as the detonations were supposed to be under where the British officers were dining, and a premature explosion killed ninety-one people. It wasn't long after that the English felt that they had had enough of Palestine and, when leaving, clearly favored the Arabs.

The hotel has hosted royalty, presidents, and many famous guests and celebrities. The staff is mixed, including Jews, Arabs, Muslims, Orthodox, and Christians. They are proud that in all of the years of their existence, they had never had an incident among the employees (they will often visit one another's homes and attend their celebrations).

When King Hussein and his entourage came to sign the peace treaty with Israel, it happened to be during Passover. The first serving was gefilte fish, and the Jordanians were so shocked by the taste that that they spit it out. "How can anyone eat cold fish?" they cried.

It must have gotten better, as on our third night at the hotel, we had the Sabbath dinner. I tasted the gefilte fish, and it was not bad.

Of course, their breakfasts, which the Israelis specialize in, were spectacular. I filled up on red and black caviar, all flavors of halvah, goat cheeses, hummus, grape leaves, and olives.

The first thing that struck me when I went to the four quarters of the Old City—Christian, Orthodox, Jewish, and Arab—was the answers I received when I asked four Palestinian merchants their frank opinions about living in Israel. Three of them had family in the territories and wished that their families were united. They felt that the Israelis made it too difficult to enter Jerusalem. When I mentioned bombings and attacks, they just shrugged. The fourth had been there from time immemorial and had been friendly with his Jewish neighbors before and after 1948 (he stayed during the '48 war). Surprising were their unanimous comments that they would prefer to live under Israeli rule. They were relatively prosperous. Their families had jobs, good educations, and medical services. They were Israeli citizens who could and did vote. They did not trust the Palestinian leaders, who, they felt, were entirely corrupt and dangerous.

The Western Wall is the only portion of the supporting wall of the Temple Mount that remained intact after the destruction of the Second Temple (70 AD). In the sixteenth century, the sultan Suleiman recovered the wall from underneath a dung heap and granted permission to the Jews to pray there. There are no Muslim sources, however, that show any interest in the Western Wall.

In the nineteenth century, the English uncovered prayer areas, Robinson's Arch, and an ancient gate, and other excavations were to follow up until today. There were many controversies regarding the wall that make interesting reading, including the British prohibition regarding the blowing of the shofar on Yom

Kippur and the prohibition after May 1948 of even looking at the wall. After nineteen years, the wall was liberated on the third day of the Six-Day war.

The lower square near the wall was where Sylvia and I separated, and we went to the men's and women's sections and placed our prayer slips in the wall.

We went to the Southern Temple Mount, where the excavations were started in 1968 and have continued to this day. A first-century street was uncovered in the mid-1990s, and you can see the stones that were pushed down by the Romans.

This was where the priests signaled the start of the Sabbath and the shofar was blown. It is awesome to stand in front of the staircase leading to the Temple Mount. The gates provided access through subterranean passageways.

Throughout our tour, we took pictures of numerous *mikvahs*, which are ritual baths. These are mandated before one enters a holy site because of purity laws (I don't think that they had hot showers and soap in those days).

In 19 BCE, King Herod doubled the area of the Temple Mount and installed four retaining walls, which remained standing after the Roman destruction in 70 AD.

Next, we went into the Western Wall tunnels, which have been recently opened to the public, and it was my most memorable experience. You are standing close (which is behind the wall and of course can't be seen) to the Holy of Holies, which is under the Dome of the Rock. You are not only close to the spot where Abraham was going to sacrifice Isaac but close to the areas when G-d created humankind. I think that anyone not affected by this would have to be made of stone itself.

This is also very close to the "Cave", which is a small synagogue. We passed the Struthion Pool, a water channel (the source of which is unknown) that goes back as far as the Maccabees (167 BCE). Our guide showed us the largest stone in the wall, which the Romans could not destroy: forty-five by eleven by fifteen feet and weighing over five hundred tons (how did they set that in the wall?). The engineering feat in the construction of the wall and the temple was amazing, and if you are interested in engineering, you should look it up in records or books.

We next went to lunch at the Mahane Yehuda Market. They had every kind of large fresh fruit, vegetable, kosher meat, spice, olive, cheese, and halvah imaginable. We loved the lunch. All the dishes were homemade from scratch, including the soup, *shashlik*, and salads. The eating tent was in a small corner of the market, owned by an older, very charming, and gracious couple.

Our next stop was Ammunition Hill. During the 1967 war, this was held by the Jordanians. The Israelis had to forgo an air attack, as they were concerned about civilian casualties (unfortunately, that was and is not the thinking of their enemies). Their intelligence was faulty, however, and the paratroopers thought that it was defended by a single platoon. The Israelis were greatly outnumbered and were ambushed in a fierce battle, but they finally took over the bunkers by unbelievable heroism.

We watched the film and saw the Jewish Nation Fund's Wall of Honor, and I was given the Paratrooper's Pin (even though I don't like jumping out of planes).

We then moved on to a JNF (Jewish National Fund, who arranged our trip) reforestation project, where I planted some trees. We couldn't find any of the trees that we had planted remotely throughout the years, as they didn't put our names on them, but I am sure that some of them have grown quite tall by now.

During breakfast at the King David, we met this lovely couple. She was from Sweden and he from South Africa. Mrs. Birgitta Yavari-Ilan is a well-known artist and poet in Israel (www.birgittayavariilan.wordpress.com). They invited us to join them for dinner with their friends, as they lived close to the hotel by the famous windmill (the Jaffa Gate is where the original city was). We were reluctant, but they insisted. So we decided to go to their home after we finished our day.

After enjoying the delicious buffet with the help of Sammy, our friendly Arab waiter, we proceeded to Yad Vashem Holocaust Museum & Memorial. We have been to many of the Holocaust memorials; the two most stunning to me were the one in Washington DC and the Anne Frank Museum. In the former, you are overwhelmed as you stare in disbelief at the absolute horror and inhumanity that took place, and the latter shows the simple beauty and humanness of a child and family. Hannah Arendt called it the "banality of evil." I for one heartily disagree. There is nothing banal about absolute evil, and ignorance is certainly no excuse.

Going through this museum, I was reminded again of the many books, films, and lectures that I had studied on this subject. You say to yourself, How in the world is it possible that there are some (maybe many) who don't want to believe that this scar on humanity happened? Then one realizes that those with hate in their hearts or closed or ignorant minds will never ever be convinced. For if they were to be convinced, their evil agenda would fail.

Among many other injustices, massacres, and tyrannical actions throughout the ages—and there were and are many—this was unique. A twisted mind took hold of a bad economic system and used his subjects in a devilish plan to wipe every trace of a people—only because, as Hitler sneeringly said, they were the "people of the book." This insane ideology became so fierce that the proponents were willing to lose their country and the war in order to fulfill their monstrous mission.

Those who say we should forget must understand that if this tragedy is forgotten, it will be repeated, perhaps in another place and another time. So it was refreshing to see so many young people there, including new military recruits, who are mandated to attend the museum. Of course, you leave stunned, but you're hopeful that at least some may learn a lesson.

We next passed by the Knesset, but it was closed because of the Israeli Memorial Day holiday (and Independence Day was coming up). The shofar blows and all of Israel stops, including ALL traffic, and the people stand outside at attention for two minutes in honor of the fallen.

The government of Israel consists of many parties, so they must govern by coalition. From what we were told, even Ben Gurion had only 39 percent of the vote when he was elected prime minister.

The Knesset consists of members of all religions, and we were told of some interesting circumstances of Israeli politics. When the Palestine Liberation Authority went to sign an agreement with Hamas, two of the Arab members of the Israeli Knesset went along to endorse the agreement. When I expressed my shock, the answer was that this is how Israel's democracy works.

Worse than that, however: when the Lebanese war broke out, an Arab member of the Knesset went to Beirut with secret Israel army tactics, which he provided to the Lebanese (he was certainly a traitor in my book). But because he is a Knesset member, he still receives his pay and his family is fully supported, including medical care and full education!

Time was running short, and we had to get back to the hotel for our dinner date at Birgitta's lovely home. She had come to Jerusalem forty years ago. She fell in love with Israel and had now made it her home.

It was an incredible evening, not only because I could smoke my cigar on her patio, but because of the warmth and fellowship of the family and guests. They were an eclectic group. The couple that eventually drove us back to the hotel was from Denmark. They come to Israel twice a year and have bought a home in Haifa. They brought their twelve grandchildren to see Israel and to counter the left-wing propaganda of Europe. The guests consisted of Europeans, Africans, Israelis, and Americans and included medical people, poets, artists, and a girl who sang religious songs, both Jewish and Christian. The food was a combination Israeli-Swedish smorgasbord, and it was excellent. The experience and conversation were unforgettable, but then there is a certain strong feeling that comes over you, a combination of awe and sacredness, when you are in Jerusalem.

The next day we were on our own, and we went to the Israel Museum. The Shrine of the Book, which houses the Dead Sea Scrolls, is past the courtyard to the right of the entrance. Miri, our wonderful guide, would take us to the Dead Sea tomorrow, and we would pass the cave area where the scrolls were discovered. She noted that the only reasons they survived were that the air was so dry and many of the scrolls were preserved in large jars.

Anything biblical that had been discovered after that time reflected a gap of a number of centuries. You cannot see everything in one visit; because of the fragility of the scrolls, they must be constantly rotated. From Qumran Cave #4, your see fragments from Ecclesiastes. There are parts of every book of the Old Testament, with the exception of Esther and Nehemiah. The book of Isaiah has been preserved in its complete form. We know that this sect of Judaism, which worshiped in the Judean desert near where Christianity was born, was different, but we are not yet sure whether they followed the twenty-four books of the Bible. The great Isaiah Scroll that is displayed is a facsimile. To the right is the model of the Second Temple just before its destruction in 70 AD.

We then retraced our steps to the left (no, I didn't get lost yet), passing the Art Garden on the right with its famous sculpture garden (Lipchitz, Moore, Picasso, etc. were displayed).

We then went on to the Archaeology Gallery with its extensive holdings from biblical times, including those of ancient peoples (from prehistoric to the Ottoman Empire). All faiths are represented, along with a complete collection of Judaica. Some of the glassware was stunning. To see small drinking and wine glasses from 500 BC was unbelievable.

We then moved on to the Jewish Art and Life Wing, where both religious and nonreligious cultures worldwide were represented, from the Middle Ages to the present. There is a Synagogue Route, which displays the interiors of synagogues from three continents. We saw everything from ritual objects, clothing, and jewelry to illuminated manuscripts. Our last stop in the museum was the art, print, drawings, and photography exhibit.

We went on to the King David Hotel to prepare for the Sabbath. We had made reservations for dinner, and as we sat in the lobby waiting for our 7:30 p.m. reservation, there was a special buzzing and feeling in the hotel. Everyone greeted us with "Shabbat shalom," and that included every staff member down to the maids. And they did this without exception until Saturday sundown.

Dinner was served by our favorite waiter, who made sure that we had prime seating and that we enjoyed our meal, which we did.

Saturday morning (Shabbat), we started early and made our way south toward the Dead Sea, with our first stop being Masada. Many know the story. The Jews had revolted against the Romans in 66 AD, and the Romans were destroying any traces of the Jewish culture, including the Second Temple (70 AD), which was rebuilt after the Babylonians completely destroyed it in 586 BCE. Masada sits on a plateau in a remote location between two ancient routes. Josephus Flavius, who fought the Romans in the Great Revolt, recorded the story. Lots of what he recorded has been borne out by later excavations. This was Herod's winter palace, and he built well-stocked storerooms, a cistern, and a defensive wall. In 66 AD, the rebels defeated the Roman garrison stationed there and built a synagogue and mikvah. Around 73 AD, the Romans laid siege, and with over eight thousand troops, they built camps around the base. After some months, they brought a tower and battering ram.

When the end was imminent, the defenders drew lots (these lots were discovered and preserved). They would rather perish than be ravaged and/or made to renounce their Judaism. Two women and five children survived and related the events to the Romans.

Note that after the Romans left during the Byzantine period, a monastery was built, and then that was destroyed when Islam rose during the seventh century.

We then went to the Dead Sea, where I floated in the buoyant and supposedly healthy mineral water. It gave me a very strange feeling.

We then had a late lunch at a nearby spa and went back to Jerusalem for a fine supper.

The following day we went to Sderot, which is less than two miles from Gaza in the western Negev. This city is not normally on the tourist map. It is poor and it has been plagued by frequent rocket attacks since 2001. You have less than twenty seconds to obtain cover once the alarm goes off. Therefore, many people and industries have moved out.

This terror brings life to a standstill. It is hard on everyone but especially the children. We were invited by the JNF to tour the police station and the JNF Indoor Recreation Center, where we took a number of pictures of the area. It is bombproof, and it is the largest indoor playground in Israel. It has sports and play facilities for all ages, along with counseling rooms for those who have suffered shock, as many have.

The Qassam rockets have a range of about twenty miles, and they are not accurate (think of V-2s during World War II). Sometimes they fall in the periphery of Arab territory, so the Israelis invite the nearby residents to send their children to the playground to be safe. So far the Gaza residents have refused, although a few have come to meetings in Sderot (anonymously, of course, as they fear retribution at home).

This facility has helped enrich the lives of the Sderot residents. Over twelve thousand rockets and mortars have been fired into this area from Gaza, killing and maiming many people and destroying many homes. We left after examining a half-spent

Qassam rocket that was filled with nails and BBs to inflict harm on civilians.

Our last stop before we headed back for last-minute shopping and then to the King David to pack was the Ayalon Institute, which was the secret bullet factory, established by the Haganah in 1945. It was situated on a kibbutz in the middle of a British army camp. The building housed a bakery and laundry on the main floor (laundry machines made enough noise to camouflage the bullet-making machinery downstairs). Forty-five people would come in from the fields, and everything was so secret they did not tell their spouses what they were actually doing downstairs. From 1946 to 1948, the secret was kept, and there was not one accident, although they were working with explosives. Almost three million bullets were made (they were nine millimeter for Sten guns). The English soldiers came from the nearby town of Rehovot to have their uniforms laundered.

Our flight was scheduled for 1:00 a.m., and we were going to be picked up at 9:30 p.m. to drive to Tel Aviv. We received calls from both our driver and El-Al. Our flight had been delayed until 4:00 a.m. El-Al efficiently arranged a late flight on Jet Blue in anticipation of missing the connection. Upon boarding the flight at 5:00 a.m. (luckily for us, our compartment had beds), we were told that due to the limited fuel supply, we were going to have to fly to Amsterdam for a couple of hours to refuel. For obvious reasons, El-Al flights are refueled in secluded parts of the airport.

When we arrived at JFK, we sat another five hours waiting for our connection and finally got to West Palm Beach and home late that afternoon. Counting the wait at the airports and flight time, this was a thirty-hour trip.

It was great to get home and get some rest, but we did miss Israel. Sylvia has been to a number of countries, and I have been to forty-plus countries—some as many forty-eight times, and I've experienced some incredible (and sometimes very frightening) happenings—but I have never visited a country like Israel. Since we have been back, we continue to reflect on this extraordinary experience, from walking on the same paths as ancient and biblical characters to recognizing places that we have been that are shown on current TV news channels.

We feel blessed to have met a number of really extraordinary and very brave people. This is a land of many contradictions: a good economy but many poor; a great agricultural base but pockets of hunger; very high technology but still using Windows 98. There is a shortage of water, which they manage to cope with. Israel has a very powerful military, but it is a very small country, about the size of New Jersey.

The people are sometimes outwardly rude and impatient, but they're very soft inside, with generally a high sense of morality coupled with a potentially vicious crime element. Israel was the cradle of many of the major religions, but it is surrounded by hate and jealousy.

Also importantly, we were able to dispel so many of the myths (which we of course suspected were myths) about Israel and their tactics. We realize that Israel is not at all perfect and has surely made numerous mistakes. We can only pray for peace in both that troubled land and the world.

Bringing You Up to Date

Happily, I am starting to close some deals, and I have some consulting assignments, which mostly are for lending and the merchant cash-advance business. We are also enjoying our summers in New Jersey and Pennsylvania with our kids and grandkids. Dan, the younger, is a junior in high school and is the starting safety on the football team. Mike is the older grand-son, and he is attending Nova Southeastern University in Fort Lauderdale, where he is making good grades studying account-ing and finance. He has been giving the family some amazing stock tips based on his research of the market.

My friends encouraged me to write this book because they claimed that many of my stories and experiences were both funny and interesting. Of course, you will be the judge of that. Although I never kept a diary and I was never a good photogra-pher (unlike my son Barry), I did save a number of newspaper and magazine articles, along with files and notes. This enabled me to make the stories as accurate as possible, noting that in the interest of not embarrassing anyone, I did make some name changes.

In doing the research, I tried to contact as many of my old colleagues as possible. Sadly, many have passed on, and I dearly miss them. My best friend, Louie Dinolfo, loved to get me in trouble but would give his life for me and my family. Gary Metzel and his wife, Jackie (still living), were close friends from Atlanta. Gary had a great sense of humor, and he could make mundane situations quite funny. Jack Hirsch (whose wife, Gladys, is also still living) was the youngest CPA in Georgia's history up until the 1950s and was our partner in our answering service in Tuscaloosa. Norman Rabinowitz, a well-known sculptor (mostly tin), was a friend in Teaneck for many years. Norman's humor could be biting and close to wicked but nevertheless hysterical at times, especially when he imitated dialects. Amalia Burgess, my controller, committed suicide because she was suffering from terminal cancer. Gene Rubin and his wife Natalie (still living) from Boston were close friends for many years. Gene always kept up my spirits. Dave Pupps, my production vice-president, was instrumental in getting some of my best people to join our company. Fred Randolph, my boss and friend from the A. S. Beck days until he died a couple of years ago. He was the gentlemen's gentleman. Arno Kuhsler owned the Ligia factory in Brazil, and he not only mentored us in the ways of Brazil but was instrumental in getting us started in that country. He left us too soon. Mike Maisel contracted fatal cancer and may have taken his own life. He left a fine family and I miss his kindness and class. Sylvia still talks to and occasionally sees some of her childhood friends. Along with them and others who are not mentioned, I dedicate this book to all of my relatives, living and dead, whom I have loved and who have loved and inspired me.

Many of the names in my old address books could no longer be located; however, I did find some, and I was gratified to either speak directly to them or correspond via mail or e-mail. One in particular turned out to be an incredible one, and it is fitting that I include him in the final chapter of the book. I mentioned the story of Larry Laurentius in an earlier chapter. I hadn't spoken to Larry in over thirty years, but since his name is not all that common, I discovered that he was listed on the LinkedIn site. LinkedIn is primarily a networking business site. When I sent him a message asking whether he was the Larry Laurentius who had worked for me at Marquesa International, the response was immediate. It was Larry, and he wanted to speak with me on the phone.

I made the call immediately, and it turned out to be an astonishing one. Larry started to relate to me that I had been his mentor and that a week did not go by in which he didn't mention my name. He then said that providence had brought us back together. He had just returned from the hospital, where he had been recovering from a liver transplant. Larry had been just a few hours from dying when his doctor called informing him that the hospital had just received the liver for his transplant and that an ambulance would soon be at his door. He had suffered greatly, with his heart stopping twice, but he would not give up. The transplant was a complete success, and his body had accepted the new liver.

Previously, he had been traveling to Columbia with his wife, who is originally from Columbia, in order to develop their shoe-manufacturing industry for export. They felt that for a number of reasons, the timing would be perfect for a new country to enter the footwear-exporting arena. They wanted my recommendation on whom to approach in the United States (remember, I've been out of the shoe business for over fourteen years).

One of the fastest-growing and most popular shoe companies is the Camuto Group, who, all told, market almost thirty million pair of shoes throughout the world. I hadn't had any contact with Vince Camuto for many years, but I sent him an e-mail explaining that this new Columbia venture might be a good opportunity for them. Vince then apparently contacted his CEO and sourcing department and a meeting was set up.

Since Larry wanted me to be part of this new venture, I agreed to go with him and his design crew to bring some prototype samples to their headquarters in Greenwich, Connecticut. It was hard to believe that after all of these years, I was showing shoe samples to a merchandising group again. Larry then (against his doctor's orders) flew to Columbia to prepare the new, corrected samples for the Camuto group.

These samples are now being finalized as I write these lines. If this new venture is successful, I guess I will have to write another book. Sylvia asked me when she could read this one, and my answer to her was, "For $14.95 I can order you a copy." She laughed because she knew I was kidding.

I'll end this book with one more, funny true story:

One night, Sylvia and I were supposed to go out for dinner with some friends. The restaurant was on the water, almost an hour's drive from our home. I had some meetings and conference calls, and we then were scheduled to leave for the restaurant at around 6:00 p.m. But at around 5:30 p.m., the sky opened up with a torrential rain.

Our friends called and suggested a restaurant that was less than ten minutes away, so we made a new reservation. They then called back and said that the weather was so bad they had to cancel altogether.

We then decided that rather than go out alone, and since the weather was so bad, we would have a meal delivered from a new local Chinese restaurant. We didn't have their menu handy, so I went online, and they had a convenient section for ordering. I filled everything in, including the details of our order and our phone number. They immediately sent back a confirmation e-mail.

After about forty-five minutes (it was still pouring rain, so I felt they might need some leeway), I called and got the following response: "What order? We don't have any order."

When I mentioned that they had confirmed the order online, she said: "Oh, our printer is broken, so we couldn't accept Internet orders, and I have a customer right now, so I will have to call you back."

After a few minutes, we had not gotten a call back, so I called them. I asked what had happened. "Oh, I tried to call you," she exclaimed, "but you gave me the wrong number!"

We were getting hungry, so I asked how long it would take to deliver an order.

"Sorry, but we don't deliver after 6:00 p.m.!"

Sylvia then said that I should have ordered from the restaurant that we had been going to for years. We have been friendly with them and their families, and they have authentic Hong Kong-style food. They don't deliver, so I called in the order for a pickup.

No sooner had I hung up the phone than the doorbell rang. I opened the door, and I couldn't believe my eyes. A young man was standing there carrying a large bag of fine-smelling Chinese food. I related the story to him and asked what was going on.

His response was that they were very busy due to the storms, but in any case, "Here is the order."

Embarrassed, I now had to call the other Chinese restaurant and cancel the order.

The food was good, but the upshot was that the next morning when I opened my e-mail, I received a cancellation notice from the original restaurant.

Like many lives, mine has had its disappointments, successes, happiness and sadness. I have tried to counteract my weaknesses, including a hot temper and impatience, with occasional acts of kindness and charity. Although I always liked the good things in life, including fine food, wine and luxurious travel accommodations I learned to respect the real worth of simple people. Many of the powerful people that I have met throughout the years were in my view empty shells, as are many celebrities and politicians. Frankly, I abhor much of the hypocrisy that I see and read about. I applaud those that opt for "good" and condemn those that opt for "evil".

Note that I have no plans to stop working, but I also have no plans to stop listening, learning, and laughing.

FINIS

Made in the USA
Middletown, DE
20 November 2017